CASEBOOK IN
ABNORMAL PSYCHOLOGY

Casebook in
Abnormal Psychology
Fourth Edition

John Vitkus
Case Western Reserve University
Medical College of Ohio

 **McGraw-Hill College**

Boston   Burr Ridge, IL   Dubuque, IA   Madison, WI
New York   San Francisco   St. Louis
Bangkok   Bogotá   Caracas   Lisbon   London   Madrid   Mexico City
Milan   New Delhi   Seoul   Singapore   Sydney   Taipei   Toronto

McGraw-Hill College

A Division of The McGraw·Hill Companies

CASEBOOK IN ABNORMAL PSYCHOLOGY, FOURTH
EDITION

This book is printed on acid-free paper.

1 2 3 4 5 6 7 8 9 0 DOC/DOC 9 0 9 8

ISBN 0-07-303473-8

www.mhhe.com

To my parents, Myles and Joyce,
who made this book possible.
To my wife, Lisa,
who made this book worthwhile.
And to my children, Allison and Ian,
who made this book necessary.

CONTENTS

Contents

PREFACE

Casebook in Abnormal Psychology, Fourth Edition consists of 14 case histories based on material supplied by psychiatric professionals. The presenting symptoms were actually observed, and the therapeutic techniques were actually administered. To maintain confidentiality, information that could identify individuals has been changed. Any resemblance to real persons is coincidental.

The 14 cases survey a variety of psychiatric diagnoses which follow the conventions of the *Diagnostic and Statistical Manual of Mental Disorders, Fourth Edition,* often abbreviated as *DSM-IV.*

Cases are presented within particular treatment approaches. **Please note:** By presenting a particular treatment with each disorder, I am *not* implying that the treatment presented is the most effective—or even the most common—treatment for that disorder.

Each case is organized into five sections: presenting complaint, personal history, conceptualization and treatment, prognosis, and discussion. These categories reflect, in a general way, how psychiatric professionals organize their cases and communicate among themselves.

This book was written with three primary goals. The first is to provide readers with a detailed and vivid account of the symptoms that characterize various disorders. The second is to highlight the differences in various therapeutic approaches. The third is to illustrate the limitations of psychiatric intervention in everyday practice.

This edition updates earlier editions with current research and treatment strategies. Most notable among these are the introduction of two new medications: sildenafil (Viagra) for male erectile disorder, and donepizil (Aricept) for Alzheimer's disease. Less dramatic but just as significant has been the introduction of many new, so-called atypical antipsychotic medications for schizophrenia. Finally, the field has been changed dramatically by the implementation of cost containment strategies known collectively as managed. The reader should keep in mind that the majority of these cases occurred before managed care was widely implemented, and many of the treatments described would be seen as quite luxurious by today's more spartan standards.

ACKNOWLEDGMENTS

I am very grateful to the following consultants for their time, help, and expertise. In addition to their professional wisdom, they provided me with a fascinating behind-the-scenes view of the therapeutic process.

Mark Bondeson, Psy.D.
VA Medical Center
Brecksville, OH

Ellie Bragar, Psy.D.
private practice
New York, NY

Howard A. Crystal, M.D.
Einstein College of Medicine
Yeshiva University
Bronx, NY

Zira DeFries, M.D.
private practice
New York, NY

John Fogelman, M.D.
St. Luke's/Roosevelt Hospital
New York, NY

David Geldmacher, M.D.
Fairhill Center for Aging
University Hospitals
Cleveland, OH

Kevin MacColl, M.A.
Beth Israel Medical Center
New York, NY

Harriet N. Mischel, Ph.D.
private practice
New York, NY

Steve Rasmussen, M.D.
Butler Hospital,
Brown University
Providence, RI

Sharon Silver-Regent, Ph.D.
private practice
New York, NY

David Spiegel, M.D.
Stanford University
Medical Center
Stanford, CA

Andrea Spungen, M.A.
Barnard College
New York, NY

B. Timothy Walsh, M.D.
Columbia/Presbyterian
Medical Center,
New York State
Psychiatric Institute
New York, NY

At McGraw-Hill, I thank Meera Dash, Susan Kunchandy, Rita Hingtgen, and Wendy Nelson for their patience, expertise, and professionalism.

CASEBOOK IN ABNORMAL PSYCHOLOGY

GENERALIZED ANXIETY DISORDER
Cognitive-Behavioral Therapy

PRESENTING COMPLAINT

Terry is a 31-year-old man living in Washington, D.C. At his initial interview, he was dressed in clean but rather shabby "college clothes" (a T-shirt, jeans, and an old, worn warm-up jacket). Terry's manner and posture revealed that he was very apprehensive about therapy; his eyes nervously scanned the interview room, he held himself stiffly rigid and stayed by the door, and his speech was barely audible and marked by hesitations and waverings. After some brief introductions, Terry and the therapist each took a seat. The therapist began the session, asking, "What is it that brings you here today?"

Terry's reply was very rapid and forced. He stated that his problems began during his residency after graduating from medical school. Being an internal medicine resident involved constant pressure and responsibilities. The schedule, involving 36-hour on-call periods, daily 6:00 a.m. rounds, and constant emergencies, was grueling and exhausting. Gradually he began to notice that he and his fellow residents were making a number of small errors and oversights in the care they provided their patients. Although none was even remotely life-threatening, still he found himself ruminating about these lapses. He began to hesitate in making decisions and taking action for fear of making some catastrophic mistake. His anxieties steadily worsened until he began calling in sick and avoiding particularly stressful situations at the hospital. As a result he was not completing many of the assignments given to him by the chief resident, who threatened to report him to the program director. As time wore on, Terry's performance continued to decline, and by the end of the year he was threatened with dismissal from his program. He resigned at the end of the year.

Before his resignation he began making plans to be transferred to a less demanding program. With some help from his father (who is a

1

physician) and some luck, he was accepted into a hospital in Washington, D.C. His second-year residency was indeed less demanding than the first, and he felt that perhaps he could manage it. After a few months, though, Terry again felt an overwhelming dread of making some terrible mistake, and he had to quit the second program after six months. He then began to work in a less stressful position as a research fellow for the Food and Drug Administration (FDA). Even in this relatively relaxed atmosphere, Terry found that he still had great difficulty carrying out his duties. He found that he could not handle any negative feelings at work, and he again began missing work to avoid trouble. Terry's contract with the FDA expired after six months and was not renewed. At this time even the prospect of having to apply for another position produced terrible anxieties, and Terry decided to live off a trust fund set up by his grandfather. For the last two years he has been supported by this trust fund and, in part at least, by his girlfriend, with whom he lives and who, according to Terry, pays "more than her share."

Besides crippling his career, Terry's incapacitating anxieties have interfered with his relationships with his family and his girlfriend. For one thing, he has avoided visiting his parents for the last three years. He states that his parents' (particularly his father's) poor opinions of him make going home "out of the question." He also confesses that he avoids discussing any potentially controversial subject with his girlfriend for fear that he may cause an irreconcilable rift. As Terry puts it, "I stay away from anything touchy because I don't want to say something wrong and blow it [the relationship]. Then what'll I do?" Even routine tasks, such as washing his clothes, shopping for groceries, and writing letters to friends are impossible to accomplish for fear that some small step may be bungled or overlooked. Terry freely acknowledges that his fears are exaggerated and irrational. He admits (after some persuasion) that he is an intelligent, capable young man. Nevertheless, he feels utterly unable to overcome his anxieties, and he takes great pains to avoid situations that may bring them on.

Along with these dysfunctional cognitions, Terry reports a number of somatic symptoms. He is very tense; he always feels nervous or "keyed up" and is easily distracted and irritated by minor problems. He complains of frequent throbbing headaches, annoying body aches and pains in his back and neck, and an almost constant feeling of fatigue. He also admits to feeling low self-esteem, describing himself as "worthless" and "lazy." On occasion he experiences brief periods of panic in which he suffers from a shortness of breath, a wildly racing heartbeat, profuse sweating, and mild dizziness. These feelings of panic tend to come on when some feared situation (e.g., having to make a decision or having to confront his girlfriend) cannot be avoided. He states that these symptoms first emerged during his first residency and have gradually intensified over the past few years.

Terry began dynamic psychotherapy soon after he lost his job with the FDA. He reports that this therapy was very complex and involved, which he found impressive in many ways. In particular, he says that his therapeutic experience gave him two important insights into the underlying causes of his paralyzing anxieties and low self-esteem: (1) his parents' expectations of him were too high and he always felt a great pressure to be perfect in their eyes, and (2) the teasing he received from his peers as a child has made him self-conscious about his weaknesses. Although Terry felt that these insights were valid, they did not seem to precipitate any significant change in his behavior. A friend suggested that Terry might benefit from a more direct form of psychotherapy and referred him to a cognitive-behavioral therapist.

PERSONAL HISTORY

Terry grew up in a small town in central Ohio. His father is a general practitioner in town and is on the staff of the county hospital. Terry's mother was an elementary school teacher until she quit her job when his older sister was born. After his younger sister was diagnosed as moderately mentally retarded, however, his mother took night courses at Ohio State University to receive training in teaching disabled children. She is now employed in the county's special education program.

Terry says that his older sister is a disappointment to their parents. After getting average grades at a small local college and working for several years as a paralegal, she now attends a small, little-known law school. Terry describes her as "not too bright." His father criticizes her for not getting into a more prestigious law school. Part of his father's anger, Terry speculates, stems from frustration at being stuck in a routine medical position in a small town. His younger lives at home and works at a sheltered workshop for mentally retarded adults run by the county special education program. According to Terry, his mother's training in special education has enabled his parents to cope fairly well with the burdens of supporting a disabled child.

According to Terry, his father early on "wrote off" his sisters (and, to a certain extent, his own stagnant career) and focused on Terry to be the "success" of the family. And Terry worked hard to fulfill this expectation. He had always earned excellent grades in school; in fact, he won full scholarships at prestigious universities that supported his undergraduate education and his training in medical school. He had always considered himself to be a good student and enjoyed studying, even in the difficult, competitive atmosphere of medical school. He described his academic achievement as something he did for himself--for his own education and improvement. In contrast, during his residencies he felt that he was toiling endlessly on what he considered to be "someone else's scum work." For the first time he began to fear his own fallibility and to avoid anxiety-provoking situations.

CONCEPTUALIZATION AND TREATMENT

Terry is a very intelligent and articulate young man who appears to be much more competent and capable than he presents himself to be. He shows no evidence of a psychotic disorder. He seems willing, even pressured, to discuss his problems, and he seems highly motivated toward reducing them. The therapist thought it reasonable, then, to take Terry's complaints at face value.

Terry's primary problem involves his excessive and unwarranted apprehension about his own fallibility and his need to perform every activity perfectly, no matter how trivial. This overriding fear has crippled his occupational and social functioning as well as his ability to perform—or even to attempt—a variety of routine, everyday tasks. This anxiety is also manifested by a number of physiological symptoms, including constant vigilance, distractibility, and irritability; pervasive muscle tension; and autonomic hyperactivity, as expressed by his occasional feelings of panic. Although he complains of periods of feeling depressed and worthless, his worries and anxieties are clearly not limited to these periods. Thus, it seems that his anxiety is his primary problem and not merely a response to his mild depression.

Terry's symptoms clearly fit the *DSM-IV* criteria for generalized anxiety disorder. People with this disorder suffer from pervasive, long-standing, and uncontrollable feelings of dread or worry that involve a number of major life activities (career, marriage, parenting, etc.). The focus of these anxieties is much broader than is the case with more circumscribed anxiety disorders such as panic disorder or simple phobia, and they are not solely associated with any other Axis I diagnosis. Thus, for example, although someone with generalized anxiety disorder might also experience a major depressive episode, his or her anxieties are not solely about being depressed. In addition, people with generalized anxiety disorder display somatic signs of their apprehension, including muscle tension, autonomic hyperactivity, fatigue, and irritability. Terry clearly fits this picture.

Terry's therapy can be organized as a process involving four general steps. The therapist's initial aim was to establish rapport with her client. To establish a better working relationship with Terry, she attempted to make him feel comfortable with her. This is no easy task with someone as tense and anxious as Terry. The first step was to explain her approach. Because cognitive-behavioral therapy requires much more direct, active participation than initially supposed by many clients (particularly those like Terry who have a history of psychodynamic treatment), it is important that the client be made fully aware of what to expect. The therapist also gave Terry encouragement that his disorder was treatable with cognitive-behavioral therapy. It is important to establish this basis of hope to foster the client's expectations for change.

The second step was to have Terry form goals for his therapy. Ideally these goals would involve some specific behaviors or attitudes. It is more effective to formulate concrete plans that address some specific feared situation, such as "I want to send my résumé to 50 prospective employers," than more general aims such as "I want to work." Like most clients with generalized anxiety disorder, though, Terry at first proposed goals that were quite vague and unfocused. He wanted to start working, to get along with his parents better, and to "not be so apprehensive about things." At first these general goals are adequate; the important point is to have the client formulate *some* goals. Overly general ones can always be specified and put into behavioral contexts as therapy progresses.

Third, relaxation training is suggested for clients who show a great deal of physical tension and seem amenable to this treatment. Therapists have developed relaxation techniques that specifically address a client's dysfunctional cognitions, muscular tension, and autonomic hyperactivity. When he began therapy, Terry showed a variety of physical manifestations of tension. Having been trained in medicine, he was attuned to the somatic aspects of healing and was very willing to try relaxation techniques that involved physiological elements.

The fourth step in therapy was a review by Terry and the therapist of the issues and goals Terry had targeted. By going over his initial complaints and plans, both the therapist and the client are assured that they understand each other fully. In addition, this review allows the client, with the aid of the therapist, to put vague initial goals into more specific and workable terms.

Therapy began by first discussing the specific issues that were of immediate concern to Terry. These topics were not necessarily a central part of Terry's goals, nor were they necessarily closely related. For example, Terry's first few sessions of therapy focused on a variety of distinct problems, including, among other things, his inability to buy a suit, his anxiety concerning needed dental work, and his dread of an upcoming visit to his parents. These loosely related issues were dealt with on a problem-by-problem basis, a process the therapist referred to as "putting out fires." This troubleshooting approach is employed for several reasons. First, cognitive-behavioral therapy is most effective if therapeutic issues are specified and well defined; individual psychological "fires" are particularly suited to this. Second, the client's enthusiasm for therapy and belief in the effectiveness of treatment is likely to be increased by initial success experiences, especially in immediate problem areas. Third, although these issues do not appear to be closely related, for the most part they share a common foundation: they are indications of Terry's tendency to avoid situations that carry a possibility of failure, however inconsequential. Over time, clients are expected to integrate these isolated issues and generalize their therapeutic gains to other areas of their lives.

The first topic Terry wanted to discuss was his inability to buy himself a suit. It had been years since Terry had shopped for clothes; he contented himself with wearing worn jeans and T-shirts. Several months ago, Terry's girlfriend made plans for the two of them to take a vacation to Boston to visit her sister. As a part of the preparation for this trip, she asked him to buy some new clothes, including "at least one decent suit." He thought about buying a suit on several occasions, but every time he was overwhelmed by the prospect of having to pick one out. He would begin shaking and sweating even as he approached a clothing store. Terry explained that he hated shopping for clothes, especially suits, because he was convinced that he would not be able to pick out the right suit. Not only would he waste his money, but everyone else would see his failure. To be at all acceptable, the suit had to be just the right color, just the right material, just the right cut, just the right price, and so on. It also had to be practical—appropriate for every possible occasion, from a sightseeing tour to a funeral. The prospect of buying the "wrong" suit made him so anxious that he could not bring himself to even enter a clothing store.

The therapist began by having Terry clarify exactly what he was and was not capable of. She then gave him clear assignments that she judged he would be able to accomplish successfully. These assignments

7

started off with small steps which Terry anticipated would be easy; gradually they became more and more complicated and difficult. The following segment of a therapy session illustrates this process:

> **Terry:** You see, I just can't go through with it [buying a suit].
>
> **Therapist:** Do you mean you are unable to, or that you'd rather avoid the whole thing?
>
> **Terry:** What do you mean?
>
> **Therapist:** Well, if I held a gun to your head, would you be able to go to the clothing store?
>
> **Terry:** Well, yeah, I suppose so.
>
> **Therapist:** So you are physically able to walk into a clothing store, right?
>
> **Terry:** Yeah, I guess I am.
>
> **Therapist:** OK. I want you to go to at least two clothing stores on your way home today. All right?
>
> **Terry:** The mall's too far away. I couldn't possibly make it to day.
>
> **Therapist:** There's no need to go to the mall. There are at least five good clothing stores right around here; three are on this street.
>
> **Terry:** Well, they're too expensive.
>
> **Therapist:** No, not really. I've shopped at most of them, and the prices are actually better than at the mall.
>
> **Terry:** I really don't know if I'll

have the time.

Therapist: It'll take a half an hour at most. Come on, Terry, no more excuses. I want you to go to two stores. Today.

Terry: But what if I buy the wrong suit?

Therapist: You don't need to buy anything. Just walk into two stores. That's it. If you feel comfortable with that, then start browsing. You might want to try one or two suits on. But for today, I just want you to take the first step and go to two stores. Agreed?

Terry: All right.

At the next session Terry was noticeably excited and pleased. He had followed the therapist's directions and had gone to a store. After he went to the first store, he found that looking for a suit was not as difficult as he had expected. In fact, he actually went to three stores and bought two suits. Unfortunately, Terry was not able to enjoy his success for long; his enthusiasm evaporated when he began to describe another problem. Several weeks ago his driver's license expired. He felt very anxious about driving with his expired license, and he knew that he had to get his license renewed, which involved taking a simple written test of basic traffic regulations. He had gotten a copy of the driver's manual and had planned to go over it several times, but each time he was struck with a terrible fear that he might miss some vital piece of information and fail his test. Terry admitted that his worries were irrational. He had missed no more than a single question on any driving test before. He realized that the test was very basic and that the chances of his actually failing the test were very remote, even if he did not study the manual at all. Still, he could not bring himself to study the manual, and the thought of taking the test "cold" terrified him.

Again, the therapist approached the problem directly and made concrete suggestions. First, she reassured him that he was a very intelligent person who graduated from medical school; he would have no trouble passing a simple driving test, even without reading the manual (which in fact he had never done before). Nevertheless, she thought that the manual would be reassuring. She suggested different ways to get him to read it, such as skimming it or just reading every other page. She explained that failing the exam was not the end of the world; even on the slight chance that he did fail the exam, he would still have two other opportunities to retake it. Finally, she reminded him that it was worse to be stopped while driving with an expired license than to just go ahead and take the test. This last warning was meant to propel Terry to action, but it was a bit risky; it could have been stopped him from driving altogether to avoid a ticket. When he mentioned this, the therapist reassured him that driving with a license that expired only a few weeks ago would most likely get him only a warning. At worst, he would have to pay a small fine. As time wore on, however, trying to explain that he "just forgot" about his license would become less and less credible. The time to take his test was now.

Again Terry followed the therapist's instructions. He read over the manual carefully and tried not to be too concerned if he did not remember every fact. Following her directions, if he felt that he could not remember some information from any particular page, he would consciously limit himself to skimming that page once. At the next session he reported, as expected, that he had passed his test without missing a question. But just like the previous session, however, his accomplishment was darkened by another "emergency" that had occurred during the week.

Over the weekend Terry lost a filling in one of his teeth when he was eating some caramel candy. He realized that he needed his filling replaced, and his girlfriend suggested her dentist, whom she recommended highly. Terry had not been to a dentist for over three years, and he was very apprehensive about the possible injury and pain a dentist could inflict. Remembering his own small mistakes as a resident, he feared that this dentist (or any dentist, for that matter) might inadvertently damage the nerve of the tooth, thus necessitating a root canal. In spite of this fear, Terry realized that he needed his filling replaced and called for an emergency appointment. He was able to make an appointment for Tuesday morning and went in for a consultation.

Although hesitant, Terry was able to make it to the dentist's office, accompanied by his girlfriend. Once in the dentist's chair, however, he became panicky and unmanageable. He clenched his mouth and made it impossible for the dentist to perform an examination. He repeatedly grabbed the dentist's hand and tried to jerk him away. Terry's girlfriend, who stayed with him throughout the appointment, told him that he made a high-pitched whistling sound resembling a drill whenever the dentist picked up one of his tools, even tools totally unrelated to the drill, such as the probing pick or the suction tube. She had never seen him this nervous before. At first the dentist refused to schedule another appointment, but Terry's girlfriend, who was a longtime patient, persuaded him to schedule an appointment for the next week.

Terry was depressed over this embarrassing experience. The worst part of it, he thought, was that his girlfriend would lose interest in him now that she saw just how anxious he could be. But because she went out of her way to schedule the appointment, Terry felt that his first priority was to learn to control his apprehensions so he could go to the dentist.

Terry's therapy that week focused on relaxation training. First, he was taught to begin by taking slow, deep breaths. After a few deep breaths, he was told to relax his body completely. He was instructed to focus on his bodily sensations. He was to move his focus slowly from head to toe, concentrating on relaxing each part of his body. He was to sense how his forehead felt, then his eyebrows, then his nose, and so on. If he noticed tension in any part of his body, he was to relax it. (Many therapists have their clients engage in *progressive relaxation* where they systematically tense and then relax various body areas. However,

Terry's therapist prefers to utilize *passive relaxation* for most clients with anxiety disorders, who are already extremely tense to begin with.) Terry was also told that if he found himself becoming distracted or had any stray thoughts, he was to "blow them away like puffy clouds" and replace them with soft, relaxing images. The therapist then asked Terry about the activities that were particularly pleasant to him. He replied that he loved the tranquility of lying in the sun on some tropical island. As a result, the therapist told him that he should try to replace any stressful thoughts with scenes of sunbathing on a Caribbean beach.

Terry was told to practice this relaxation technique two or three times a day. To get her clients to do this practice, Terry's therapist makes relaxation tapes that gently and calmly guide the clients in these exercises. The tapes are made individually, with the clients' names and special instructions tailored for them. To help ensure that her clients do not lose interest in these relaxation exercises, the tapes are only 10 to 15 minutes long. Because of his impending dental appointment, Terry's therapist made his tape right after their session. She also wrote out the rationale for not continuing to avoid the various things that he needs to accomplish, as well as the role of relaxation in reducing his anxiety so that entering into these situations would be possible. He expressed gratitude for her effort and her personal concern when he picked these up the next morning.

Terry began the next session by proudly exclaiming, "I survived!" He reported that he used the relaxation training to divert his attention throughout the appointment, and this distraction was very successful. (In fact, he reported that he focused on his feet.) Terry's therapist, who herself had a filling replaced just two months before, acknowledged that it was a stressful and difficult procedure and that he should be congratulated on his accomplishment. During the session Terry reported that he had also used the relaxation training in a completely different situation. While he was having lunch with some friends, Terry began to feel that his friends were ignoring him. He became upset and irritated at them and began worrying that his companions were no longer interested in maintaining their friendship with him. Instead of leaving the restaurant, however, he decided to use the relaxation training to relieve his tension and to replace these negative anxieties with more pleasant scenes. As a result he was able to remain calm during lunch, which turned out to be a pleasant experience after all.

The next several sessions focused on different individual topics. For example, Terry had not done any laundry in over a year. He avoided this chore because he could not bring himself to go through the effort of sorting the clothes properly, making sure each load of clothes had the correct amount of detergent and was run under the right cycle, and so forth. He also dreaded folding the laundry, lining up each crease exactly and folding the T-shirts just right to avoid any wrinkles. Nevertheless, he wanted to surprise his girlfriend by doing their laundry, and he asked the therapist for her help. First, the task of doing the laundry was broken down into manageable tasks (sorting, selecting the cycle, etc.). Terry was then instructed to approach each task individually and to proceed to the next step only if he felt calm and relaxed after the previous step. He was also told that most people find that their first instincts are best, so once he made a decision about sorting or folding, he was to go through with it. Prior to starting, Terry wrote out careful instructions on exactly how to wash the clothes and put them away. It took Terry quite a while to accomplish this job, but he was able to control his anxieties and move steadily from task to task. When he reported completing the job at the next session, he was complimented and encouraged to attempt other avoided activities.

Another source of apprehension concerned writing a letter to an old roommate from college. They had exchanged correspondence for years, but Terry had not responded to this friend's last three letters for fear that he might look foolish through some mistake in his grammar or spelling. He worried that the friend, who was a journalist, would then lose respect for him. Terry's anxieties were heightened after his friend's last letter. In it, the friend jokingly wondered whether Terry had forgotten how to write. This comment made Terry wonder if he had indeed lost his ability to compose a letter that would be acceptable to his friend. Like everything else, his therapist had Terry approach this problem in gradual steps. First, he was to make a brief outline of what he would put in a letter. Next, he was to write a letter that they could go over during the next session. As was the case with shopping for a suit, renewing his license, and doing the laundry, Terry found that just starting an avoided activity greatly diminished his apprehensions, and he finished and sent the letter without ever showing it to the therapist.

Terry found that after each "fire" was put out, he felt much less anxiety about that topic the next time he attempted it. It also required fewer steps to complete these tasks. After several sessions of "putting out fires," Terry's therapy began to focus on more global interpersonal issues. At one session Terry discussed his fears that his girlfriend was planning to leave him. During the previous week she said that a special project came up at work (she worked in an architectural firm) and that they would have to postpone their vacation to Boston for a month. Terry, who constantly harbored fears that she would end their relationship, took this as a sign that she was ready to leave him. He asked the therapist what he could do to make her stay. The therapist told him that no one could guarantee that their relationship would last forever and began to discuss whether it was likely that Terry's fears were accurate. Initially Terry refused to discuss this possibility, saying "Don't tell me anything about her leaving. I don't want to hear it!" His therapist persisted, however, and reminded him of the importance of not avoiding important topics. Over the next two sessions he gradually became able to discuss the possibility of her leaving him. He even made some plans if indeed this occurred. But like most of his worries, this too was in vain. She finished her project, and they went to Boston on the postponed date.

While they were in Boston, Terry's mother fell and broke her hip. When his father asked when Terry would be coming to visit, Terry made a feeble excuse about his schedule. He knew he was expected to visit her, but he dreaded going home and interacting with his parents, particularly his father, who would undoubtedly ask him about what he has been doing over the past few years. He pleaded with his therapist, "Tell me what to say."

The therapist engaged Terry in a role-playing exercise. First, she instructed him to enact his father while she modeled effective responses to the father's comments and criticisms. Terry was told to pay close attention to her while she modeled these behaviors; he was to remember her posture, the color of her blouse, everything. These details were not important in themselves; they were meant to give Terry a clear, visual reference that would help him remember the modeled responses. After going over several responses, the roles were changed. Now the therapist enacted the role of Terry's parents, and Terry discussed possible responses from his own viewpoint. Because it was felt that maintaining a good interaction with his parents was just as important as dealing with a bad interaction, Terry practiced responding to many different types of comments, both positive and negative.

When Terry returned from Ohio, he reported that his father was indeed as critical as he had suspected. His father was very disappointed that he had "thrown away" a career in medicine, and he kept asking Terry what he had been doing for the past three years. His father felt that every man should at least support himself by the time he was finished with his education. Although these interactions made Terry very anxious, he was able to maintain control over his feelings and was able to stay in the family home for the entire 10-day visit. Terry stated that his interactions with his mother and older sister were generally positive. He found, somewhat to his surprise, that he really enjoyed their company. Although he still felt nervous about visiting his parents, he felt that he could have an adequate interaction with them and decided not to wait so long before visiting them again. (Six months later Terry was more comfortable about discussing a visit with his parents, but he had not actually visited them again.)

Terry felt that much of his father's disappointment was justified, and the next focus of therapy was for Terry to apply for jobs. When Terry began therapy, he reported "getting back to work" as a goal, although in reality he seemed perfectly happy to keep on living off of the trust fund. But now Terry felt enough confidence to begin a true job search.

Like every other aspect of therapy, Terry and his therapist approached this task one step at a time. First, they discussed the sorts of jobs he would be interested in and capable of performing. Terry's estimations of his own abilities were consistently lower than his

Case 1

therapist's. He also wanted to avoid any job that involved pressure and responsibility. At first, he thought of becoming a library researcher for some government agency. His therapist, who also thought it wise to avoid any high-pressure positions, told him that he could probably do better, perhaps something that would enable him to use his medical training. They finally decided that he should seek employment that involved medical issues but was outside a hospital or clinic setting. The therapist's instructions were concrete and firm: by the next week he was to have his résumé compiled, and one week later he was to have it printed. She then directed him to send out at least 10 applications per week until he heard something. During this time they rehearsed possible interview questions through role-playing. After eight weeks (and by making use of a few old contacts), he was offered a part-time position at the Food and Drug Administration as a research assistant. He found that he enjoyed working and could do his job well. After six months he was offered a full-time staff position.

Terry discontinued therapy at about the time that he was hired full-time. His therapy had involved an eight-month process of directly approaching various psychological "fires" and learning to cope with his fears. With these success experiences, he was able to slowly develop a sense of himself that was more in line with his actual abilities. Over the past few months he reported that his self-esteem had gradually improved and that his risk-avoidance habits were starting to decline. He still worried about performing various tasks and duties well, but he was now able to attempt these activities in spite of his apprehensions. Only rarely did his fears cause him to avoid these situations entirely. He was able to discuss possible negative consequences of his own and other people's actions. In short, although he stated that he still felt anxious about some situations, he felt that he was learning to control his fears. He felt better about himself and his work. Most noticeably, he was working steadily and routinely engaging in a wide variety of activities that he would not have even attempted just six months before.

PROGNOSIS

Terry's prognosis is excellent. When he began therapy, he had very low self-esteem and very little confidence in his abilities to perform even the most trivial task. Consequently he avoided situations that involved any amount of pressure or responsibility. His constant fears of being embarrassed or rejected also interfered with his interpersonal relationships. Without treatment, it is possible that Terry would have become severely agoraphobic, that is, so overwhelmed by his anxieties that he would be unable to leave his home or interact with other people. At the very least, it is likely that his ability to carry out his day-to-day tasks and his ability to maintain his relationships with his family, friends, and girlfriend would have continued to deteriorate.

Terry has reversed this trend. His paralyzing anxieties are greatly diminished, and his avoidance behavior for the most part has ended. By encouraging him to face feared situations directly and in small increments, Terry's therapy seems to have enabled him to approach a variety of previously avoided situations. In addition, he is able to apply this step-by-step approach and the relaxation training he received to problem areas that were never directly discussed in therapy. He also has been able to integrate the therapeutic gains of these isolated tasks and make progress in his more global problems involving his interpersonal relationships and his career. In addition to his behavioral gains, Terry has also built up his self-esteem and self-confidence, as evidenced by a shift in his therapy goals. Terry's initial aim in therapy was to avoid any pain, rejection, or pressure in his career or his interpersonal relationships. Now, however, his goal is to attempt to work through difficult tasks and to avoid situations only if they may be unduly stressful. This shift appears to be a good indication that Terry will maintain his therapeutic gains.

DISCUSSION

Terry's presenting complaints suggest the presence of a number of different anxiety disorders. For example, his refusal to engage in everyday tasks for fear of being ridiculed may be taken as evidence of a social phobia (a strict avoidance of potentially embarrassing or humiliating situations). However, he also fears a variety of situations that have no obvious evaluative component (e.g., washing his clothes), and he seems to be more apprehensive about actual failures than about the negative evaluations of these failures. Similarly, Terry's panicky feelings and obsessive thoughts about his fallibility might indicate the presence of panic disorder or obsessive-compulsive disorder, respectively. However, these symptoms are not sufficiently marked to fulfill the *DSM-IV* criteria for these diagnoses.

Terry is not unique. Researchers have noted an overlap between generalized anxiety disorder (GAD) and other anxiety disorders and mood disorders (Kent & Gorman, 1997; Newman & Bland, 1994; Weissman, 1990). Furthermore, research has linked greater comorbidity with poorer outcome (Borkovec, Abel, & Newman, 1995; Durham, Allen, & Hackett, 1997). Gorman (1987) suggests that GAD is often used as a residual category; that is, it provides a diagnosis for people who show symptoms of other anxiety disorders but who don't fulfill the *DSM-IV* criteria for any particular one. In any case, the therapist must take care to determine the appropriate diagnosis for each case.

In addition to his anxiety disorder, Terry's attitudes seem to reflect an underlying obsessive-compulsive personality disorder. His perfectionism, his preoccupation with details, his indecisiveness, and his conviction that other people are incompetent all indicate the presence of this personality disorder. In fact, it could be said that Terry's anxiety disorder first emerged when he became overwhelmed by these compulsive characteristics.

There are three atypical features in Terry's case. First, most people diagnosed with GAD suffer from diffuse, vaguely formed anxiety; rarely are they able to identify the exact source of their pervasive worries. Terry's fears, on the other hand, seem to be organized around issues clearly associated with his compulsive traits. In fact, this type of compulsive thinking occurs in only a small minority of the cases.

Second, GAD rarely becomes so thoroughly crippling. Most clients with this disorder report feeling "unhappy" or "uncomfortable" with their lives, and some suffer some minor disruption of their occupational and/or interpersonal functioning (for example, they might be passed over for promotion because of their tendency to hesitate, or their spouses might become irritated by their constant fears and worries). However, most people with GAD are usually able to function. In fact, it is estimated that over half of those who suffer from GAD never seek treatment (Weissman & Merikangas, 1986; Whitaker, et al., 1990). In contrast, in the course of a few years Terry had stopped working completely and was on the verge of becoming a total recluse. He was unable to complete even the simplest everyday tasks. In his therapist's words, "Terry didn't just suffer from severe anxiety, he really wasn't living a life."

Third, with the advent of cost-cutting efforts by third-party payers (generally known as managed care), eight months of weekly sessions is a luxury few clients would receive. Even liberal plans pay for no more than 26 sessions per year, but more commonly the cap is set at 6 to 12 sessions. Some authorize as few as 3! As a result, pharmacotherapy is becoming more common because it requires only periodic 15-minute updates with the psychiatrist. Psychotherapists typically respond to these limitations by focusing on major issues quickly and assigning more "homework." Harvey and Rapee (1995) assert that short-term cognitive-behavioral treatment for GAD might even be a cost-effective alternative to treatment with anxiolytics.

Research on Generalized Anxiety Disorder

Epidemiologic surveys have reported that GAD is a commonly observed anxiety disorder with prevalence rates ranging from 5.7 to 10.0 percent (Karno, et al., 1989; Newman & Bland, 1994; Whitaker et al., 1990).

Researchers have suggested a variety of biological causes for GAD, including genetic factors (Kendler, et al., 1991; Weissman, 1990), blunted hormone response (Abelson, et al., 1991), and neurological abnormalities (Wu, et al., 1991). Other researchers have suggested that GAD can be triggered by an environmental trauma such as rape (Frank & Anderson, 1987) or the death of a spouse (Jacobs & Kim, 1990). To date, the origins of GAD are unclear.

Generally speaking, three approaches are commonly used to treat GAD: cognitive-behavioral treatment, psychodynamic treatment, and pharmacological treatment. A variety of antianxiety medications have been found to be effective in reducing the anxiety of GAD patients (Downing & Rickels, 1985; Kragh-Sorensen, et al., 1990; Rickels, et al., 1988). Recent studies indicate that antidepressants (Hedges, et al., 1996; Rickels, Downing, Schweitzer, & Hassman, 1993) and even low-dose administrations of antipsychotic medications (Wurthmann, Klieser, & Lehmann, 1997) are also efficacious.

Of the two psychological treatments, cognitive-behavioral therapy is quite different from more traditional psychodynamic therapy. Cognitive-behavioral therapists have little interest in their clients' family histories or in their interpretations of past events, and consequently the histories they obtain tend to be limited to objective, factual information such as the chronology of the person's symptoms and the situations that seem to exacerbate these symptoms. Instead of investigating the clients' early traumas and dynamic interpretations of events, they take a more active role in directly modifying their clients' actual behaviors. That is, a client's specific complaints are not considered superficial or defensive but are usually taken at face value; seemingly minor, specific problems ("I can't buy myself a suit") are considered part of the "real problem" and addressed directly. Eventually the treatment of these individual concerns will be generalized to other life situations. Research has generally shown that cognitive-behavioral treatment for GAD is highly effective. For example, a recent meta-analysis of 35 studies published between 1974 and 1996 (Gould, Otto, Pollack, & Yap, 1997) found cognitive-behavioral therapy to be as effective as pharmacotherapy. In addition, cognitive-behavioral therapy showed greater maintenance of gains, whereas pharmacotherapy decreased in efficacy after discontinuation of medication.

Often this direct perspective is exactly what the clients are seeking. In other cases, though, clients become very uncomfortable with this approach. They feel that direct therapy is too "trivial" or "superficial," and they fear that they will never get to the "real problem." Most therapists feel strongly that a client's beliefs about the effectiveness of therapy is an important part of the treatment. At the present time, there is mounting evidence that cognitive-behavioral therapy is the most efficacious psychological treatment (Borkovec & Costello, 1993; Durham & Allan, 1993).

OBSESSIVE-COMPULSIVE DISORDER
Pharmacotherapy with Behavioral Therapy

PRESENTING COMPLAINT

Mary is a 68-year-old married homemaker in a middle-class suburb of Pittsburgh. She and her husband have been married for 46 years and have four children (three sons and a daughter) and 10 grandchildren; three children and eight grandchildren live in the same town. Mary and her husband are both the children of Polish immigrants and were raised in strict religious homes. They have continued this tradition in their own family, and Mary describes herself and her family as devout Catholics.

Throughout her life Mary has been neat and orderly. She has always valued cleanliness and has quite a disdain for dirt and clutter. She put great effort into keeping her house clean and tidy (which was quite a job with three sons). In addition, she has always been very careful in her personal habits. In the course of a typical day Mary would brush her teeth three or four times and wash her hands perhaps six to eight times.

Mary has also been very disciplined in her religious practices. For example, she often worried about whether she had confessed completely or whether she had performed various rituals correctly. Over the past few years, however, her religious worries have become markedly more intense, leading her to perform rituals that occupy several hours every day. Her increased anxiety seems to focus primarily on one issue: the taking of the wafer during holy communion.

The worship service of most Christian denominations includes some form of communion, a ritual where the congregation members partake of the body of Christ (usually symbolized by a small piece of bread or a wafer) and the blood of Christ (usually symbolized by wine or juice). According to traditional Catholic doctrine, the wafer and wine are not merely symbolic but are actually part of the Host and are themselves holy. As a result, only someone who is absolved of sin (a

23

priest) can touch the sacramental elements without contaminating them, and he must place the wafer directly into the mouth of the parishioner. Then in 1969, Pope Paul VI declared that this procedure was no longer necessary. This pronouncement caused great anxiety for many older, traditional Catholics; it was particularly distressing for Mary with her heightened fears of dirt. She dreaded contaminating the Host by touching the wafer. Much to her relief, her priest was very conservative in his practices and continued to place the wafers into the mouths of his parishioners.

But about 10 years ago this priest retired and was replaced by a younger man who encouraged his parishioners to take their wafers directly. Mary, along with a few others, insisted that he continue to feed her the wafer, and he honored her request. However, Mary's husband, children, and friends now took their wafers directly. Interestingly, Mary did not see her family members as contaminating the Host; rather, their contact with the Holy Spirit allowed the Host to be transferred to everything they touched. This idea began with their drive home from mass. The steering wheel, the door handles, and eventually the entire car was now holy and could not be contaminated. Any object at home that was touched, be it a chair, a table, the kitchen sink, and even the toilet, was imbued with the Holy Spirit and had to be avoided. At first Mary tried to keep track of what was touched and what wasn't, but she couldn't keep up. She also realized that her family could touch many things without her knowing it. Gradually she became agoraphobic and spent much of her time shut up in her room for fear of her contaminating touch. Yet her devotion to her husband and household compelled her to inhabit the common (now holy) areas of the house.

Eventually the extreme anxiety generated by this situation became too much to bear, and Mary settled on a compromise that entailed two types of responses. One response was to make herself as clean as possible before she touched the Holy Spirit, thus minimizing her contamination of the Host. Her handwashing became more frequent until she was at the point of washing her hands for six to eight *hours* every day. Not surprisingly her hands became cracked, raw, and bloody, which only exacerbated her anxiety. The other response was to try to rid an object of the Host before it could be contaminated with her touch. Mary's washing compulsions gradually escalated to the point where she would spend hours busily scrubbing fixtures that were already gleaming and wiping furniture that had no visible signs of dust. Mary mentioned that the most baffling problem was the faucet, which left her with a dilemma: she couldn't touch the faucet handles without first washing her hands, but she couldn't wash her hands without touching the faucet handles.

Perhaps the most tragic aspect of Mary's illness concerned her relationship with her family. She had to limit her contact with her loved ones, because they themselves were holy and would carry the Holy Spirit to other objects. When Mary insisted that they constantly wash their hands and take frequent showers (which was her attempt to rid the Host from their bodies), they responded with annoyance and resentment. It has been three years since she last kissed or hugged her husband or any of her children and grandchildren, and she has had no contact at all with her grandchildren for the past several months.

Mary was well aware of the illogical nature of her obsessions and the compulsive behavior needed to reduce her level of anxiety, but out of embarrassment she kept her religious anxieties to herself. Along with these anxieties, Mary suffered from intermittent periods of depression as a result of the uncontrollable nature of her compulsions and the increasingly limited contact with her family. Mary had always been in fairly good health, which was fortunate given her wariness of doctors. Because she lacked a primary-care physician, her raw hands and depressed affect went undiagnosed and untreated. Eventually her anxieties and depression became overwhelming, and Mary began to have persistent suicidal thoughts, which themselves were the height of sinfulness. Finally she confided in her husband. After hearing her concerns over contaminating the Holy Spirit, he urged her to discuss this problem with their priest. Entering a place of such intense holiness as their church was unthinkable for Mary, so they asked the priest to make a house call. It was not his first; he had been concerned over Mary's absence for some time and had made many visits (which always heightened her obsessions). On the priest's recommendation, Mary decided to seek help at a clinic.

PERSONAL HISTORY

Mary's childhood appears to be unremarkable. She is the second of five children, with an older brother, two younger brothers, and a younger sister. Her older brother served in World War II and one younger brother served in Korea, but neither was injured or seems to have been noticeably affected by their wartime experiences. This same younger brother died of a heart attack eight years before her admission to the clinic. Her other siblings are alive and keep in regular communication.

Although Mary described her upbringing as strict, she denies any cruelty or abuse, or even that it was oppressive. In Mary's words, "When I said a 'strict' upbringing, I meant disciplined, not mean or vindictive or anything like that." Mary could not think of any particularly upsetting event in her childhood or adolescence; instead, she said she had "the usual ups and downs children have."

As noted in her presenting complaint, Mary has a long history of mild obsessions and rituals. For example, she frequently had notions that some numbers were good and others were bad, which would lead her to perform minor compulsions such as turning light switches off or on a certain number of times or buying a certain number of items at a store or inviting a certain number of guests to a party. Mary is an avid gardener and enjoys growing many types of flowers. But after seeing petunias at a friend's funeral, she stopped growing them because "they would bring bad luck." (It is interesting that Mary had no fear of dirt or germs, particularly since her obsessions involve themes of contamination.) Mary also admits to having several minor phobias, including spiders, snakes, and electricity. Mary's problems with her anxieties have waxed and waned over the course of her lifetime, but generally these have not interfered with her duties as wife and mother. The one exception occurred when she was 22, when her first child was

15 months old and she was pregnant with her second. At that time she began having obsessional ideas about harming her son and did not want to be left in charge of him. Mary's mother moved in and took care of the son for about three months. Mary's obsessions gradually diminished as her pregnancy progressed, and she had no further obsessions after the birth of her second son.

Mary's family history shows no evidence of any mental illness. Mary's daughter, however, has been in therapy for depression and continues to take antidepressant medication. In addition, Mary's oldest son has intermittently suffered from periods of anxiety. From Mary's description, he seems to suffer from panic attacks, but because he has never sought treatment, no diagnosis of panic disorder can be confirmed.

CONCEPTUALIZATION AND TREATMENT

DSM-IV defines obsessive-compulsive disorder (OCD) as the existence of recurrent obsessions or compulsions (or both) of such severity that they cause distress or interfere with everyday activities and relationships.

Obsessions are unwanted, intrusive thoughts, ideas, or impulses, usually of a disturbing or senseless nature. Initially the person tries to ignore the obsession or mask it with some other thought, but the obsession persists. Obsessions take many forms (Baer, 1994; Henderson & Pollard, 1988; Leckman, Grice, Boardman, & Zhang, 1997); some of the more common obsessions are contamination (fear of dirt, germs, infection), doubt (wondering if one has completed simple tasks or has violated a law), somatic illness (fear that one will become ill), need for symmetry, saving/hoarding (fearing that items can't be thrown out), violence (fear of harming a spouse, killing a child), and promiscuity (fear that one might not control one's sexual behavior). About 60 percent suffer from multiple obsessions. Obsessions are almost always greatly anxiety-provoking, both because of their inherently upsetting nature and because in most cases they lead more or less directly to specific compulsions. The person understands that the obsessional thoughts are illogical but nevertheless feels unable to control them.

Compulsions are ritualized, repetitive behaviors performed to reduce anxiety, often the anxiety generated by obsessional thoughts. Sometimes, though, compulsions are performed in a stereotyped way or simply because the person somehow feels that the behavior must be performed. The most common compulsions are checking, washing, counting, asking advice and/or confessing, needing symmetry and precision, repeating, counting, and hoarding (Baer, 1994; Henderson & Pollard, 1988; Leckman et al., 1997). About half of those who suffer from OCD have multiple compulsions. Not all compulsions are expressed in observable behavior, though. Some people engage in covert rituals, such as silently reciting stereotyped statements or counting to themselves. Covert compulsions are harder to recognize, but once they are identified they can be treated in the same manner as overt rituals. For a small group of patients, such as those who suffer from obsessional perfectionism, obsessions do not lead to identifiable rituals. These cases are the most resistant to behavior therapy.

As they are with their obsessions, most people are greatly distressed by their compulsive behavior. The person recognizes that the compulsive behavior serves little practical function and is excessive and disruptive. Usually the person attempts to resist the compulsion, at least initially, but anxiety increases to the point where the compulsion must be performed. People with OCD do not enjoy the compulsive behavior. Behavior patterns that are initially enjoyable but become uncontrollable, such as compulsive gambling, are not true compulsions and are probably better thought of as addictions.

Mary's deep-seated and persistent fear of contaminating the Holy Spirit followed the pattern of a classic contamination obsession, but with one unusual twist: Mary wasn't afraid of being contaminated; instead, she was afraid of being the contaminating agent through her own impure nature. This obsession led her to perform the typical washing compulsions of excessive handwashing and persistent washing and wiping of everything (and everyone) in her home.

Goodman and his associates (Goodman, Price, Rasmussen, Mazure, Fleischmann, et al., 1989; Goodman, Price, Rasmussen, Mazure, Delgado, et al., 1989) developed the Yale-Brown Obsessive-Compulsive Scale (Y-BOCS), which provides an objective measure of the severity of OCD that is independent of the content of the obsessions and compulsions and is not affected by other disorders the person might suffer concurrently. It has been demonstrated to be an accurate and sensitive measure of OCD (Nakagawa, et al., 1996). The Y-BOCS is administered by the therapist and consists of 10 questions, 5 concerning the severity of obsessions and 5 concerning the severity of compulsions. The therapist scores each item from 0 (no pathology) to 4 (extreme pathology). Thus, total scores can range from 0 to 40.

During Mary's initial interview she detailed the intrusiveness of her obsessions and compulsions and the anxiety they provoked. She scored a 32 on the Y-BOCS, indicating severe to extreme problems with virtually every aspect of her obsessions and compulsions. Of more immediate concern, however, was Mary's severe depression, as indicated by her depressed mood, lethargy, and suicidal ideas. Her score of 34 on the Hamilton Rating Scale for Depression (HRSD) (Hamilton, 1967) indicated severely depressed mood. At this point it was important to determine whether Mary suffered from a concurrent major depressive episode or whether her depression was secondary to her OCD. Because Mary had no history of previous depressed episodes, and because her depression appeared to result from her inability to control her compulsions and from her consequent estrangement from her family, her therapist concluded that her depression was most likely secondary to her OCD.

The majority of OCD patients are treated on a five- to eight-week outpatient treatment program. However, the severity of Mary's depressed mood, including her inability to care for herself and her suicidal thoughts, warranted her admission as an inpatient.

The initial goal of therapy was to relieve Mary's depression. She was prescribed clomipramine (known by the trade name Anafranil). Anafranil is one of the family of drugs known as tricylic antidepressants and is especially indicated for patients suffering from obsessional ideas.

As is true with most cases involving pharmacological treatment, care must be taken to avoid or at least minimize the side effects of medication. This is particularly important with elderly patients. Mary's dose was gradually increased until she was taking 150 milligrams per day, which is a moderate dose. Fluoxetine (Prozac) is also commonly prescribed for OCD and has been shown to be effective in double-blind, placebo controlled studies (Tollefson et al., 1994). Both are roughly equal in their efficaciousness; use is determined primarily by the consideration of side effects.

During her stay at the hospital, Mary participated in milieu therapy, which consisted of general supportive care, group discussion sessions, and education as to the nature of OCD. At the same time, Mary's husband and her children still living nearby were also provided with education explaining OCD as a disorder and suggestions for supportive care at home, including information on the action and possible side effects of Mary's medication.

Once Mary's suicidal thoughts receded, she was discharged home. Her depression began to lift after about four weeks, and at this time behavior therapy began. It is common practice with severely depressed patients that behavior therapy is delayed until their depression begins to abate. Mary's behavior therapy consisted of two elements: exposure therapy and behavioral contracting.

As the name suggests, exposure therapy calls for the patient to be exposed to the object of the obsessions and then prevented from performing the compulsion. Gradually the patient's anxiety will begin to decrease without having resorted to the compulsion, and through extinction the connection between the obsession and the compulsion will be weakened and eventually broken.

In Mary's case the object of the obsession was the Holy Spirit, so her therapist arranged for a priest to come to her home and begin imbuing objects with the Holy Spirit. Because Mary's obsessions began with the holy wafer, this was used in her therapy. At first the priest handled a wafer and then placed his hands on the kitchen table. She was not allowed to wash the table beforehand, nor was she allowed to wipe the Host away. Mary was able to tolerate this situation surprisingly easily, perhaps because of her four weeks on Anafranil. As she became accustomed to the Host on the table, the therapist then had Mary touch the table herself. Again, Mary was not allowed to wash her hands or the table. At first Mary showed moderate levels of anxiety to this procedure, but gradually her fears subsided. Finally Mary was asked to hold a wafer herself. After a few sessions she was able to do this with little anxiety, and the exposure portion of her treatment was considered complete.

The second stage of Mary's behavior therapy was behavior contracting. Mary was instructed to make specific agreements that would limit her compulsive behavior. These contracts were to be in writing and signed by Mary, her husband, and her therapist. One of her initial contracts was that she would wash her hands no more than 10 times a day. Soon this agreement was amended to allow only five daily handwashings. Another contract was to plant petunias in her garden. Generally these behavior contracts provide the patient with a formal way to resist the need to perform compulsions and with support from others to aid in this resistance.

After eight weekly sessions of behavior therapy, Mary's obsessional thoughts and compulsive behaviors were reduced dramatically. She washed her hands fewer than five times a day, and she made no attempt to clean objects around the home. Most importantly, she no longer felt the need to avoid her family members. Her scores on both the Y-BOCS and the HRSD were 9, showing mild, subclinical levels of disturbance on both measures. Her medication dose was reduced to a maintenance level of 50 milligrams per day, and her therapy was reduced to "checkup" sessions every 90 days.

PROGNOSIS

Mary was seen for follow-up one year after treatment. She reported relatively little disturbance from her obsessional thoughts and a virtual absence of compulsive behavior. She had little difficulty fulfilling her various behavioral contracts during the year. Mary was most pleased with her relationships with her family, which she described as close and supportive. Her contracting was discontinued, as were her checkup sessions. A follow-up session one year later revealed no substantial changes in the intervening year. At both her one-year and her two-year follow-up session, she scored below 10 on the Y-BOCS and the HRSD.

Mary died of a massive heart attack about five years later. In those five years there was little evidence of any relapse of her OCD symptoms. Her husband reported that she continued to have mild obsessional thoughts, mostly related to doubt concerning her participation in religious rituals. However, he stated that as far as he could tell, Mary's obsessions had become less severe and less frequent over time. He could not think of a clear instance of a compulsion in the past few years.

DISCUSSION

OCD has long been thought of as a very rare disorder, but recent evidence indicates that it is much more common than previously believed (Henderson & Pollard, 1988; Rasmussen & Eisen, 1990; Regier, Narrow, & Rae, 1990). Community surveys have reported prevalence rates ranging from 2.2 percent (Kramer et al., 1986) to 2.8 percent (Henderson & Pollard, 1988) in the general population. Rasmussen and Eisen outlined four reasons why OCD might have been underdiagnosed in the past. First, as was true with Mary, patients realize how "crazy" their obsessions and compulsions would sound to others and therefore hesitate to discuss their symptoms. Second, many professionals have a narrow view of OCD as including only certain types of obsessions and compulsions and thus fail to recognize OCD in some of their patients. Third, many OCD cases, particularly those that involve bizarre obsessions, might simply be misdiagnosed, usually as schizophrenia. An associated problem is that OCD is often overlooked in the presence of other psychiatric disorders. For example, researchers (Rasmussen & Eisen, 1989; Weissman & Merikangas, 1986) reported high rates of concurrent anxiety and mood disorders in their OCD patients. Baer et al. (1990) found that over half of their sample of OCD patients also suffered from at least one personality disorder; McKay, Neziroglu, Todaro, and Yaryura-Tobias (1996) found an average of four personality disorders in their sample. Interestingly, the most common personality disorders were borderline and histrionic; only 7 percent of their sample were diagnosed as having obsessive-compulsive personality disorder (OCPD). The link between OCPD and OCD appears to be more phenomenological than genetic (Diaferia et al., 1997). Finally, because OCD was believed to be so rare, most professionals did not routinely screen for it in their initial patient evaluations. Weissman and Merikangus (1986) suggested that many family members of patients with anxiety disorders might also suffer from an anxiety disorder but go untreated, and they recommended that professionals routinely inquire as to the status of the family members of patients with anxiety disorders. Recent research confirms this family link. In a study of 466 first-degree relatives of 100 OCD patients, Pauls et al. (1995) reported a 10.3 percent rate of OCD among the relatives, with a further 7.9 percent showing subclinical OCD symptoms. The corresponding rates for 133 relatives of 33 control subjects were 1.9 percent and 2.0 percent, respectively.

OCD prevalence rates do not vary significantly between the sexes (Karno, Golding, Sorenson, & Burnam, 1988) or across different cultures and nationalities (Marks, 1986). OCD also remains stable over time, with roughly equal prevalence rates being reported among adolescents (Flament et al. 1988; Weissman & Merikangas, 1986) and the elderly (Kramer et al., 1986).

Research on OCD shows that Mary's case was typical in many ways. She first developed obsessional thoughts and compulsive behaviors in adolescence, and these patterns continued off and on for the rest of her life. Although it is unusual for someone to first seek treatment at such an advanced age, historical events provide an explanation. Like many people with mild to moderate obsessional thoughts, Mary was able to remain in control, though undoubtedly she suffered persistent anxiety. But this control was built on the relatively fragile foundation of strictly observing numerous small rules and rituals; her defenses collapsed after the seemingly minor change in the communion service.

Mary's case was typical in other ways. She suffered from a secondary depression, which is quite common among OCD patients, affecting perhaps 60 percent. At Mary's clinic, 17 of 18 patients with severe OCD symptoms who did not respond to drugs or psychotherapy had comorbid major depressive disorder; the one remaining had dysthymia (S. A. Rasmussen, personal communication, September 1990). Mary received a combined treatment involving medication and exposure therapy, which is also quite typical. Between 80 to 85 percent of OCD patients receive both medications and behavior therapy (S. A. Rasmussen, personal communication, May 1992). As is true with many OCD patients, other family members showed signs of mental illness. Although there was no evidence of mental illness in Mary's family history, her daughter and one of her sons showed signs of depression and panic disorder, respectively. Finally, Mary suffered from a contamination obsession and washing compulsions, which are very common among OCD patients.

A typical outpatient program would consist of four weeks of education, two weeks of family discussion, and two weeks of exposure therapy and behavior contracting. Most programs entail a total of 15 to 20 hours of direct treatment and have been shown to be effective in controlled studies (Lindsey, Crino, & Andrews, 1997; Van Noppen, Steketee, McCorkle, & Pato, 1997).

A wide variety of antianxiety and antidepressant medications have been prescribed to combat the anxiety and depression that accompany OCD, as well as the OCD symptoms themselves. These may be employed with or without cognitive-behavioral therapy. When these patients do not respond to medications or behavioral therapy, neurosurgery in the form of cingulotomy is available. Baer et al. (1995) reported that of 18 OCD patients receiving neurosurgery, 5 showed good improvement and 3 showed partial improvement. These authors warn, however, that neurosurgery is used only for severe cases that do not respond to aggressive pharmacological and behavioral treatments.

Mary's case was unique in that her contamination obsession took a curious form: she saw herself as the source of the contamination and was afraid of desecrating the objects and people around her. Thus her handwashing ritual was aimed at preventing her from infecting others instead of vice versa. Mary developed a compromise compulsion of wiping and washing all affected surfaces, which ironically resulted in washing the sacred Host down the drain. This behavior takes the form of a classical washing compulsion.

Religiousness and OCD

Cases where the person is reacting to religious beliefs and ideals naturally raise the following question: To what extent does religion contribute to psychopathology? This is an interesting and important question that merits examination.

In his work with OCD patients, S. A. Rasmussen (personal communication, May 1992) has found that religious beliefs tend to influence the types of obsessions a person may develop. Deeply religious patients are more likely than other patients to report obsessional thoughts involving religious blasphemies, sexual promiscuity, and uncontrolled violence. However, these patients do not differ from other patients in the overall severity of their symptoms. Greenberg (1984) has found that for a number of different forms of psychopathology, religiousness affects the *content* of a person's disturbance rather than its incidence or severity. Historically, a rise and fall of religious themes in psychopathology corresponds to the fluctuating importance of organized religion in the general culture. A similar result was reported by Muris, Merckelbach, & Clavan (1997), who noted that although pathological obsessions and compulsions are more intense and more frequent than normal ruminations and rituals, they were not fundamentally different in content.

DISSOCIATIVE IDENTITY DISORDER
Psychotherapy with Hypnosis

PRESENTING COMPLAINT

Sherry is a 31-year-old nurse's aide who has received inpatient psychiatric care off and on for the past five years. Approximately two weeks after her most recent readmission, she became very confused about her surroundings and complained that "everything had changed." She demanded to know who had rearranged the hospital and the grounds, and she repeatedly asked to see people who didn't exist, both patients and staff members. When staff members attempted to calm her, she became verbally and physically abusive, shouting obscenities and swinging her fists.

Sherry had been admitted with a diagnosis of schizophrenia, disorganized type. She had a history of previous hospitalizations, and her strange and irrational behavior seemed to be clear evidence of yet another psychotic episode. Other therapists, however, believed that Sherry's behavior might be evidence of a dissociative state, a state of consciousness where one part of her awareness is split off from another. Sherry was given the Hypnotic Induction Profile (HIP) and was found to be highly hypnotizable, scoring a 4 out of a possible 5. While in a hypnotic trance, she gave the present date as being eight months earlier than it in fact was and stated that she was at a hospital over a thousand miles away. The date she gave and her description of the hospital corresponded to a clinic she attended just prior to her most recent admission. The therapist who hypnotized her found that she had no memory of anything after leaving this clinic; it was as if she had lost the last eight months of her life. Through hypnosis, Sherry was able to experience age regression (a reliving of the past as though it were the present) to the time of her earlier hospitalization. After the session involving age regression, she was able to reorient herself to her present time and location, and her "psychotic" behavior diminished.

Amnesic periods were not new to Sherry; she frequently complained of episodes for which she had no memory. Sherry is a quiet, demure, and conscientious person, but her behavior often changes during her amnesic episodes. According to the reports of her friends, family, and past therapists, her behavior during these blackouts was often hostile, angry, and self-destructive. Although Sherry could not remember what she did during these episodes, she would often find physical evidence of odd behavior. Sometimes she would notice new cuts and bruises, and on several occasions she woke up to find herself in bed with a strange man after having had unprotected sex. For Sherry, the knowledge that she could not control her own behavior was positively frightening.

A recent blackout period occurred about three weeks ago. Under hypnosis Sherry experienced age regression back three weeks to the time of this amnesic episode. After a minute or so, she suddenly looked up at the therapist and sneered, "What the hell do you want?" Her voice and tone had changed completely from the shy woman who had gone into the hypnotic trance; she was now hostile, angry, and sarcastic. The therapist was somewhat startled by Sherry's sudden change in tone, but he remained calm and asked Sherry who she was. She responded, "Why should I answer you; I don't owe you anything. But what the hell; it doesn't make any difference. You can call me Karla."

The therapist then asked "Karla" what had happened just now (that is, during the amnesic episode Sherry experienced three weeks ago). Karla made it clear that she was irritated at the intrusion on her time and gruffly explained what happened. She had just picked up a man at a bar with the intention of going back to his apartment. But Sherry had spoiled her fun by crying at the bar, causing the man to lose interest. Determined to punish Sherry, Karla threatened to inflict a deep cut on Sherry's leg. With intense hatred and bitterness, Karla ran an imaginary knife over a recently healed cut on her leg, shouting, "I'll show her; I'll really cut her this time! I'll go to sleep and let her find it!" She then closed her eyes. When her eyes reopened, her voice and manner were those of Sherry. Sherry gently touched the wound and sobbed quietly. When the therapist asked her how she got this cut, she appeared to be confused and hesitantly replied, "Well, I . . . I don't know. I guess I ran into something."

PERSONAL HISTORY

Sherry has a twin sister. They both had suffered numerous episodes of physical abuse and neglect throughout their childhoods. At one time their mother bloodied Sherry's nose, and on another occasion she broke Sherry's tooth with her fist. Both of these events occurred before the age of 4. Once Sherry's mother also threw a pot of boiling water at her in a fit of rage, leaving her with second-degree burns on her arms and chest. Sherry's parents divorced after a bitter marriage lasting five years. Two years later her mother remarried. Unfortunately for the twins, their new stepfather was also violent; as his primary form of punishment he would beat the twins using a board studded with nails. After three or four years Sherry and her sister moved in with their biological father. Although he was more caring than the mother and stepfather, he nevertheless was capable of abuse, particularly during his frequent alcoholic binges. On these occasions he would beat the twin girls with a belt buckle. After several years Sherry's mother obtained a court order that gave her custody of the children. Immediately after winning their custody, however, the mother sent the twins off to live at a strict boarding school. Sherry's mediocre grades precluded any realistic chance of being admitted to a good college, so after graduation she joined the Army and was separated from her sister for the first time.

For most of her life, Sherry dealt with the anxiety of this abuse and neglect by dissociating the traumas onto her sister. That is, she frequently experienced her physical and psychological pain as having happened to her twin sister instead of to herself. For example, Sherry stated that her mother once threw boiling water at her sister. However, her mother's and sister's testimony (the former describing an "accident"), as well as her medical records, show that in actuality Sherry was the one who was scalded as a child. It was not until she was separated from her

39

sister, however, that she began to experience uncontrollable amnesic periods.

When Sherry joined the Army, she had hopes of being trained as a nurse, but her Army career had barely begun when trouble arose. During basic training she began to notice long periods of time that she could not remember. Her behavior during these periods was reported to be wild and unpredictable; she would often begin violent arguments with other recruits, and on several occasions she had sexual relations with male soldiers on the base or with strange men she would pick up at one of the local bars. Sherry had no recollection of these actions, and at the time suspected that she was being singled out unfairly, though she was never able to provide an alibi due to her frequent blackouts. She also made several suicidal gestures during her amnesic episodes, usually in the form of cutting herself on the forearms and/or taking overdoses of tranquilizers. In addition, she had gone to the camp infirmary on several occasions and complained of auditory hallucinations and depression. As a result of her bizarre and disruptive behavior, Sherry received a psychiatric discharge and was hospitalized with a diagnosis of schizophrenia, disorganized type. While in the hospital she was given chlorpromazine (Thorazine), an antipsychotic medication, which did little to relieve her symptoms.

Over the next five years Sherry was admitted to several different psychiatric institutions and received several different diagnoses, including bipolar disorder, major depression, schizophrenia, and borderline personality disorder. As a result she has been treated with lithium and a variety of antidepressant and antipsychotic medications. All of these efforts, however, had little lasting effect.

CONCEPTUALIZATION AND TREATMENT

Three aspects of Sherry's history were fundamental in the conceptualization of her case. First, Sherry has a strong dissociative capacity, as evidenced by her high hypnotizability. Second, she suffered relatively severe and persistent abuse and neglect as a child. Third, and most crucial, consciousness was split between two very different personalities ("Sherry" and "Karla"). These characteristics are the hallmarks of someone suffering from dissociative identity disorder (DID), formerly called multiple personality disorder.

People with strong dissociative capacities, even those who have suffered significant childhood traumas, do not necessarily develop alter personalities. Generally they will utilize their dissociation skill as a defense against particularly painful experiences, a sort of emotional buffer, simply by "zoning out." In some cases, however, the dissociation processes themselves become involuntary and uncontrollable. Blackout periods and reports of uncharacteristic behavior are indications of these involuntary dissociations. Finding themselves unable to control their behavior, these people are then compelled (either by their own fears or by the insistence of others) to seek psychological help. This seems to be the case with Sherry. Based on this conceptualization, the therapist, a psychiatirst, established a diagnosis of DID with histrionic, psychotic, and depressive features and discontinued her anti-psychotic medication, which in any event did not seem to be effective.

Sherry's therapy was organized into five stages. The first was aimed at recognizing and eventually controlling her dissociations. Using Sherry's hypnotizability as a therapeutic tool, the therapist attempted to provide structure to her spontaneous dissociative states through formal hypnosis. The therapist regularly contacted Karla during hypnotic trances. As therapy progressed, Sherry was gradually trained in self-hypnosis techniques, which gave her a measure of control over her dissociative states.

The second stage of psychotherapy involved setting limits on her self-destructive tendencies. Using self-hypnosis, she was taught to reexperience her past psychological traumas and urged to not blame herself for her past abuse. Sherry was also taught to express her emotions more openly in an attempt to increase outlets for her hostility other than through her dissociative states. On a more behavioral level, Sherry was frequently hospitalized for short periods to prevent her from carrying out her suicidal threats. In addition, antidepressant medication was administered to counteract her depressive symptoms.

The third stage of therapy focused on the transference between the patient and the therapist. Given Sherry's history of almost continuous abuse and neglect, one would not expect her to trust her therapist fully and to believe that he truly cared for her welfare. Indeed, initially she suspected that the therapist was interested in her only because she was a fascinating case that would lend him prestige if he could cure her. In this light her frequent suicidal gestures were seen as tests of his commitment. Would he remain concerned for her welfare even at the risk of professional failure? At this stage it was essential for the therapist to face the possibility of failure as well as to convey a genuine interest in her well-being in spite of her suicidal gestures and her resistance to therapy.

The fourth, and perhaps the most crucial, stage of therapy involved integrating the two personalities into one being. To accomplish this, Sherry first had to be convinced that the hostile and disruptive aspects of her subconscious were valuable and should not be suppressed. Indeed, the assertiveness and self-confidence expressed by Karla were assets that should be incorporated into a more well-rounded personality. One technique that promoted this integration was giving "equal time" to both "Sherry" and "Karla." In this way, Sherry learned to tolerate Karla's more aggressive emotions, thus reducing the need for Karla to rebel and undermine Sherry. Similarly, Karla was taught that Sherry's good-natured attributes could be quite useful in forming and maintaining relationships with others. Over a period of years, both personalities gradually incorporated elements of the other, and the shifts between them became smoother and less disruptive. After approximately three years of therapy, Sherry reported that she was aware of Karla for the first time. She described this realization as "opening a door in myself." Karla then added, "I'm in here too. We're both here. It's not one or the other; we're together."

Another important aspect of this integration was to have the patient understand the traumatic memories and events that caused the dissociations in the first place. However, the therapist must be cautious in this endeavor. On the one hand, rushing a patient to relive early traumas too quickly can exacerbate the dissociations. On the other hand, failing to deal with repressed traumas may perpetuate the need for dissociations in the future. In general, these patients are encouraged to confront and accept their painful memories, to gain control over these memories, and to restructure these memories in a way that is consistent with their emerging unified self-image.

In Sherry's case, her mother's persistent manipulation and neglect engendered extreme emotional dependence, which led to persistent feelings of guilt and obligation. One example of Sherry's sense of obligation toward her mother is that she currently pays her mother's bills and provides her mother with a rent-free room in her apartment, this in spite of the fact that her mother is financially secure. In fact, because Sherry has spent a great deal of the past 10 years in psychiatric hospitals, her mother is much better off than she is. To add insult to injury, Sherry's mother shows little appreciation for this help. She rarely attends family therapy sessions with Sherry, and when she does, she usually shows much more concern for her own interests (e.g., vacation plans, clothing purchases) than for her daughter's improvement. Understandably, Sherry was very resentful of her mother's callous selfishness, yet she felt unable to challenge her directly. Instead she would criticize herself for being so weak and dependent. Often this self-derogation and repressed anger was expressed by Karla, who would cut Sherry's wrists or perform other acts of self-mutilation to punish Sherry for being so weak. Many times after paying her mother's bills, Sherry would emerge from the bathroom with her arms dripping blood. She was saying to her mother symbolically what she couldn't say directly: "You are bleeding me to death."

To prevent Sherry from venting her frustration in self-destructive ways in the future, her therapist urged her to ask her mother to pay her own bills and move out of her apartment. This confrontation was not without some cost; Sherry entered a severe depression after this episode. However, she responded well to antidepressant medication and began to function better after her recovery.

Finally, the fifth stage of Sherry's therapy involved interaction management as a means of helping her to avoid the pathologic compliance and repressed resentment that characterized her previous relationships. Interaction management is a therapy technique used to teach the patient more effective ways of dealing with other people through the use of role-playing and modeling. As a part of this therapy, Sherry attended conjoint sessions with her mother, her sister, and, later, her boyfriend. The therapist then provided Sherry with ways to react to the various interpersonal demands of these people more assertively.

The course of Sherry's therapy was very gradual. For several months she received intensive treatment as an inpatient before she was released and continued psychotherapy on an outpatient basis. After three years both personalities had finally recognized each other, and shortly thereafter she began a relationship with a man. Her outpatient therapy, which took the form of frequent office consultations and occasional active interventions, continued for two more years. During this time Sherry broke up with her boyfriend and entered a severe depressive episode. However, she made no serious suicide attempts; she was given antidepressant medication and was able to remain an outpatient. Her outpatient therapy drew to a close about one year later. Approximately three years later Sherry was raped. At that time she was brought to the hospital in a confused and agitated state. Hypnotic regression enabled her to relive the painful events of the rape and to convince herself that she was not responsible for the trauma. She was released from the hospital after two weeks. For the past few years Sherry has received supportive psychotherapy off and on at her own request.

PROGNOSIS

Sherry has made steady progress since the beginning of therapy. Over the course of several years, her uncontrolled bursts of anger and self-mutilating behaviors for the most part have ceased, she has developed a more equitable relationship with her mother, and her therapy has progressed from inpatient care to outpatient care to intermittent support sessions. However, she remains vulnerable to future dissociative episodes in response to severe stress, particularly if it involves sexual or financial exploitation. An example of this vulnerability was evidenced after her rape. Although Sherry had been in therapy for years, she suffered from uncontrollable dissociations as a result of this painful trauma.

Sherry's power to dissociate is a two-edged sword. While her ability to separate and repress the traumatic events of her life might insulate her from severely painful experiences, it can also leave her open to uncontrollable dissociations that frequently result in self-damaging acts or unacceptable behavior. Sherry's continued adjustment will depend on her ability to learn to use her powers of self-hypnosis to gain mastery over her intrapsychic processes through integrating her two personalities. Ellason and Ross (1996, 1997) found that treatment for multiples was especially efficacious after an integration had been achieved. Although the prognosis for Sherry is generally good, her therapist remains cautious about her ability to cope independently with painful, traumatic experiences. It remains to be seen whether Sherry will be able to control her dissociations in the face of severe life pressures.

DISCUSSION

Historically DID has been only rarely diagnosed. However, the prevalence rates in the United States and Canada (but not elsewhere) have grown dramatically in recent years. Ross (1997) goes so far as to assert that DID, or at least pathological dissociative features, are "quite common." But this is a minority view. Until recently, little has been known about this disorder aside from anecdotal clinical reports. Some researchers have begun to specialize in treating DID patients (often called "multiples"), and they are beginning to publish data based on their own samples (Bliss, 1984; Coons, Bowman, & Milstein, 1988; Ellason & Ross, 1995). Still, the number of multiples seen at any one clinic is usually relatively small; therefoe it requires much effort to collect usable samples. For example, Philip Coons (Coons et al., 1988) reported that it took 13 years to collect data on 50 multiples from his personal practice! To speed up data collection on samples large enough to generate reliable results, researchers have utilized some innovative techniques. One strategy is to survey many different therapists, each of whom might have treated only one or two multiples (Putnam et al., 1986). Another strategy is to combine data from different clinics that specialize in DID. In this way Ross et al. (1990) collected a sample of 102 multiples across four sites.

Common Characteristics

Research findings from the studies cited above have been remarkably consistent. Most multiples are women in their twenties and thirties who first experienced dissociation in childhood or early adolescence. The vast majority have suffered some form of severe abuse or trauma. Putnam et al. (1986) report that during childhood 45 percent of their sample personally witnessed someone's violent death. Coons and Milstein (1986) recorded the following types of abuse:

Types of Abuse or Trauma in 20 DID Patients

Patient	Age	Sex	Abuse	Abuser(s)	Frequency
1	15	M	incest, beating	father	repeatedly
2	28	M	severe toileting	mother	repeatedly
3	47	M	beating	father	repeatedly
4	14	F	incest, beating	father	repeatedly
5	17	F	incest	father	repeatedly
6	19	F	incest	father	once
			beating	stepfather	repeatedly
7	21	F	incest	father, brothers	repeatedly
			beating	father	repeatedly
8	22	F	sexual fondling	grmoth's friend	repeatedly
9	23	F	neglect	parents	repeatedly
			incest	uncle	once
10	23	F	incest	father,bro,uncle	repeatedly
			beating	father, brothers	repeatedly

11	26	F	incest	stepfather	once
			uncle, cousin	once	
12	29	F	verbal abuse	father	repeatedly
13	31	F	incest,beating	father, brother	repeatedly
14	32	F	incest	father	repeatedly
15	32	F	beating	mother	repeatedly
16	33	F	beating	husband	repeatedly
17	35	F	sexual fondling	father, brother	once
			watched sister burn to death		
18	42	F	incest	uncle	once
			beating	father	repeatedly
19	44	F	incest, burned	father	repeatedly
20	46	F	sexual fondling	stepfather	repeatedly
			pushed dn stairs	stepfather	once

From *The Journal of Clinical Psychiatry, 47:3,*106–110
Copyright 1986, Physicians Postgraduate Press.

Another common characteristic of multiples is that they are highly hypnotizable. This characteristic is shared by patients who suffer from other dissociative disorders such as amnesia (memory loss) and fugue (forgetting one's identity and assuming a new identity). Many therapists see the ability to be hypnotized as a fundamental marker for the ability to dissociate, and some have advocated its use in diagnostic screening and treatment (Peterson, 1996; Spiegel, 1986). A related point is that multiples typically developed elaborate fantasy worlds in childhood, which often contained imaginary playmates that shared the child's pain. In Sherry's case, her twin sister may have fulfilled this role.

Some researchers argue that the concepts of hypnosis and dissociation are unclear and urge caution in the use of hypnotizability as a clinical tool (e.g., Frankel, 1990; Hilgard, 1988). Others note that memories are unstable and susceptible to suggestion (e.g., Loftus, 1993), thus casting doubts on the accuracy of repressed memories and, by extension, the validity of DID as a diagnostic category (Merskey, 1995; Spanos, 1996).

Drawing on the common characteristics he observed in multiples, Kluft (1984) developed a four-factor theory of DID. First, children who have the ability to dissociate their experiences are particularly vulnerable to develop DID. Second, traumatic events or circumstances can trigger these dissociative abilities into action as a way of escaping these painful experiences. Third, children will use available psychological resources such as imaginary companions as models for their alter personalities. Finally, lack of healthy experiences with role models will fixate the pattern of dissociation. Initially, alter personalities serve to shield the child from painful trauma, but eventually they might take on lives of their own to the point where the person loses control over his or her behavior.

The Organization of Multiple Identities

In DID, consciousness is divided among two or more distinct and unique personalities, each with its own system of social relationships and behavior patterns. Different personalities have even shown different allergic reactions, food preferences, alcohol tolerances, and medication side effects (Putnam et al., 1986). In a particularly intriguing study, Miller et al. (1991) had an ophthalmologist who was blind to subject condition conduct detailed eye examinations on the different personalities of 20 DID patients and a matched group of 20 control subjects who role-played different personalities. There was much more variation among the personalities of DID patients than among the role-played personalities of the controls on a number of objective measurements and clinical assessments.

The number of alter personalities varies widely among multiples, ranging from 1 (as in Sherry's case) to 60 (Putnam et al., 1986). Although the average number of alter personalities is around 15, this figure is thrown off somewhat by a few patients with very many alter personalities. For example, Putnam et al. (1986) report an average of 13.3 alter personalities, but the most commonly reported (i.e., modal) number was only 3. They also found an association between the number of reported childhood traumas and the number of reported personalities.

There is a wide variation in the characteristics of alter personalities. Most multiples report one or more personalities who are children under age 12, and over half have personalities of the opposite sex. At any one time only one personality tends to dominate the person's consciousness. As was true in Sherry's case, the shifts between these different personalities can be quite abrupt. Putnam et al. (1986) found that the switch between personalities often takes just seconds, and for over 90 percent of their sample the average duration of a personality switch was less than five minutes.

Generally speaking, alter personalities form three basic clusters: "core" personalities, aggressive personalities, and intermediary personalities. Core personalities contain the characteristics that describe the patient as he or she is generally known to most people. These personalities are usually meek, passive, and obedient, and they aim to please others and avoid pain.

A second cluster consists of one or more personalities that are self-confident, outgoing, and assertive. Sometimes these personalities become aggressive, reckless, and/or promiscuous. Many times these personalities attack the people who have mistreated them in their lives (e.g., abusive or exploitive parents, spouses, bosses), but usually their anger is directed toward the core personality. Sometimes they might attempt to "punish" the core personality through suicide attempts or by inflicting painful wounds. At other times these aggressive personalities may take advantage of the core personality in more subtle ways. In one case, a man's aggressive personality wrecked a car the core personality had borrowed from a friend. Subsequently, this alternate let the core personality "wake up" at the scene of the accident to explain the wreck to the police and the irate owner.

A third cluster includes personalities that act as intermediaries between the submissive and the aggressive personalities. Often these intermediaries serve as referees to reconcile the different needs of the other personalities. They also seem to function as rational spokespersons who can sympathize with the meek core personalities and yet understand the wild and disruptive actions of the aggressive personalities. Therapists using hypnosis find it helpful to make use of these intermediary personalities at the beginning stages of therapy. These personalities tend to be fully aware of the actions of all other personalities, and they are relatively receptive to treatment.

The present case is somewhat unusual in that only two distinct personalities, "Sherry" and "Karla," emerged. In one sense, it was fortunate that Sherry had only one alter personality. Generally, the more complex and varied the personalities, the more difficult the therapy. On the other hand, the absence of any intermediary personality may have impeded the initial reconciliation.

Interactions among different personalities have two common properties (Spiegel, 1996). First, these interactions are characterized by *asymmetric amnesia*, also called directional awareness. There are many patterns of asymmetric amnesia. Typically the core personality has no direct knowledge of the other personalities, whereas these other personalities have at least a limited knowledge of the core. In most cases at least one personality (typically an intermediary personality) is omniscient; this personality becomes the focus of therapeutic attempts at integration. Karla knew all about Sherry, her thoughts and feelings as well as her actions. In contrast, Sherry experienced amnesic periods when Karla took over, and she knew nothing about Karla's existence except for physical signs or reports from other people. Although Karla was a hostile personality who was difficult to work with, her omniscience provided the therapist with the best pathway toward integration.

A second characteristic of the interaction between personalities is *trance logic*, a suspension of the rules of logic and reason. Alter personalities often revert to trance logic to explain their attempts to harm the core personality. Putnam et al. (1986) found that 53 percent of the suicide attempts in their sample resulted from an alter personality's attempt to kill the core personality, a process these researchers refer to as "internal homicide." The alter personality seems unconcerned (or unaware) that a completed suicide will result in his or her own demise. After Sherry made a suicide attempt, her therapist asked Karla whether she was worried about what would happen if Sherry actually died. Karla responded, "It doesn't matter. I could just float to some other body. But for now I've got to be with her."

Distinguishing DID from Other Diagnoses

One difficulty in diagnosing DID is that it shares many features with other diagnoses. The hostile, disruptive, and uncontrolled behaviors of the aggressive personality could indicate an oppositional disorder, an antisocial personality disorder, or a borderline personality disorder. The frequently observed depressed behavior and suicidal attempts lead many therapists to diagnose major depression. In some cases, the aggressive personality is so uncontrolled and delusional that a diagnosis of schizophrenia or delusional disorder is indicated. In fact, Ellason and Ross (1995) found that multiples scored much higher on a measure of positive symptoms of schizophrenia than did a matched group of schizophrenics. In contrast, multiples showed almost no negative symptoms of schizophrenia. Thus, establishing these psychotic and depressive symptoms as resulting from a dissociation is no easy task. Typically multiples experience six to seven years of therapy and receive two or three other diagnoses before they are finally diagnosed with DID. Among the most common prior diagnoses are depression, personality disorder, anxiety, substance abuse, and schizophrenia. Help may be on the way, though. A recent test of the Structured Clinical Interview for *DSM-IV* Dissociative Disorders (SCID-D) reliably distinguishes multiples from patients with schizophrenia and schizoaffective disorder (Steinberg et al., 1994; Steinberg & Hall, 1997). Although multiples might concurrently suffer from other psychiatric disorders, these are usually secondary to their problems with multiple personalities. Generally, a diagnosis of DID is greatly facilitated by a therapist who is experienced in recognizing and treating dissociative disorders. Many therapists have found that special training in techniques involving hypnosis has greatly enhanced their ability to identify this condition.

On the other hand, this special training might bias clinicians to see dissociation where none exists, and many professionals remain skeptical about the current popularity of dissociative disorders (Hilgard, 1988; Merskey, 1995; Spanos, 1996). Although this hypothesis is intriguing, it has not gone unchallenged. Gleaves (1996) notes that many of the assumptions of this theory are untenable. Furthermore, research has not supported it. Putnam et al. (1986) found no differences between patients whose therapists used hypnosis at any point during diagnosis or treatment and patients whose therapists did not. Although the use of hypnosis in the diagnosis and treatment of DID remains controversial, as does the validity of DID as a useful diagnostic category, a growing number of therapists are diagnosing DID and employing hypnosis in their treatment strategies. At the present time it is unclear whether this growth merely reflects an increased awareness of DID, an actual increase in its incidence, or merely a diagnostic artifact based on the heightened suggestability of potential DID patients.

BIPOLAR I DISORDER
MANIC EPISODE WITH PSYCHOTIC FEATURES
Eclectic Therapy

PRESENTING COMPLAINT

Julie is a 20-year-old sophomore at a small midwestern college. For the last five days she has gone without any sleep whatsoever; she has spent this time in a heightened state of activity which she describes as "out of control." For the most part, her behavior is characterized by strange and grandiose ideas that often take on a mystical or sexual tone. For example, recently she proclaimed to a group of friends that she did not menstruate because she was "of a third sex, a gender above the two human sexes." When they asked her what she meant, she explained that she is a "superwoman" who can avoid human sexuality and still give birth. That is, she is a woman who does not require sex to fulfill her place on earth.

Some of Julie's bizarre ideation took on a political tone. One instance of this political theme involved global disarmament. She felt that she had somehow switched souls with the senior senator from her state. From his thoughts and memories, she developed six theories of government that would allow her to save the world from nuclear destruction. She proclaimed these six theories to friends and even to professors, and she began to campaign for an elected position in the U.S. government (even though no elections were scheduled at that time). Nevertheless, she felt that her recent experiences made her particularly well suited for a position high in the government, perhaps even president.

During this time Julie was worried that she would forget some of her thoughts, and she began writing these thoughts everywhere: in her notebooks, on her personal computer, and even on the walls of her dormitory room. Julie's family and friends, who had always known her to be extremely tidy and organized, were shocked to find her room in total disarray with hundreds of frantic and often incoherent messages written all over the walls and furniture. By and large these messages reflected her disorganized, grandiose thinking about spiritual and sexual themes.

By the end of the week Julie was beginning to feel increasingly irritated and fatigued. She began having difficulty walking, claiming that her right leg was numb. At this point her dormitory resident assistant brought her to the college health service, and she was seen by the therapist on call.

Julie spoke very rapidly in a rambling, loose style. Finally, when Julie's delusions (strange systems of thought based on false or bizarre foundations) were clarified to her, she realized that she was in need of help and did not resist the therapist's recommendation that she be hospitalized immediately.

Therapist: Well, Julie, what brings you here?

Julie: I have a lot of trouble walking and I need to walk because I have so many things to do before the election like make up posters and TV spots and interviews and all that stuff.

Therapist: What did you say about your leg? You said something's wrong with it, didn't you?

Julie: Oh, yeah. Well, sometimes I can't feel it because it's really another person's leg and I can't always control it.

Therapist: You just said that your leg is really another person's leg. It that right?

Julie: I did? You know, this has happened to me before, the leg thing, I mean. I had a lot of strange thoughts then, too. I had to go to the hospital.

Therapist: I think this may be the same sort of thing, and you may need to go to the hospital again, OK?

Julie: All right.

Previous Episodes

In the course of therapy, Julie described two earlier episodes of wild and bizarre behavior. These manic episodes alternated with periods of intense depression.

Julie's first manic episode occurred during high school. In the summer between her junior and senior years, Julie went to a tennis summer camp with several other boys and girls her own age. During the trip she began to develop a strong attraction toward one of the boys. She had never had these feelings before, and they frightened her. She became extremely self-conscious about her sexual thoughts, and she became convinced that everyone else was constantly watching her and could read her mind. Although she never developed a relationship with the boy, she felt that she could not stand to be so near to him and had to leave. She returned home after one week. She felt "safe" at home, and her agitation quickly subsided. She did not date during the remainder of the summer or during her senior year, which passed with no further incidents.

At the end of the summer, Julie went off to a private university in the east. After being away at college for 10 days, she developed a severe depression as a result of not coping with being on her own. She could not bring herself to attend classes or any campus activities. She suffered from a number of somatic difficulties characteristic of depression, including poor appetite, insomnia, an inability to concentrate, and psychomotor retardation. After two weeks Julie left school and was admitted to a psychiatric hospital near her parents' home. While in the hospital she was given an antipsychotic medication, haloperidol (Haldol). She also attended psychodynamically oriented group and individual therapy. Gradually her depressed symptoms dissipated, and she was discharged after seven weeks.

At the beginning of the next school term, Julie enrolled in a private university in the Midwest. Her past anxious and depressed episodes made her feel as though she had missed many social opportunities commonly experienced by people her age, and she decided to make a change and to have a "real college experience." Julie made friends with a group of students who smoked, drank, used recreational drugs, and engaged in casual sex, including group masturbation, lesbian encounters, and unprotected intercourse. Over the next several weeks she became increasingly irritable and restless, and she had difficulty sleeping and concentrating. Her use of marijuana and cocaine increased, as did her reckless behavior. Her most disturbing memory was of the morning when she awoke in the lounge of a fraternity wearing only a sheet, without any memory of what she might have done the night before.

After half a semester she entered her second, and most severe, manic episode. She developed clearly bizarre thoughts and behaviors that revolved around themes of responsibility, sexuality, and religion. First she acquired several compulsive rituals. She washed her hands whenever she thought about sex, and she found herself compelled to hold her hands together to prevent her middle finger from curving, which she was convinced would publicly signal her masturbation experiences. She believed that everyone was watching her and knew about her encounters with drugs and sex. She was deathly afraid that someone would somehow expose her. Paradoxically, she often felt as if she could control the world; at times she felt that she could prevent nuclear war, and at other times she felt personally responsible for nuclear explosions that she believed she felt through slight ground tremors. She also suffered from what she described as a "Jesus Christ delirium." She felt a special empathy with Christ, and she experienced vivid episodes where Christ talked directly to her. She wanted to "merge with the higher spirits," and at times she felt her body "floating up to heaven." Her delusions often included ideas about the special significance of parts of her body. For example, she felt that the follicles on the left side of her head were "sensitized" to receive thought messages from Christ. Many times she also attempted to include other people in these delusions. Once her boyfriend saw her pressing her legs together and caressing her breasts with her hand. When he teased her about how "sexy" she looked, she tried to convince him that her right leg and hand were actually his, and thus it was he who was really stroking her body.

As she gradually lost control over her psychotic behaviors, she began to get the attention of university officials. Several students complained to her resident assistant after they watched her repeatedly chanting "work . . . work . . . work." Finally she was hospitalized after she began babbling about finding the biblical garden during a lecture she was attending. At first she only muttered to herself, but eventually her incoherent babbling became audible to the entire class. Suddenly she ran out of the classroom, and security officers found her wandering around the campus.

Julie was admitted to the university hospital where she was put on antipsychotic medication and lithium. She was again enrolled in psychodynamically oriented group and individual therapy, where she developed a good relationship with her psychotherapist. After about a month of intensive group and individual therapy, her bizarre ideation gradually diminished, and she was released and returned to school. Although she was told to continue taking lithium, she complained of the nausea and diarrhea it caused and soon discontinued taking it.

Approximately a month after leaving the hospital, Julie began to feel depressed. Again, she experienced difficulty with eating, sleeping, and concentrating. She discontinued her favorite pastime, painting, and stopped going to classes. Finally, she withdrew from the university and returned home to the Midwest. She was not treated for her depression, which gradually lifted during the summer. At the insistence of her parents, Julie then enrolled in a small college near her home.

PERSONAL HISTORY

Julie grew up in what she termed was a "traditional Irish Catholic home," with overprotective and demanding parents. Of the five children, she was the one who always obeyed her parents and played the role of the good girl of the family, a role she describes as "being the Little Miss Perfect." Julie described herself as being quite dependent on her parents, who treated her as if she were much younger than she actually was. In contrast to her passive obedience, Julie describes her siblings as rebellious. Her older brother openly defied the Catholic church by announcing his atheism, and her older sister had made it known to her parents that she was sexually active while she was still in high school. Julie also describes her two younger sisters as defiant, but to a lesser extent.

Julie describes her parents as exceptionally strict with respect to sexual matters; they never discussed issues related to sex except to make it clear that their children are to remain virgins until they are married. Throughout high school her mother forbade her to wear makeup. Julie describes herself as a "tomboy who played with trucks, fished, and always wore pants." She detested wearing dresses because they somehow made her feel a lack of control. She remembers being shocked and frightened when she began menstruating; she was especially distressed at the loss of control this entailed. Julie did not date during high school, and until recently has not had a steady boy-friend in college.

Julie's family history shows evidence of mood disorders: her maternal grandfather received electroconvulsive therapy (ECT) for depression, and her father's aunt was diagnosed with a "nervous breakdown" which apparently was a depressive episode at menopause.

CONCEPTUALIZATION AND TREATMENT

Julie suffers from episodes of wild and reckless manic behavior alternating with episodes of moderate to severe depression. This pattern is a prime indication of manic-depressive illness, which *DSM-IV* terms bipolar I disorder, often abbreviated as BP-I. (Bipolar II diorder involves episodes of depression and hypomania, which is less severe than mania.) To many therapists her grandiose and bizarre delusions would be taken as signs of a psychotic disorder like schizophrenia. However, her history of alternating manic and depressed episodes and the correspondence between her psychotic symptoms and her disor-dered mood (i.e., the delusions that appear during her manic episodes are primarily grandiose and/or mystical; those that manifest during the depressed episodes are critical and judgmental) point toward a diagnosis of BP-I with severe psychotic features, or, to use a former and still commonly used term, manic-depressive psychosis.

Eclectic therapy draws on the assumptions of many different theoretical approaches and makes use of a variety of therapeutic techniques. Aspects of the biomedical, psychoanalytic, humanistic, and behavioral schools, among others, may be employed. Typically, eclectic therapists are trained in one of the prevailing theoretical approaches and later combine elements and techniques from different schools in ways that they feel provide the best explanation for the etiology of a particular case and the most effective treatment for that patient. By and large, eclectic therapists focus initially on their patients' presenting complaints and on ways to control these problems. Once these immediate issues are addressed, therapy can begin to explore possible underlying causes. Typically, a patient's personal history is investigated to help the patient delineate important events that may have shaped his or her life. Next, the ways in which these events may contribute to the patient's present problems are discussed in individual or group therapy, or both. Finally, the therapist and the patient discuss how these insights can help the patient's long-term functioning. Thus, the aim of eclectic therapy is to provide patients with a pragmatic and flexible approach to their problems.

In Julie's case, the initial consideration of her therapist is to control and, in time, eliminate her florid psychotic symptoms. Her initial treatment consisted of psychopharmacological therapy in a controlled environment. Once Julie's therapist became aware of her history of past manic and depressed episodes, she decided to hospitalize Julie and prescribe a combination of antipsychotic medication (in this case haloperidol, because it had been shown to be effective previously) and lithium carbonate. Antipsychotics work to diminish a patient's psychotic behaviors; lithium carbonate, usually referred to simply as "lithium," is a mood stabilizer used to reduce the wild mood swings of bipolar patients. Once the bizarre psychotic features abate, Julie will gradually be taken off halperodol. However, she will most likely remain on prophylactic mood stabilizer treatment indefinitely to prevent the recurrence of her wild mood swings. Julie's therapist maintains her lithium level at approximately 0.5 milliequivalent per liter of blood, confirmed by biweekly blood tests. For Julie, this amounts to a dose of 1200 milligrams per day.

The next stage for Julie's therapy is to examine her past experiences to identify some potential causes of her disorder. In all likelihood Julie's problems, at least in part, might stem from her overprotective and strict upbringing. Julie describes her father not only as having strict values but also as being overbearing and demanding; she describes her mother as having perfectionist standards bordering on compulsiveness. One interpretation of Julie's behavior is that she developed a series of compulsive defenses to help her reduce the anxiety caused by her parents' high expectations. For example, in an attempt to meet her parents' high standards of sexual purity (a task made even more difficult by the more open sexual mores of her sister), Julie denied her own sexual urges and feelings. An unfortunate result of this strategy was that she developed a great confusion about her own sexuality, and to some extent her gender identity. As was seen above, these themes pervade her psychotic delusions.

To fulfill her parents' other strict expectations, Julie attempted to be "Little Miss Perfect." She has always been a very conscientious daughter. She received straight A's throughout school, she has very neat personal habits, and she has always had a willingness to take on duty and responsibility. Her psychotic compulsions, the most striking of which was her chanting "work . . . work . . . work" around campus, are further indications of this defense. Her grandiose delusions of being able to single-handedly bring about world peace are symbolic expressions of her need to fulfill her responsibilities. These compulsive defenses were also prevalent during her recent hospitalization. For example, despite the fact that she had already withdrawn from school, Julie insisted on having her books with her in the hospital so that she could keep up in her classes.

Adopting the identity of "Little Miss Perfect" also implies a repression of the sexual component of Julie's subconscious, and describing herself with this term is another of her compulsive defenses.

Her attempts to deny her sexuality began with her childhood tomboy behavior. It is significant that wearing dresses made her feel a "lack of control" as a child. At age 13 she was understandably shocked and frightened when she began to menstruate, probably because it conflicted so directly with her need for cleanliness and her desire to deny her emerging sexuality. In fact, her first manic episode, which appeared during her summer tennis camp experience, apparently resulted from her first strong feelings of sexual attraction. Later, when she was away at college, she was determined to rebel against her parents' strict expectations. Unfortunately, her experiments with drugs and sex seemed to overwhelm her compulsive defenses, resulting in a severe episode of manic psychosis. The themes of her psychotic delusions clearly illustrate her ambivalent feelings toward her own sexuality. On the one hand, her delusions about being a third gender convey her continued attempts to deny her sexuality, especially the physical symbol of her sexuality, her menstruation. On the other hand, many of her other thoughts express some attempt to reconcile her sexual feelings with her strict upbringing. Most notable among these is her explanation to her friends that she was a superwoman who could fulfill traditional sex roles without having to degrade herself with sex.

In addition to her problems in coping with her sexuality, Julie's psychotic ideation about spiritual themes seems to reflect her anxiety over trying to meet the relatively strict demands of the Catholic church while at the same time coping with the social pressures of modern college life. For many patients it is not uncommon for psychotic manifestations to incorporate a spiritual component, particularly for people with traditional religious backgrounds.

Often patients have a difficult time accepting the fact that they have repressed conflicts over their beliefs. Many firmly hold on to their (often unreasonable) principles and ideals and fail to understand how their internal standards may have contributed to their problems. In contrast, Julie recognized that her parents were very strict and at some level realized that she had not completely adopted their values. However, Julie did not understand the difficulty she had in defying the expectations of her upbringing. In a sense, Julie underestimated how strongly she still held her parents' values. Only gradually did she comprehend the extent of her own ambivalent feelings and how they might have an impact on her therapy.

Once the patient's underlying issues have been identified, the next step of therapy is to adjust self-expectations in ways that reduce anxiety without overwhelming neurotic defenses. In Julie's case, her experimentation with drugs and sex was an attempt to change her self-image, but these experiences created neurotic conflicts that were too strong for her to cope with. Still, Julie seemed to have a need to free herself of at least some of the strict constraints imposed by her parents and her faith. With this in mind, Julie's therapist had her engage in a "mini-rebellion." After her hospitalization, Julie had to decide whether to stay at home for a while or to return to school. She was encouraged to return to school as a way of developing a sense of separation from her parents. This she did. Julie was also told to think about the conflict between her wants and her duties and how she might resolve these problems. A question Julie was told to keep in her mind was "When is Little Miss Perfect right, and when is she wrong?"

Julie's therapist also suggested concrete ways to diminish her neurotic defenses. For instance, Julie was told to try to become less concerned about her grades and to "loosen up" socially. At first, Julie had difficulty with this prescription. While she was still in the hospital, she had her parents bring her books so that she could study, even though it was already decided that she would not finish the semester. After she was released from the hospital, she refused to date and went out with her friends only rarely. The therapist frequently encouraged her to go out and enjoy life, to let herself be more relaxed. Only gradually did Julie's social activities increase. After about four months, Julie mentioned that she had a boyfriend. She was urged to continue seeing him, provided he understood her needs and was supportive of her. In fact, the therapist saw the boyfriend with Julie for two sessions so that he could get a better understanding of exactly what her needs were.

In addition to her individual therapy, Julie was also involved in a depression therapy group. Julie found the supportive atmosphere of the group to be extremely helpful in letting her overcome her shyness about telling people about her illness. Because Julie was the only bipolar in the group and had by far the most unusual experiences, the other group members treated her with respect and a certain degree of celebrity. Julie told her therapist that it felt good being able to help other people just by being open and friendly.

The focus of therapy then shifted to altering Julie's impressions of the demands of her parents and the church. For this the therapist employed a process of cognitive restructuring. One issue involved Julie's perception of sex. In therapy Julie frequently admonished herself for having sexual fantasies and for her past sexual behavior. Her therapist tried to convince her that sex was not evil and that having sexual thoughts, and even engaging in sexual behavior, did not mean that she would automatically be sent to hell. The therapist emphasized that sexual feelings are common to everyone, particularly young people her age, and that having sexual feelings was not something to be ashamed or afraid of. A second issue was Julie's dependence on her parents' approval. Julie often refrained from doing something she would have enjoyed for fear that her parents might disapprove. To counter these thoughts, Julie was told that her mother was old-fashioned and had different ideas about life. In all likelihood, her mother's standards were not as strict as Julie guessed. But even if they were, it was probable that her mother did not fully understand Julie's feelings, thus creating standards that were impossible for Julie to meet. It was emphasized that Julie should not deny her mother's values; rather she was encouraged to accept them for what they are: another person's ideas that are different from her own.

The final stage of Julie's therapy involved support and maintenance. Julie's weekly visits now dealt primarily with supporting her sense of autonomy from her parents, especially in the areas in which they disagree. Just as important as her psychological support, these visits helped her maintain a proper level of lithium in her system. Every other week she has the lithium level of her blood analyzed to ensure that she maintains an effective yet safe lithium blood level.

PROGNOSIS

As is the case with the many patients with bipolar disorder, Julie responded well to lithium treatment. At the present time (13 months after her most recent manic episode), Julie appears to be doing well. She is still in supportive therapy, which has now been reduced to a biweekly basis. Julie is still somewhat tense and anxious, but she has had no psychotic symptoms since her last episode. Julie is very bright (so far she has earned a 3.9 GPA in college in spite of the disruptions caused by her illness) and has a great deal of insight into the causes of her problems. She describes her boyfriend as supportive and undemanding, and her relationship with him seems to be going well. Julie describes their sexual behavior as "a lot of necking and heavy petting"; they have not engaged in intercourse. Although Julie wants to keep sex at bay for the time being, she has begun to think about her future plans with her boyfriend and the possibility of getting married. Her main concern does not seem to be with her moral standards but rather with the possibility of a future pregnancy. Lithium is contraindicated for pregnant women, so she will need to interrupt her lithium therapy if she decides to become pregnant, and she fears that she might relapse into another manic episode when she interrupts her therapy. This is a legitimate concern. However, at the same time it shows the progress Julie has made in coming to terms with her own sexuality and reconciling her underlying gender confusion.

In general the early onset of Julie's disease and the severity of the psychotic symptoms Julie manifested would lead one to be rather pessimistic about her long-term prognosis (Cohen, Khan, & Cox, 1989; Solomon et al., 1995). However, Julie's rapid response to lithium, her complete lack of residual psychotic features between episodes, her abstention from illicit drugs, and her keen insight into the causes of her disorder all argue against a diagnosis of an underlying psychotic pathology. Thus, the prognosis for Julie seems quite good provided she continues to respond to lithium, utilizes supportive psychotherapy, and remains in a supportive relationship.

DISCUSSION

Julie's case was typical in many ways. Most people with bipolar disorder begin to experience symptoms in late adolescence; the average age of onset is about 20, a figure that has remained stable over the past century (Burke, Burke, Rae, & Regier, 1991; Weissman et al., 1988). Julie's age of onset was a bit younger, but not unusually so. In addition, Julie responded well to lithium. Although some studies on the effectiveness of lithium for bipolar patients have reported a success rate of 80 percent (e.g., O'Connell et al., 1991), recent research paints a more sobering picture. Studies of hospitalized bipolars with follow-up periods ranging from 2 to 5 years yield relapse rates ranging between 42 and 64 percent (Goldberg, Harrow, & Grossman, 1995; Solomon et al., 1995.) Finally, Julie has a family history of affective disorders. Compared with the general population, bipolar patients are much more likely to have first- and second-degree relatives with a history of mood disorders (Klein, Depue, & Slater, 1985). The rate of mood disorders among these relatives ranges from 8 percent to 29 percent in different studies (Dwyer & DeLong, 1987; Gershon et al., 1982), and this rate triples or quadruples in children whose parents both suffer from an affective disturbance. These figures lead many researchers to believe that bipolar disorder is transmitted genetically (Gershon & Nurnberger, 1995; Pardes, Kaufman, Pincus, & West, 1989). However, the genetic link is not direct; relatives of bipolar patients have increased rates of *some* mood disorder, but not necessarily bipolar disorder. Thus, bipolar disorder is thought of as a "spectrum disease" inherited through multiple genetic factors that have not been identified.

Compared with the incidence of other mood disorders, the incidence of bipolar I disorder in the general population is low; the reported lifetime prevalence rates range from 0.4 to 1.2 percent, and the disorder is equally common in males and females (Kessler et al., 1997; Weissman et al., 1988; Winokur & Crowe, 1983). This rate has been slowly increasing over the past few decades, but it is unclear whether this rise reflects a true increase in the prevalence rate or merely an improvement in the diagnostic standards and procedures employed in epidemiologic research. The latter may be particularly applicable to cases like Julie's. In the past, psychotic features of bipolar disorder were often seen as evidence of a purely psychotic disorder such as schizophrenia, delusional (paranoid) disorder, or schizoaffective disorder. These categories are difficult to tease apart unless the diagnostician has a reliable patient history and a clear indication that the psychotic features are congruent with the manic mood (Carlson, 1996).

Finally, it should be noted that manic-depressives must be handled with special care. As a group they have a higher mortality rate than patients who suffer from other mood disorders (Goldring & Fieve, 1984; Weeke & Vaeth, 1986), with a suicide rate about twice as high as those who suffer unipolar depression or other mental disorders (Chen & Dilsaver, 1996). Special efforts should be made to bring these people to treatment, especially because they tend to be resistant to the idea of therapy.

However, the problems are not over once treatment begins. Lithium carbonate is a strong psychoactive agent that has many potentially serious side effects. Gastrointestinal difficulties such as nausea and diarrhea are common. Worse, prolonged elevated levels of lithium can result in irreversible kidney and/or thyroid damage. For these reasons lithium treatment must be closely regulated. Yet despite these side effects and the availability of alternative treatments, lithium remains the most commonly prescribed treatment for bipolar disorder (Howland, 1997) and remains the treatment of choice (Schou, 1997).

Because of these potentially dangerous side effects, other mood stabilizers have gained in popularity in recent years. Most notable among these are anticonvulsant medications originally design to treat epilepsy: carbamazepine (Tegretol), divalproex (Depakote), gabapentin (Neurotin), and valproate (valproic acid, Depakene). All are useful treatments, though psychiatrists must keep a close eye on dosing strategies and response (Bowden, 1996; McElroy, Soutullo, Keck, & Kmetz, 1997).

Finally, manic-depressives tend to have a very difficult adjustment after treatment, and psychiatric professionals, family members, and friends should make special attempts to provide a comprehensive, supportive treatment (Kusumakar et al., 1997; Solomon et al., 1995).

MAJOR DEPRESSIVE DISORDER, SINGLE EPISODE
Interpersonal Therapy with Pharmacotherapy

PRESENTING COMPLAINT

Like many Americans, Jeff has loved cars for as long as he can remember. Throughout his childhood he collected toy cars and built models. As he grew older, his infatuation became a passion. About ten years ago he bought a dilapidated 1956 Chevy two-door hardtop. Over the next several years he lovingly restored it to show-winning condition. Last year he bought a Corvette of the same vintage, which, though drivable, will require significant restoration work in his specially prepared garage workshop. He is a car fanatic outside his garage as well. He watches at least one car race every weekend, subcribes to eleven car magazines, and serves as vice president of the Motor City Chapter of the Tri-Chevy Association. He doesn't mind the winter planning meetings with other club officers, but he lives for the frequent summer events, where he can live and breathe Detroit iron.

This weekend his club met at Mid-Ohio Raceway, but he didn't go. In the last two months he had missed three similar events and one planning meeting. His favorite parts stores went unvisited, races went unwatched, magazines piled up unread, his Vette languished untouched. He hadn't even driven his pristine hardtop for over a month. The cars he had loved so fervently before now held nothing for him. As he said, "My give-a-crap meter is on zero."

Work was pretty much the same story. He used to feel lucky; he designed cars and got paid for it. He even got a promotion a few months ago, from design engineer to project manager. At first things seemed to go well, but soon he started having trouble getting his new staff organized, and they fell behind on their deadlines. The more he was pushed to make his group productive, the more out of control things got. One engineer transferred to another department, and others were looking to leave. Even his secretary was being resentful and defensive. He knew his group was doing badly, but he had no idea what he should do. So he did nothing, and gradually he stopped caring. He called in sick as much as he dared. He wasn't turning out to be such a great manager after all.

Nor was he a great father. It used to be that dinner was always family time, and after dinner he always made time for the girls, bathing them (until they got too old for that), reading them stories, or playing computer games. Only after they were tucked in bed did he retreat to his sacred workshop downstairs. But in the last few months he had barely talked to his children. He cannot remember at what point their games became annoying and irritating, or the point at which he began stare at the TV all evening, not really caring what was on. Eventually he gave up the TV too, because he couldn't stand Renee's accusing looks when she passed by. Now when he came home he just went to the garage and sat.

He stared blankly at his two '56 Chevys. Once they had been his pride and joys. Now when he looked at them he felt nothing. Nothing seemed to matter anymore: his cars, his job, his family. His life? Thoughts about his death occurred frequently in the past few weeks, and they returned now. It was hard to see the point of living. There was his family, but he had life insurance. Would it be enough to support them? Probably. Would Renee remarry? Undoubtedly. And no doubt to a much better husband and father than he was. But a suicide might be hard on Renee and the girls. It would be better if it were an accident. Walk in front of a bus? Crash into a bridge support? He wouldn't use his Chevys, that would be wasteful. The Camaro would do. It used to be that thoughts of his death made him a little scared, but lately they seemed to have a calming effect. As he was sitting there calmly contemplating his suicide, the phone rang.

Jeff: Hello?

Bill: Hey, Jeff, it's Bill! We missed you this weekend. I haven't seen you in a while.

Jeff: Yes, well. . .

Bill: How's the Vette coming?

Jeff: About the same; I haven't done much. I haven't done anything. Nothing.

Bill: You know, you don't sound too good. Is everything alright?

Jeff: I don't know.

Bill: You know, Jeff, you sound pretty down. Are you feeling OK? Do you want to talk to somebody or something? Is there anything I can do?

Jeff: I don't know. Maybe there is something.

Bill: Name it.

Jeff: What's the name of your friend in the Psych Department, the one at the clinic?

Five minutes later the phone rang again, and a man introduced himself as "Bill's friend from the clinic." After some brief introductions he asked Jeff to describe what led to his referral for therapy. After Jeff recounted his thoughts that night, the therapist asked Jeff to meet him at the university hospital in twenty minutes. He then asked Jeff to put Renee on the phone. He explained who he was and that Jeff needed to go to the hospital, maybe for a few days. And, he added, she was to drive.

PERSONAL HISTORY

Jeff is a 37-year-old mechanical engineer employed as a design manager for an automobile corporation in Detroit. Renee is an assistant principal of an elementary school. They and their two daughters live in an upper-middle-class suburb.

Jeff grew up in a middle-class suburb of Cleveland. His father was the vice president and general manager of a small manufacturing firm until his retirement seven years ago. His mother held a series of part-time secretarial jobs. Jeff has two older sisters. The elder is an oncologist in San Francisco; she is divorced. The younger is married to a real estate broker and does not work outside the home.

Jeff's father ran his company with a firm hand, and he did the same with his family, especially his only son. He rarely gave praise for work well done, though he was quick to criticize any mistake. He made little fuss when Jeff graduated with his master's degree, nor even when Jeff's sister graduated from medical school. He was a stern but fair disciplinarian; he could be harsh in his punishments, but they were usually deserved. According to Jeff, his father's most central characteristic is his stubbornness. He was convinced of his own correctness and never waivered. His father seems to have mellowed in his old age, though, and is generally an amicable, though still strict, Grandpa during visits with Jeff's family.

Jeff's mother was a relative nonentity in the house who was completely dominated by her overbearing husband. His older sister was often bossy with her friends and siblings, though perfectly subservient to their father. His younger sister was something of a rebel in high school, but she seems to have settled down when she started her family. Jeff remains close to this sister and maintains a distant but cordial relationship with the elder sibling.

Jeff estimates that his childhood experiences were fairly normal. Although he did not have a close relationship with his parents or his older sister, he and his younger sister shared many close experiences. He described several typical childhood mishaps, such as when he broke his leg falling out of a tree, but he denied any psychologically traumatic episodes or instances of abuse. His father did use corporal punishment, but Jeff never saw it as excessive or unwarranted. "He'd pop us once in a while, but he never lost control, and we generally knew what we were in for before it happened."

When asked to describe his marriage, at first he could only talk about what a poor father and husband he was; how he found almost everything Renee and the girls did was annoying and pointless. Lately they interacted very little, and when they did they treated him with a mixture of concern, frustration, and contempt. When he described some fun family event, his attitude took on a wistful tone, as if he was remembering a pleasant vacation long past. Later in therapy Jeff was able to describe his marriage more fully and more objectively. He and Renee met while in graduate school, and they married a few months after graduating with their master's degrees. He described their marriage, as a "real partnership" where both shared in the domestic duties. He had probably changed more diapers and cooked more dinners than she had, he observed. His only real complaint was that sometimes she took on a dominant, bossy attitude. In some ways she was like his father and older sister, always having to have her way. He resented this, especially after spending all day being harangued by his section chief and hassled by his secretaries and coworkers.

Jeff's description of his job followed a similar pattern. Before the past few months, Jeff's generally enjoyed his job. He had the unavoidable conflicts with demanding bosses and disgruntled subordinates, but on the whole he looked forward to work. But things changed after his promotion. The productivity of his group declined rapidly, but the section chief became more insistent that Jeff's group be productive. He felt trapped and overwhelmed. On the one hand, he recognized a lot of the inefficiencies and redundancies of his group, but he felt he couldn't get them to adopt his plans. They showed him little respect. One member had already transferred to another project, and most everyone else wanted to follow. On the other hand, Jeff felt too humiliated to ask someone for help in managing his project group. It made sense to talk to other project managers, as Renee had often told him to do, but he couldn't bring himself to bother them with his own problems.

When asked about his friendships, Jeff remarked that he really didn't have any. Renee seemed to have many friends who were teachers and administrators, and he had several casual acquaintances at his job, at least he did until recently. They knew several parents of their children's classmates, but no one well. He could not call anyone a close friend.

"What about Bill?" asked the therapist? Jeff thought of his fellow club members primarily as fellow car fanatics, not as friends. But he remembered Bill's concern, and he had received calls and cards from other club members. He thought he might have some friends after all.

CONCEPTUALIZATION AND TREATMENT

Of primary importance for interpersonal therapy (IPT) is an analysis of the client's social interactions and their possible role in the development and maintenance of symptoms. Hence, much of the personal history focuses on current relationships, particularly those involving marriage and employment. Most clinicians, like Jeff's therapist, make an informal assessment of interpersonal problems, called an "interpersonal inventory," from information taken from the personal history.

IPT conceptualizes depression as having three constituent processes: (1) *symptom formation* (psychological and/or biological factors that lead to depression), (2) *social functioning* (current interpersonal interactions involved in depression), and (3) *personality* (enduring characteristics that might contribute to and/or underlie depression). Although attention is given to all three of these factors in the course of therapy, they receive predominant focus roughly in their numerical order.

When Jeff and Renee arrived at the hospital (a neighbor agreed to sit with the girls), they met the therapist in the emergency room. They soon moved to an examination room, where Jeff was given two depression questionnaires: the Beck Depression Inventory (BDI) (Beck et al., 1961) and the Hamilton Rating Scale for Depression (HRSD) (M. Hamilton, 1967). Jeff's scores of 31 and 29, respectively, confirmed his severe depression. With Renee waiting outside, the therapist also had Jeff discuss in greater detail the issues they had mentioned on the phone, particularly his suicidal thoughts. They also discussed specific details of his symptomatic picture. His depressed mood had been more or less continuous, and worsening, throughout the episode. He never cried, but he usually felt hopeless and dejected. He had lost interest in his children and his beloved Chevys. His appetite, sleep, and sexual desire had all greatly decreased. He had never had a previous episode he would call depression, although from time to time he had felt down, discouraged, and low. He could remember no evidence of depressive symptoms with any family member, though if there were any, he added, no one in his family would be likely to admit it. After this, a psychiatry resident performed a brief physical exam while a nurse took a brief medical history.

In consultation with the resident and the supervising psychiatry attending physician, it was agreed that Jeff suffered from major depressive disorder, single episode, melancholic type. He also described several features of avoidant personality disorder, including a marked fear of evaluation, self-criticsm, and social isolation, including a solitary hobby. At the time of his initial evaluation, it was unclear to what extent these features were a consequence of his depressed mood and to what extent they may have contributed to it.

Despite his severe depressive symptoms and his suicidal thoughts, it was agreed that he was probably not in any immediate danger of suicide. Jeff was started on fluoxetine (Prozac) at 20 milligrams per day, which would be monitored by the attending psychiatrist weekly. For psychotherapy he was scheduled for weekly sessions at the therapist's office. It was suggested that Jeff talk to his boss and arrange a brief leave of absence, two or three weeks, if possible. Before going home, Jeff signed a behavioral contract in which he promised to contact the therapist if he felt any suicidal urges, or, if that were not possible, to go immediately to the emergency room.

Jeff arrived at the first therapy session on time. He was neatly dressed, but he had prominent beard stubble, disheveled hair, and a look of complete exhaustion.

Consistent with the standard IPT model, therapy focused initially on interpersonal factors associated with the onset of his depression. From his notes, it struck the therapist that Jeff's depressive symptoms first began to appear shortly after his promotion to project manager. Was there something, he asked Jeff, about your job change that you found upsetting?

"Everything was upsetting," Jeff wailed. His responsibilities increased tremendously, but he felt no more authority. Now he had to answer for the performance of the entire project group, a group he felt little control over. Worse, he was expected to solve endless disagreements and squabbles within the group. He felt like he worked for two bosses, and no one worked for him. He described several instances of his boss's demanding explosions and his subordinates' near mutinies. Everyone, it seemed, was dissatisfied with him. And everyone was probably right. "Some people can manage," he reflected, "and some can't. I can't."

In the next session Jeff described similar interpersonal problems with his marriage, his family, and even his club. He became vice president of the club, he explained, just to help out. But it turned out to be a repeat of work: once again he was saddled with the responsibility to settle personality conflicts without having any authority to do anything constructive. The therapist liked this example because the small size and limited involvement of the group made for a particularly simple and clear illustration. The first few sessions were devoted to gathering information about Jeff's depression, his interpersonal interactions, and his personal history.

At Jeff's third session, he reported feeling much less depressed and that his suicidal ideation had virtually ceased. These were good signs, for they indicated that Jeff was responding to his medication. His improvement also indicated that it was likely that he would continue treatment. Discussing the effectiveness of antidepressant medication does not take away from the value of IPT; to the contrary, it often facilitates improvement because it provides a biological cause for depression. Sometimes the ability to "medicalize" the disorder can relieve the client from the guilt and shame they may feel if they think of depression as a personal weakness rather than an illness.

At the end of this session, the therapist was optimistic. He felt he understood Jeff's situation moderately well, at least in a general sense, and Jeff seemed to be making good progress. It was time to clarify the issues that would be the focus of therapy and to make a therapy contract. The issues they would focus on would be his management role at work, his interpersonal interactions with his family, and his perceptions of what was and was not appropriate in various interpersonal situations. Their contract specified, among other things, (1) these three central treatment issues, (2) the limited nature of the treatment (16 weeks, 50 minutes per week), and (3) the roles of the therapist and the psychiatrist in managing his case.

At this point the therapist felt that the therapeutic alliance had developed to the point where he was comfortable suggesting interpretations that could challenge some of Jeff's long-held beliefs. However, he was careful to avoid phrasing these interpretations in a way that diminished Jeff's sense of control in the therapeutic process. For example, if he had stated a definite conclusion ("You shouldn't let everyone push you around."), the therapist would have risked two failures: first, that Jeff would feel guilty for his weakness and thus feel even less empowered at work, and second, that Jeff would see therapy as yet another situation where he has no control. Instead, the therapist was careful to bolster Jeff's role within the therapeutic alliance while empowering him at work. He asked Jeff, "I get the sense that you care a great deal for your subordinates and want to help and protect them. Is that right?" From this gentle beginning, the therapist directed the discussion to the crux of the issue: Jeff's inappropriate, and ineffectual, adoption of a submissive role with his subordinates. But the path to this goal always maintained Jeff's sense of authority and appropriate responsibility. He was gradually prodded to realize (and, eventually, suggest himself) that establishing himself as leader, issuing clear expectations, and holding employees responsible will work to everyone's benefit.

The therapist also discussed the opposite end of Jeff's work dilemma: his overly passive responses to his superiors. As he did with his subordinates (and apparently his father, older sister, and wife as well), Jeff habitually adopted a submissive interpersonal role. For example, one particularly humiliating experience occurred when his project group submitted an unusable design. Although the design flaw was clearly not his fault (it resulted from a change in specifications that was never relayed to the group), he nevertheless took sole responsibility and apologized for the error. It is difficult to say whether this habitual submissive interaction pattern resulted from an immediate reaction to his superiors or from his habitual submissiveness, which prompted others to take control. In all likelihood both of these factors were at work. The end result was that Jeff trapped himself in a position where he accepted criticism of his work without question, yet he did not see any legitimate way to assert his own perspective. It is little wonder, then, that he felt helpless and worthless. Again, through carefully phrased interpretations, the therapist attempted to get Jeff to recognize his often self-defeating interpersonal style and to find ways to assert his proper authority. One particularly helpful technique was role playing. First the therapist would portray Jeff's role and model possible responses Jeff could make to his superiors. Jeff then played himself and practiced responses he felt might be particularly useful. In keeping with the interpersonal approach, the suggestion of possible responses and the determination of which responses might be most effective involved a collaborative effort, with Jeff having the ultimate say.

The remainder of the sessions during the middle stages of therapy were used to discuss interpersonal issues related to Jeff's marriage, family life, and interactions with his parents and sisters. Analyses of interpersonal exchanges and role playing were utilized throughout. Jeff was quite responsive to these techniques, and his depression continued to lift. He suggested that Renee accompany him for one or two sessions, and the therapist agreed. Typically IPT is either individual or conjoint, but there was no reason not to mix the two here. The possible benefits were that Renee would be more sensitive and aware of their marital dynamics, thus increasing the likelihood of maintaining gains after therapy. Renee joined Jeff for sessions 11 and 12. The therapist noted that Jeff was careful not to criticize Renee for her "bossy" behavior; rather he phrased the discussion in such a way that Renee was induced to discover for herself many of the communication patterns that characterized their marriage.

At session 14 the therapist brought up the issue of termination, which would occur after session 16, as agreed in their contract. Before doing so, though, Jeff again completed the BDI and HRSD, scoring 8 on each, which were well within the normal ranges. With this clear sign of improvement before him, Jeff was encouraged about his ability to remain well after therapy. The therapist mentioned that he would discuss Jeff's medication with the psychiatrist, given Jeff's clinical improvement. Concurring in this decision, Jeff discontinued Prozac soon thereafter.

At the final two sessions Jeff and his therapist reviewed his progress over the last four months. Virtually all of his somatic complaints had ceased, except that his sleep was still somewhat disturbed, perhaps due to his medication. He no longer had suicidal thoughts. There were significant improvements in virtually all topics covered by their contract. He again spent evenings with the family and helped with family chores and duties, and his relationship with Renee was much improved. Although his job was still a source of moderate stress, he no longer found it overwhelming and is making plans to transfer to a position within the company with reduced managment duties. And finally, as Bill corroborates, Jeff is back at his Tri-Chevy meetings. Although Jeff states that he has not regained the concentration and focus needed to resume the reconstruction of the Vette, he once again enjoys attending club events, and just cruising around town, with the hardtop. Once again he finds fulfillment in the two loves of his life: his family and his cars.

PROGNOSIS

Jeff's prognosis is good. The development of a single episode following a stressful life event (his job change) is quite typical, and the course of his recovery is common for individuals who respond well to treatment. At termination he no longer met any criteria for depression. He has a stable and supportive nuclear family and no identifiable family history of mood disorders. It is possible that his successful therapy will provide some long-term protection, but this remains speculative; long-term follow-up studies for IPT have yet to be run.

Despite the factors in his favor, it is likely that Jeff will experience another depressive episode at some point in the future. *DSM-IV* reports that the probability of developing a subsequent episode following a single episode is about 50 to 60 percent, and the severity of his presenting symptoms argue that his chances of relapse might be higher still. Fortunately, his successful response to treatment means that effective measures are available should he experience a relapse.

A particular cause for concern is his avoidant characteristics, which are not likely to diminish over time. Interpersonally, it is possible, if not likely, that his avoidant personality will lead to persistent feelings of low self-esteem, which will translate to yet more self-defeating interpersonal encounters.

DISCUSSION

Major depression is among the most common of psychiatric complaints, the so-called "bread and butter" of clinical psychology. Based on a number of large-scale epidemiological studies, *DSM-IV* provides lifetime prevalence estimates ranging from 10 to 25 percent for women and 5 to 12 percent for men. The point prevalence—that is, the proportion of the general population suffering from major depression at any one time—has been estimated to be from 5 to 9 percent of women and 2 to 3 percent of men.

This 2:1 sex ratio is a low figure based on community samples (surveys of the general population). Epidemiologic studies using clinical samples (those already seeking treatment and diagnosed as depressed) report somewhat higher female-to-male ratios (e.g, Regier et al., 1988). A number of reasons for this gender differential have been proposed, including actual differences in incidence, differences in coping and problem solving, and differences in willingness to report symptoms (Nolen-Hoeksema, 1990). Interestingly, in their study of mood disorder among the Amish (whose religious and cultural values forbid drugs and alcohol), Egeland and Hostetter (1983) report no sex differences. It is possible that in the general population, many depressed men mask their symptoms through substance use.

Besides sex, many other risk factors for depression have been identified, including stressful life events (Newman & Bland, 1994), comorbid dysthymia ("double depression") (Keller, Hirschfield, & Hanks, 1997; Sotsky et al., 1991), anxiety (Rodney et al., 1997), personality disorders (Shea et al., 1990), and a family history of mood disorders (Benkelfat et al., 1994).

IPT and interpersonal models of personality

"Interpersonal therapy" is a general term that includes a variety of specific underlying assumptions and therapeutic techniques, ranging from psychodynamically based psychotherapies (Blatt & Felson, 1993; Mahler, 1968) to behaviorally based reciprocity models (Coyne, 1976; Kiesler, 1983). IPT is middle-ground clinical approach that has been standardized for clinical trials (Craighead, Craighead, & Ilardi, 1998; Klerman, Weissman, Rounsaville, & Chevron, 1984). The one uniting factor of interpersonal therapies is their shared emphasis on the importance of interpersonal processes as fundamental in the development and maintenance of personality and mental health, first clarified decades ago by prominent personality theorists such as Sullivan (1953), Leary (1957), and Meyer (1957).

Although Jeff's therapist generally followed the structure and procedure of standardized IPT, his conceptualization and treatment emphasis leaned toward the reciprocity model. The basis of this model is that interpersonal relationships are based on certain predictable behavior exchanges. For example, a passive statement will tend to evoke a controlling response and vice versa. These behavior pairs, which are termed "complementary" (Carson, 1969; Kiesler, 1983), are natural and more or less automatic. Moreover, they tend to engender self-perpetuating behavior exchanges, where an initial submissive comment receives a dominant reply, which elicits a second submissive comment, which evokes further dominance, and so on. With the exception of escalating hostile arguments, researchers have found general support for this complementary pattern in naturalistic interactions (Orford, 1986; Van Denberg, Schmidt, & Kiesler, 1992).

Applied to cases of depression (Coyne, 1976; Horowitz & Vitkus, 1986), interaction sequences follow this typical pattern: depressed persons are likely to begin conversations by soliciting help, disclosing personal problems, or complaining; others are likely to reply with controlling responses (giving advice and suggestions, criticizing), which exacerbate the depressed person's initial feelings of weakness and incompetence. Eventually partners become frustrated and reject depressed persons, compounding their sense of failure and isolation. Clinical observations (Coates & Wortman, 1980) and controlled research (McMullen & Conway, 1997; Tan & Stoppard, 1994) have supported this model.

Jeff's therapist makes use of this knowledge in his practice. He makes sure to phrase his questions and comments in a submissive way to prompt Jeff to respond with authority. In most cases the spouse is the client's most important interaction partner; here Renee was enrolled in therapy both to assess her typical interpersonal responses and to make her more aware and sensitive to Jeff's interpersonal needs. The therapist's interpersonal orientation is shown in many other ways, even by his use of the term *client*, which emphasises Jeff's ultimate control over the therapeutic relationship.

Interpersonal therapy has been shown to be effective in treating depression, both in its standard IPT format (Elkin et al., 1990; Frank, 1996) and by specifically focusing on complementary behavior exchanges (Kiesler, 1986; Teichman, 1997). IPT can be easily adapted to treat a variety of patient populations, including adolescents, the elderly, couples, and clients suffering from grief reactions, dysthymia, anxiety, personality disorders, eating disorders, and a variety of medical conditions, including HIV infection (Hinrichsen, 1997; Moreau & Mufson, 1997; Mufson, Moreau, Weissman, & Klerman, 1994; Weissman & Markowitz, 1994). It may be particularly helpful when pharmacotherapy is contraindicated (e.g., during pregnancy) or simply undesired (Stuart & O'Hara, 1995).

Pharmacotherapy for depression

Perhaps the most common treatment for mood disorders is pharmacotherapy. For unipolar depressive disorders (MDD and dysthymia), a variety of medications is available; the decision of which particular antidepressant to prescribe is based on a number of factors: potential side effects, presenting symptoms, response history, and therapist experience and confidence. Until recently, a typical pharmacotherapy treatment for major depression began with tricyclic antidepressants such as imipramine (Tofanil), amitryptyline (Elavil), or trazodone (Desyrel) because of their demonstrated effectiveness and fairly mild side effects. If the depression does not respond to initial tricyclic medication, MAO inhibitors such as tranylcypromine (Parnate) and phenylzine (Nardil) are tried, though they remain a second choice because they require a restricted diet and have more severe side effects. Recently, second-generation antidepressants were introduced, including bupropion (Wellbutrin), sertraline (Zoloft), fluoxetine (Prozac), fluvoxetine (Luvox), and paroxetine (Paxil). These have become very popular due to their limited side effects and broad effectiveness. Despite the public controversy surrounding Prozac (see Kramer, 1993), controlled studies have found it to be relatively safe and effective in treating MDD (Fava et al., 1995). Furthermore, fluoxetine has been associated with a lower rate of direct health care costs when compared to other antidepressants (Hylan et al., 1998). Prozac may be particularly suited to Jeff, who has underlying avoidant symptoms.

The National Institute of Mental Health Collaborative Research Program, a large, multi-site comparison of therapy (cognitive-behavioral therapy, CBT, and IPT) to imipramine and placebo controls revealed that all forms of treatment were roughly equivalent and more effective than no treatment (e.g., Imber et al., 1990). However, investigators did find a difference in the the course of effectiveness: medication had a faster effect (usually after about 10 to 21 days) than did psychotherapy (usually after about 4 to 6 weeks), but following psychotherapy improvement was more sustained with fewer relapses. Many clinicians recommend a treatment involving pharmacotherapy for fast improvement plus psychotherapy for sustained effectiveness. This double dose gives depressed clients the best chance for rapid relief and long-term improvement.

BORDERLINE PERSONALITY DISORDER
Psychodynamic Therapy

PRESENTING COMPLAINT

Debbie is a 34-year-old married homemaker. Her husband, Mark, is a 37-year-old corporate lawyer who specializes in international law. Debbie and Mark met each other 11 years ago, shortly after he was hired by her father's firm. They have been married for seven years and have no children. They divide their time among three residences: a lavishly decorated townhouse in Boston, a 14-room summer home in New Hampshire, and a large condominium in Zurich, where Mark stays during his frequent business trips to Europe.

The therapist made first contact with Debbie one afternoon in February when she called in a panic about a "marital crisis." She was clearly agitated and sounded as if she had been sobbing. After briefly introducing herself, she described her crisis. She and Mark had gotten into an argument just as he finished packing for a business trip. She accused him of abandoning her and began to insult and berate him. In the heat of the fight she threw several porcelain figurines at him, each one costing several hundred dollars. None had struck him or even come close. As she continued to fight with him, he slapped her with enough force to knock her off balance. She then started sobbing. When he saw that she was not injured, he began to leave. Debbie threatened to kill herself if he left her alone, but he walked out the door. After a little while Debbie called a friend. The friend was a former patient of the therapist and suggested that Debbie call him.

The therapist was extremely concerned over several aspects of the call. The first was the mention of suicide. He asked Debbie if she really wanted to die. She seemed a little surprised by the urgency in his voice. No, she said, she didn't really want to die. But she often got so angry with Mark that she said things like that. The therapist continued. Did she have a concrete plan? Had she made any previous attempts?

When her answers were again negative, the therapist felt assured that she was in no immediate danger and did not require hospitalization.

He was also concerned about domestic violence. Debbie was taken aback by this phrase even more than the talk about suicide. No, neither she nor Mark ever really got hurt. Of course she had no desire to file charges. Once again convinced that there was no immediate danger, he arranged an initial consultation during lunch the next day.

Debbie arrived right on time. She began by thanking the therapist for his concern the day before. His concerns were not over, though, and he began by asking her once again about her ideas of suicide and her feelings of depression. She repeated that suicide was a frequent threat, but that she had no real intention of dying. He then asked her about her mood. Had she been depressed? Irritable? Bored? She reacted to the latter, saying that for the last several years she has felt apathetic and lethargic. This was especially noticeable when Mark was away, but it persisted to some extent most of the time when he was home, too.

He then asked her whether she had spoken to Mark since their argument. She had called him in Switzerland to apologize and to say how important he was to her. Mostly she didn't want him to worry. According to Debbie, this switch from anger to concern was common.

> I have these lightning-fast changes in my feelings for Mark. It's like there's a little switch inside me that moves from NICE to MEAN. I remember one time when we took an elevator to a business party. I was feeling fond of him and proud of his success. But then, the moment he walked out of the elevator and into the hall, I suddenly hated him. I started saying that he only had his job because he married me, that he was living off my father's money. It's not true, you know. Anyway, I said that he was manipulative and controlling and arrogant. There we were in the hallway: I was yelling at him, and he was yelling back. We had to just turn around and leave. This happens all the time; I suddenly get mean and vindictive. I really worry that one day I'll just drive him away.

The therapist again asked Debbie about domestic violence. Mark struck her yesterday; had he hit her before? She replied that he had slapped her once before. It was a slap like yesterday's. She had also slapped him on occasion, but usually she throws things at him. She claims that she doesn't really want to hit him. In fact, she never really aims. The violence has never escalated beyond this level. The therapist then asked her about other aspects of their relationship.

Therapist: How is your sexual relationship with Mark?

Debbie: Do you mean how much or how good?

Therapist: Both.

Debbie: Well, it's pretty dismal. I guess we make love twice a month, on average. But remember, he's not home a lot.

Therapist: Do you enjoy it?

Debbie: He seems to, but I don't, really. I don't think I was meant to enjoy it. I used to get excited by sex, but I haven't for a long time now. I feel like I'm sexually dead.

Therapist: Do you have any plans for a family?

Debbie: God, no. We used to talk about it, but we usually ended up fighting. I'd get so angry at Mark that I'd swear I'd never have his children. I didn't think he deserved any. You know, I've had two abortions. I scheduled them for when he was away, and I don't think he knows. I mean really, why should I go through all that just for him? First of all, I don't know if I could take the pain of having children.   But that's just the beginning. I don't think I could stand them always being around, needing me, depending on me. I suppose I would get a nanny, like my mother did for my brothers. But I'd still be their *mother*. They would always be needing things and wanting things. I don't want that. And then think of the money they'll cost.

Therapist: Would the money be a problem?

Debbie: Well, you can't just throw it away. Now, Mark does that. His younger brother is always asking for a handout of one kind or another, and there's Mark, Mr. Generous, always shelling out. I feel robbed. You know, sometimes I think his brother is out to take us. I really do. But I try not to think about it. I have Mark's accountant look after all the money. I was never good with numbers myself.

The therapist scheduled Debbie for two sessions a week.

PERSONAL HISTORY

Debbie is the oldest of four children. She has three brothers who are 12, 15, and 17 years younger. Debbie had persistent problems with mathematics and writing throughout school. She graduated from high school without distinction and did not attend college. Debbie had a moderately successful career as a fashion model until her marriage to Mark.

Debbie's parents are from a poor manufacturing town in Connecticut. They were married in their teens when her mother became pregnant with Debbie. For the first few years of her life, Debbie lived in Cambridge, Massachusetts, where her father went to engineering school. Soon after graduating he founded a small company that designed and manufactured medical equipment. This business has grown into a large corporation with three plants in the United States and two in Europe. Debbie's mother has never been employed outside the home. Debbie describes her as a "professional hostess" who is very involved in entertaining clients and socializing at company events.

Debbie describes her father as a strict, demanding tyrant who gets his way through intimidation and reproach. She also describes him as opinionated and bigoted. He was very proud of his rags-to-riches rise in business, and he expected his children to show similar successes. Debbie recalls that he would stand over her while she did her homework and criticize her whenever she had any trouble. Countless times he asked, "Why can't you get it?" or "What's the matter with you?" Debbie describes her mother as a "nonentity" who passively submitted to her husband's overpowering will. She rarely offered Debbie any encouragement or compassion; she seemed consumed with trying to perform to her husband's stringent expectations and by her growing dependence on alcohol and barbiturates. Over the years Debbie's parents spent less and less time with her, and by the time her brothers were born, they had little interest in child care. They hired professional sitters to care for the boys and saw them very little.

None of the four children is close to either parent. The oldest boy was always the nonconformist of the family. He is now a graduate student working toward his Ph.D. in history. At first their father was proud of his eldest son's academic accomplishments, but his pride turned to dismay when the son opted for a career as a history professor. His father would ask him, "Why don't you get a real job?" Two years ago this son married a Jewish woman. Not only did her parents refuse to attend the wedding, they disowned the son outright. The middle son has always had considerable difficulty in school. Like Debbie, he seems to have particular trouble with mathematics. Unlike his older brother, he felt intimidated by his father and constantly tried to please him. He is now attending a local junior college and plans to work in the company after he graduates. The youngest brother is a senior in high school. Debbie believes that he is the smartest of the three boys but has always gotten mediocre grades. She describes him as spoiled and apathetic. Debbie feels close to the eldest brother but not the younger two.

CONCEPTUALIZATION AND TREATMENT

Over the next several weeks, Debbie provided descriptions of events and feelings that reaffirmed and amplified her presenting complaints. She mentioned that Mark is a highly successful corporate lawyer. He speaks fluent French, German, and Italian; is a wonderful negotiator; and was the key figure in establishing the overseas plants in Belgium and Switzerland. He is also a workaholic who is in the country less than half the time, and even then spends about 70 hours per week at the office. This information made Debbie's virulent suggestions of nepotism all the more dramatic, while also setting a context for their relationship and making her fears of abandonment more understandable.

Borderline personality disorder is defined as a long-standing character disturbance marked by sudden and dramatic shifts in mood, unstable and intense relationships, and inconsistencies in the evaluations of oneself and others. *DSM-IV* lists nine specfic criteria that define borderline personality disorder; a person must demonstrate at least five to warrant a diagnosis. Instances that fit each of these nine criteria can be found in Debbie's behavior. The nine criteria are:
1. unstable, intense interpersonal relationships
2. impulsiveness that is potentially self-damaging
3. unstable mood
4. inappropriate and/or uncontrolled anger
5. recurrent suicidal threats
6. persistent identity disturbance
7. feelings of emptiness and boredom
8. efforts to avoid abandonment
9. stress-related paranoid ideation

Consistent with traditional psychodynamic theory, the roots of Debbie's character disturbance lay in her relationship with her parents. According to self psychology (Kohut, 1977) and object relations theory (Mahler, 1968), children are utterly dependent on their parents early in life and require a certain degree of love, support, and encouragement from them to form a healthy ego. Furthermore, the Oedipal drama that is central to Freud's theories requires an appealing opposite-sex parent and a threatening same-sex parent, or their symbolic equivalents. Without these elements, the Oedipal conflict will not be resolved, resulting in a disruption of ego identity and a failure to sublimate libidinal urges. Debbie's passive, uninvolved mother and her domineering, critical father possessed none of the qualities Debbie required for normal ego development. As a result Debbie's emotional and social development was severely impaired. Because her mother gave her no emotional support, Debbie became overly dependent on others and was terrified of abandonment. At the same time, though, she was wary of this dependence and feared intimacy. Because of her father's abusive style, she never learned to channel her libidinal urges into sexual or career pursuits. Instead, she introjected her father's abusive style, which led to low self-esteem and prevented her from developing clear goals and ambitions. She also projects this hostility onto men, in particular her husband and, as the therapeutic relationship developed, her therapist as well. Her immature superego fails to control the expression of this rage, which often comes across as irrational.

It will take some time, perhaps several years, to overcome these deficiencies and develop an ego healthy enough to tolerate, let alone integrate, the positive and negative qualities she recognizes in herself and in others. In the meantime, Debbie's therapist set up a structured, goal-oriented treatment program to cope with her immediate concerns. The first and primary goal of this program was to develop a trusting, therapeutic alliance. But establishing this trusting relationship with a borderline patient is easier said than done. Borderlines tend to be very difficult patients, and Debbie was no exception. However, once she developed a trusting alliance with her therapist, she was then able to focus on a goal-oriented program that directly addressed many problem areas in her life. Debbie's treatment program has five primary goals:

1. Improve impulse control
2. Increase self-esteem
3. Increase sexual contact with her husband
4. Reduce depressed mood
5. Diminish paranoid ideation

1. Improving impulse control. When Debbie began therapy, she had very little impulse control. This was expressed most dramatically in her sudden outbursts aimed at her husband, though it came out in other ways too, including spree shopping and reckless driving. One effective technique was to tap into Debbie's expressed interest in money. Once her therapist recognized this interest, he developed an economy metaphor. For each altercation with her husband, Debbie was to ask herself what it would cost her in terms of anger, bitterness, and Mark's potential rejection of her, versus what she will gain from controlling her anger in terms of pleasure, self-esteem, and security. When she felt the need to castigate Mark, she was to stop and first calculate the benefits and liabilities. Simply stopping to calculate this econometric helped Debbie avoid many of her impulsive behaviors.

2. Increasing self-esteem. Debbie's therapist found two ways to increase her self-esteem. The first involved focusing on Debbie's strengths, many of which had been glossed over. For example, Debbie works on many charity boards and organizations. She is very attractive and sophisticated, and she can be remarkably charming. As a result she is quite successful at fund-raising and dealing with corporate donors. However, she usually dismisses the value of her efforts by saying that it is "only" charity work. In therapy she was urged to recognize the value of her contributions.

A second approach to bolstering self-esteem was to diagnose specific conditions that Debbie had always interpreted as signs of general failure. Debbie's school history and her description of her middle brother's academic problems suggested the posibility of an undiagnosed learning disability. The therapist arranged to have Debbie tested by a specialist in learning disabilities, and sure enough, she met the criteria for mathematics disorder. By explaining her limitations as diseases (which may have genetic links), the therapist instructed her to no longer see herself as generally stupid but merely as someone who suffers from rather a common, specific learning disability, sort of like a specific disability such as being nearsighted. And just as nearsighted people are prescribed corrective lenses, she was given some practical advice for how to live with her limitations, such as using a calculator.

3. Increasing sexual contact. As therapy progressed, Debbie occasionally described elements of her sex life that she found particularly pleasing. It turned out that most of these experiences occurred with her husband. These pleasant memories were pointed out to her to highlight the positive aspects of her relationship with her husband, which were often forgotten when she went into a rage and focused only on his negative qualities. The approach to increasing her sexual behavior took much the same form as the treatment to control her impulses. She was asked to think of how much a pleasurable sexual encounter was worth to her. What would she get out of it? What would Mark get? How would it contribute to their sexual relationship as a whole?

Debbie was also encouraged to have open discussions with Mark about her problems with intimacy. In the beginning she was unable to tolerate more than a cursory exchange without feeling overly threatened, but at least Mark was beginning to understand that her somewhat hot-and-cold sexual behavior was not really meant as a personal rejection.

Progress in this dimension was somewhat erratic. Certainly the quantity of her sexual activity with her husband increased, but often she felt threatened by the increased intimacy and recoiled. This would be expressed by her making preparations for a sexual encounter (making a special dinner, buying new lingerie) but then suddenly deciding to sleep in a different room, leaving her husband confused and frustrated. But even this was an improvement. In the past she would drive Mark away with a stream of hostile remarks when she felt threatened by intimacy. More and more, she signaled her refusal to have sex by relatively benign behaviors, such as sleeping in a different room. Only when she began to make real progress in her ego integration did she really come to accept the intimacy that comes with sex and show a significant improvement in the quality of her sex life.

4. Reducing depressed mood. Aside from Debbie's rather alarming mention of suicide during her initial telephone call, she showed few overt symptoms of depression. As therapy progressed, however, a consistent pattern of dysphoria began to reveal itself. Although Debbie remained fairly active socially, she regarded many of these activities as dull and monotonous. It became clear that most of her everyday activities were initiated by friends, relatives, or other external demands, such as business dinners and deadlines for charity drives. Much of her boredom and apathy stemmed from her identity disturbance: until she developed a coherent sense of self, the events in her life continued to lack meaning.

Debbie was referred to a psychiatrist for a medication evaluation, and he prescribed the antidepressant bupropion (Wellbutrin), which increased her general activity level and her interest in her outside activities. It also improved her willingness to complete some of the treatment recommendations suggested by her therapist.

5. Diminishing paranoid ideation. Sometimes Debbie's wariness of intimacy and her desperate need not to be abandoned combined to produce behaviors that had a paranoid quality. One indication of her deep mistrust was her extreme jealousy, expressed by her frequent accusations to Mark of his "screwing around," to use one of her least vulgar terms. While it was true that Mark's travel schedule and long hours provided him with ample opportunity for extramarital affairs, in actuality he had never given Debbie good cause to doubt his fidelity. Nevertheless, she frequently confronted him with jealous accusations. At a recent dinner dance, Debbie saw a coworker whom she suspected was one of Mark's lovers. Mark made no comment concerning this woman; in fact he hadn't even known she was at the dance. Suddenly Debbie began sobbing and making quiet but audible comments that she "knew all about that bitch." Mark quickly led Debbie out. A loud argument began in the hallway and lasted through the ride home. In therapy Debbie admitted that Mark had given her no reason to suspect this woman, but still Debbie could not control herself.

Another sign of Debbie's paranoid ideation was her manner of holding grudges. Once Debbie called her therapist to reschedule an appointment she had to miss. He was ending a session with another patient at the time and asked her to hold for a few minutes. She hung up 30 seconds later. Being familiar with her inflated sense of entitlement, he was not particularly surprised by this. But he was surprised when she brought up this phone call four weeks later as evidence that he habitually takes advantage of her.

The therapist's method for having Debbie gain control over her paranoid ideation had two steps. First, Debbie was asked to analyze as objectively as possible the evidence that supports her suspicions. Second, she was reminded that her accusations were not "free"; they carried certain costs, such as embarrassing and aggravating the accused as well as starting a hostile interaction. She was told to be responsible for her accusations. Together these suggestions had the effect of making Debbie think before pointing her finger, which greatly reduced the number of impulsive rages.

When Debbie began therapy, she was always prompt and attentive. Gradually, however, she began arriving late—first by a few minutes, but then by as much as half an hour. After three months she began skipping an appointment now and again, and then after four and a half months she discontinued therapy for a period of three weeks.

Up to this time Debbie and the therapist had made great gains toward establishing a therapeutic alliance; Debbie's comments became more open, revealing, and personal. At the same time, her level of hostility toward the therapist gradually increased. She never failed to question the latest bill he sent her, even though nothing had changed since the first one. But the most interesting expression of her hostility toward him was her grooming habits. It began when Debbie brushed her hair during a session. She brushed her hair again at the next session, but this time she pulled the hair out of the brush and let it fall on the couch. She quickly began to perform more and more of these grooming habits, and with each one the residue left behind wound up on the therapist's couch: used tissues, cotton balls, and even clipped toenails. The therapist became more and more annoyed, but he suppressed his anger and tried as best he could to remain cool and professional. Finally he decided to point out this behavior and discuss its underlying meaning.

Having been a fashion model, Debbie was careful to manage her appearance. She would be particularly careful with a male authority figure, whom she would naturally associate with her hypercritical father. By putting on makeup in front of the therapist, Debbie symbolically conveyed that she was willing to have him see the "real her" without her first needing to cover her faults. But by leaving her litter behind her, she was also asking him to "clean up her garbage." Thus, she saw him as both savior and servant. As they developed a closer alliance, however, she felt threatened by the increasing intimacy and tried to drive him away, in this case with her rude, inconsiderate behavior. She was transferring her ambivalent feelings about her father, and to a lesser extent her husband, onto the therapist. She needed him to accept the "real" her, yet she feared that he might abandon her once he saw her faults. Her behavior was a test to see what he would put up with and how much he really cared.

When the therapist discussed this transference reaction with Debbie, she reacted with a blank look. She was unaware of performing her grooming behaviors, let alone their underlying meaning. Though she had no immediate reaction to his interpretation, she seemed to think about it as she left. She arrived on time for the next session and has attended regularly ever since. At the next session she was very interested in the concept of transference and the way it revealed her underlying motives. Whether this experience will lead to a significant insight remains to be seen.

PROGNOSIS

Debbie has been in therapy for about eight months, and her therapist is optimistic about her prognosis. She has many innate strengths, including a high IQ and a demonstrated capacity for ego integration. She was successful in establishing a therapeutic alliance, and she has begun to be more tolerant of intimacy with her husband. Her impulse control problems have diminished markedly, and they will most likely continue to recede. Most noticeably, her self-esteem has improved.

Still, personality disorders are notoriously persistent, and doubtless many problems will continue. It will take a number of years before she matures emotionally and is able to accept her hostile and libidinal urges. Until then, she will remain dependent on a man, both financially and emotionally. In addition, she will be limited by her developmental disabilities, though she has learned to make allowances for them.

Whether Debbie continues to show ego integration depends on several factors, the primary one being how long she stays in her present therapy. If she stays for at least another year, she will probably continue to do well. If her present therapy is discontinued much earlier than that, most likely her fragile ego could not take the stress of abandonment. Fortunately for Debbie, she can afford to pay for her therapy. The typical managed care plan would pay for only a handful of sessions, but Debbie can afford to continue indefinitely. Her final termination from treatment will depend on life events as well as her therapeutic progress.

DISCUSSION

Borderline personality disorder is considered to be one of the most severe of all the personality disorders (Arntz, 1994; Gunderson, 1996; Kroll, 1988; Linehan, 1993), and treating borderline patients is not a task for the faint of heart. They are extremely demanding in terms of the therapist's time and energy. Two issues predominate in treatment with borderlines. The first is establishing a therapeutic alliance. As Debbie's case demonstrates, this can be a difficult process. In fact, this case is a relatively uncomplicated example. Many borderlines are treated for years without establishing a positive alliance. Others make frequent inappropriate demands on therapist, such as late-night phone calls. One therapist received a phone call at home from a borderline client. His 10-year-old son answered, only to hear the client threaten to kill his father. Still other clients switch from therapist to therapist (or from hospital to hospital) in their efforts to avoid emotional intimacy.

The second issue that predominates in treatment involves transference and countertransference. Debbie's case provides a good example of the transference process. Because transferences are often negative and persistent, therapists must be especially careful in managing their own countertransference reactions.

Debbie is quite a provocative person, both in her physical attractiveness and in her hostile rages. Although her therapist is generally a very easygoing and calm man, she often brings out the worst in him. On several occasions her therapist felt like he "wanted to sock her." Although he does not condone the fact that Mark had struck her, after treating her for several months he understood Mark's frustration and even feels that Mark is to be commended for showing such restraint over the past 11 years.

In addition to the demands of building a therapeutic alliance and managing transference and countertransference reactions, therapists who treat borderlines must contend with three additional problems. First, change tends to be slow and gradual, and therapeutic plateaus are frequent. Second, borderlines are generally unable to project their thoughts into the future, and thus they often fail to grasp their own improvement and how it might have an impact on their lives. Finally, most borderline patients have limited ego strength and weak impulse control, and they have little reason to expect positive change.

Recently researchers have begun to report some limited success with borderlines using cognitive-behavioral treatments (e.g., Arntz, 1994) and dialectic behavior therapy, a form of cognitive-behavioral therapy with a specific focus on modifying behavior through group skills training (Linehan, Heard, & Armstrong, 1993). Although these treatments tend to be long (e.g., Marsha Linehan puts one year as the minimum treatment), they have nevertheless been shown to be cost-effective (Gabbard, 1997; Gabbard, Lazar, Hornberger, & Spiegel, 1997). Success has also been reported with the use of antianxiety, antidepressant, antipsychotic, and even antiepileptic medication.

Conducting research on borderline patients is also a fascinating but frustrating enterprise. There are two main difficulties: a failure of the field to settle on one set definition of borderline personality, and the overlap between borderline personality disorder and other forms of psychopathology.

Historically the concept of "borderline syndrome" was broader than the current *DSM-IV* usage of the term. Thought disorder was a central element to a borderline diagnosis. Thus, a person was thought to be on the "borderline" between a neurotic and a psychotic disorder. In *DSM-III* in 1980, borderline syndrome was divided into two personality disorders: borderline personality, which mainly described problems in self-image and mood, and schizotypal personality, which emphasized thought disorder (Swartz et al., 1989). Many researchers

(Edell, 1984; Kroll, 1988; Kullgren, 1987) disagreed with this decision. *DSM-IV* has made a move toward the original meaning by adding criterion #9 (paranoid ideation) but many feel this still gives insufficient emphasis to the thought disorder common among borderlines.

Several measures for borderline personality have been developed based on these different notions, including the Borderline Syndrome Index (BSI) (Conte, Plutchik, Karasu, & Jerrett, 1980; Edell, 1984), the Diagnostic Index for Borderlines (DIB) (Gunderson, Kolb, & Austin, 1981), and the Diagnostic Interview Schedule/Borderline Index (DIS) (Robins, Helzer, Crougham, & Ratcliff, 1981). Of these three, the DIS most closely adheres to the definition of borderline personality as described by *DSM-IV*. The use of different diagnostic tools complicates research because inconsistent results are based on different methodologies.

A further complication is that people with borderline personalities are likely to suffer from a number of other psychiatric conditions, including substance use (Inman, Bascue, & Skoloda, 1985; Nace, Saxon, & Shore, 1983), eating disorders (Pope & Hudson, 1989), dysthymia and depression (Pepper et al., 1995), and especially other personality disorders, particularly schizotypal personality disorder (Edell, 1984; Spitzer, Endicott, & Gibbon, 1979). This overlap makes it difficult to estimate the prevalence rate accurately. One piece of good news is that the historical association between borderline personality and schizophrenia has been severed, as the two can be distinguished reliably (Kullgren, 1987).

Despite this complicated picture, some generalizations concerning the epidemiology and demographics of borderline personality disorder can be made. Using the DIS, Swartz, Blazer, George, and Winfield (1990) found that 1.8 percent of a community sample met the criteria for borderline personality. Generally, studies (e.g., Swartz et al., 1990) conclude that borderline personality is more common in women, though this is not always found (Golomb et al., 1995). Information on race, marital status, and socioeconomic status (SES) is inconsistent. More research is needed to better understand this fascinating but complicated disorder.

ALCOHOL DEPENDENCE
Alcoholics Anonymous

PRESENTING COMPLAINT

It had been an insanely wild summer. Grace had gotten drunk and high virtually everyday, if not every single day. She and Conrad, her boyfriend, had a cool bunch of friends who shared a daily ritual. They'd get up around noon, usually with a hangover, and get together in the afternoon. They would get high and make plans for the night. At 10:00 or 11:00 p.m. she would sneak out to meet them, and they would spend the night drinking and doing drugs. Maybe they would go to some clubs, or maybe they would just hang out. Rad would (hopefully) drive her home around 3:00 or 4:00 a.m., when she would crash, limp and wasted. But by noon the next day she was ready for more. It was fun, exciting, and liberating.

But it could be dangerous, too. Rad didn't always manage to take her home. About a month ago he had left her at a club in San Francisco's seedy SOMA district (he had either gotten mad at her or just forgotten her, neither could remember which), and she stumbled around the warehouses and bars for three hours wearing only a ripped T-shirt. Finally a security guard, fearing she might have been raped, called SFPD, who took her to a local hospital. When the police were satisfied that she had not been assaulted, they called Grace's mother to pick her up. Her mother, who thought Grace had been safely tucked in bed, was flabbergasted. Grace earnestly protested that it was the first time she had ever done anything like that and promised that it would never happen again. Her protests weren't necessary; her mother was too frightened and confused to think of punishment.

Grace decided to cut down on how much she drank and to cut out the drugs altogether, and for a few days she did. But soon her daily intake of alcohol was back up to her usual amounts, if not more. After a few more days she started smoking pot again, then using acid, and within two weeks her drug use was up to its old level.

Then one night she had a strange, almost spiritual revelation. It was a typical party-frenzy night just like any other, and she was intoxicated as usual, but it kept bothering her that she couldn't quit drugs. While she and Rad were driving to yet another club, she asked him why she couldn't stop, why she gave up on her plan so quickly, why she kept getting high every night. Rad, who was a veteran of many Alcoholics Anonymous and Narcotics Anonymous meetings, knew what the answer was. Like him, she was an alcoholic and a drug addict, and she was obviously in denial herself. His answer, "Because you can't control it. Duh!" stated what was obvious to everyone who knew her, except of course Grace's mother and Grace herself. The simple truth of Conrad's statement turned on a light in her head, and for the first time it struck her that she might have a problem. If she really wanted to quit drugs, Conrad added, she'd have to quit everything. And she couldn't do it herself; she would need a detox program, and then some recovery group like AA or NA.

Grace took Conrad's advice to heart and entered an inpatient rehabilitation program at a local hospital; Conrad entered a similar program across town. Both were typical inpatient programs: a few days of detoxification, several days of psychoeducation and group meetings, and then a couple days of skills training and planning for relapse prevention.

One component of treatment that began on the first day was attendance at AA meetings. Grace was surprised that there was no indoctrination, no twelve-steps lecture, no pressure to confess. The only awkward part was the end of the meeting, when everyone formed a circle, held hands, and recited the Lord's prayer. The speaker at the meeting was a young woman, about 25 years old, who introduced herself by saying, "My name is Pat, and I'm an alcoholic." "Hi, Pat!" was the traditional, friendly refrain. Pat described a life of alcohol and drug use that gradually escalated into a series of uncontrollable binges. She had made three attempts to quit at rehab programs. At the last program she met a terrific man; they were married six months later. On their wedding night they celebrated by ordering a bottle of champagne with dinner. Then they ordered another, and then split a bottle of whiskey before passing out. Within a week they were drinking every-day, and soon they started using drugs again; she tended to hold back, but her husband engaged in frequent cocaine binges. Then one night about three months ago he had a massive heart attack and died. This week would have been their first anniversary.

At the meeting the next day, three people got up and described lives ruined by drugs and alcohol. Other meetings introduced the AA Twelve Steps and the Twelve Traditions, and after these Grace picked up some AA literature and read through it in her room. She felt a sense of connection with the group almost immediately, and she was closely involved in the meetings for the rest of her stay. Before she left the inpatient program, the meeting coordinator gave her a list of contact people who were members of groups in her neighborhood.

Grace's mother assumed that once Grace was released from the hospital, her treatment was over. "Oh, no," Grace replied, "sobriety is a lifelong struggle." Then Conrad, newly released himself, came by and drove her to a meeting, leaving a startled mother behind. When Grace got home, her mother forbade her to attend any more meetings. She refused to see young Grace as an alcoholic, and she had a vague fear that she would lose Grace to a fanatical, cultlike group. She also forbade Grace to see Conrad, whom she considered to be the cause of Grace's drug use in the first place. Grace and Conrad were undeterred, however, and they developed a system of code names and neutral pickup locations so they could continue attending meetings every day. When he drove her home, he made sure to park at least two blocks from Grace's house. After attending a couple of meetings at one of the groups, Grace approached the meeting organizer, introduced herself, and said that she would like to get up and talk. The next week she told her story. Although most of the meeting veterans thought they had seen it all before (and most had), still many in the audience felt a lump in their throats when a small Chinese girl walked up to the front of the room and lowered the microphone to her level. In her high, wavering, but determined voice, she announced, "My name is Grace, and I'm an alco-holic." She was 13 years old.

PERSONAL HISTORY

Grace is the youngest of three children. Her sister is five years older; her brother is three years older. Grace's parents are both second-generation Chinese. Her father, a successful importer who now owns a chain of three small leather goods shops, abandoned the family when Grace was 4 years old, and she has little recollection of him. Ever since the separation, Grace's mother has supported the family through her job as a secretary for an importing firm in Chinatown, where she met her ex-husband. Despite help from her family and friends, being a single mother has been difficult, as evidenced by their moves within San Francisco: first from the elegant townhouse in Pacific Heights to a six-room apartment in the Marina, and then to a modest bungalow in the Sunset District. For the past six months Grace's mother has been dating a buyer for a local department store who does business with her company. Grace describes her relationship with her mother as "distant." Although Grace does not openly rebel against her mother, as her sister does, their relationship is nevertheless characterized by continuing animosity in the form of almost constant bickering and accusations.

Grace's sister is extremely intelligent but has always been a rebellious child. She has frequent fights with their mother over a variety of topics, ranging from dating and drug use to clothing and hairstyles. Her oppositional disposition is not solely instigated by her reactions to authority; she has just as many arguments with her siblings.

Grace's brother is also rebellious, but his quest for autonomy takes the form of aggressive behavior and drug abuse. He has not been as discreet or judicious as Grace, though, and his drug use has resulted in more serious brushes with the authorities. He has been suspended from school on three occasions, once for fighting and twice for having drug paraphernalia. He has also been arrested twice, once for vandalism and once for drug possession. His sentence for the latter was mandatory enrollment in an inpatient detox/rehab program and one year of weekly AA meetings. He was sober less than 24 hours after his release from detox, and he attended few AA meetings, usually while intoxicated.

Grace met most of her friends, including Conrad, through her brother. This put her in company with peers three to five years her senior. Ironically, this same age disparity allowed Grace to maintain her grades at a B+ average. Because her drug-abusing friends were at least three years older, they were in junior high school when Grace was still in elementary school, and she mostly saw them only at night and on weekends. Grace developed a pattern of drug use she termed her "double life." She never used drugs while she was in school or with her mother, and to most authority figures she was the picture of innocence. According to Grace, she just showed up on time at the designated location, and she was never suspected. Her active masquerading even overcame incriminating evidence. Once her teacher noticed drug paraphernalia (a bong) in her purse and confronted Grace and even informed her mother. But Grace explained that her brother must have put it there as a joke, and she was readily believed. Grace's mother had other warning signs, such as finding some marijuana and condoms in her room, but again Grace shifted the blame onto her brother.

Grace's innocent public image contrasted with her nighttime persona. Grace had her first alcohol when she was 10 years old. When her mother had gone out and left the children home alone, they raided her liquor cabinet and got drunk. Soon after this she met her brother's friends, and they started going out together. At first she mostly had beer, malt liquor, and cheap wine, but gradually she became less discriminating, drinking whatever was available. She began to spend more and more time getting drunk with her brother's friends. Then boys in the group introduced her to pot. Starting from there, Grace quickly increased the frequency and variety of her drug use. By the time she joined AA, Grace used pot, opium, and LSD regularly, and she dabbled with other substances, including speed, hashish, and PCP. Interestingly, she always avoided cocaine, and especially crack, out of fear of getting hooked, a worry that remained effective in the midst of her wildest drug use.

Grace was on acid when she had her first visit to the hospital emergency room at age 11. She doesn't remember the event. Apparently while she was tripping she cut her wrists with a carving knife at a party. Her friends were terrified and called an ambulance. The wounds themselves were superficial, but the suicidal implications were very serious. She saw a psychodynamic therapist once a week. Her therapy had little impact on her substance abuse; she was still seeing this therapist when she entered her inpatient program.

Grace was taken to the hospital again the next year when she suffered a sudden paralysis lasting for two days, which she believed to be an aftereffect of acid. Nevertheless, she continued her drug use unabated.

Grace also experimented with sex. On most nights she had sex with Conrad, but they were by no means monogamous. She often had sex with other friends, and sometimes with strangers. Sex was usually unprotected. When she thought about it, she got very scared: scared of getting pregnant and scared of catching herpes, or AIDS, or God knows what else. She didn't like being scared, so she got high, which led to more sex, which caused more fear, and the cycle continued.

Denial also obscured her mother's view of Grace's behavior. Despite Grace's hospital emergencies, finding Grace with drug and sex paraphernalia, and watching Grace come home drunk and high, her mother never suspected any serious drug use. Between the financial and family strains of single parenting, her new romance, and her difficult first two children, there was little opportunity for close supervision. Grace's mother expressed her utter surprise at their first family session: "I still can't get over that we're here because of Grace. She was the one I didn't have to worry about."

CONCEPTUALIZATION AND TREATMENT

Grace demonstrated a clear case of substance dependence. For over three years she had gotten drunk and high every weekend and many weeknights. Of all the substances she abused, she pointed to alcohol as causing most of the problems in her life, and alcohol dependence became the focus of treatment. The *DSM-IV* criteria for alcohol dependence are (1) tolerance, a need for more alcohol to get the same level of intoxication, (2) withdrawal, symptoms experienced after discontinuing use or the need to take more of the substance to counteract withdrawal feelings, (3) consumption in larger amounts and/or more often than intended, (4) unsuccessful attempts to cut down, (5) a great deal of time spent obtaining, using, and/or recovering from alcohol, (6) social or recreational activities given up, and (7) continued alcohol use despite knowing it may cause physical or psychological problems. It is possible that Grace met all seven criteria. She failed to quit her alcohol use, or even to cut down on her alcohol consumption; she usually drank more than she intended, often passing out in strange places; she spent every afternoon and night getting drunk; she limited her social sphere to her drug-using friends; and she continued to drink and use drugs even after two hospital visits which she herself had attributed to complications from drug use. Over the course of her drug use, she gradually increased the amount of alcohol and drugs she consumed, until by the time of her treatment she was using amounts that would have killed her only a year before. But these fine points of diagnosis were lost on Grace. She was an alcoholic, plain and simple.

Grace quickly learned the process of recovery according to AA, which is summarized in The Twelve Steps. These first appeared in *Alcoholics Anonymous* (usually referred to as *The Big Book*) in 1939. They are:
1. We admitted we are powerless over alcohol—that our lives had become unmanageable.
2. Came to believe that a Power greater than ourselves could restore us to sanity.
3. Made a decision to turn our will and our lives over to the care of God *as we understood Him.*
4. Made a searching and fearless moral inventory of ourselves.
5. Admitted to God, to ourselves, and to another human being the exact nature of our wrongs.
6. Were entirely ready to have God remove all these defects of character.
7. Humbly asked Him to remove our shortcomings.

8. Made a list of all persons we had harmed, and became willing
    to make amends to them all.
9. Made direct amends to such people wherever possible, except
    when to do so would injure them or others.
10. Continued to take personal inventory and when we were wrong
    promptly admitted it.
11. Sought through prayer and meditation to improve our conscious
    contact with God *as we understood Him,* praying only for knowl-
    edge of His will for us and the power to carry that out.
12. Having had a spiritual awakening as a result of these steps, we
    tried to carry this message to alcoholics, and to practice these
    principles in all our affairs.

These twelve steps, in turn, are based on the Twelve Traditions, first
printed in 1945. A short form of the Twelve Traditions, used
commonly today, is as follows:

1. Our common welfare should come first; personal recovery depends
    on AA unity.
2. For our group purpose there is but one ultimate authority--a
    loving God as He may express Himself in our group conscience.
3. The only requirement for AA membership is a desire to stop
    drinking.
4. Each group should be autonomous except in matters affecting
    other groups or AA as a whole.
5. Each group has but one primary purpose--to carry its message
    to the alcoholic who still suffers.
6. An AA group ought never endorse, finance, or lend the AA
    name to any related facility or outside enterprise, lest problems
    of money, property, and prestige divert us from our primary
    purpose.
7. Every AA group ought to be fully self-supporting, declining
    outside contributions.
8. Alcoholics Anonymous should remain forever nonprofessional,
    but our service centers may employ special workers.

9. AA, as such, ought never be organized; but we may create service boards or committees directly responsible to those they serve.
10. Alcoholics Anonymous has no opinion on outside issues; hence the AA name ought never be drawn into public controversy.
11. Our public relations policy is based on attraction rather than promotion; we need always maintain personal anonymity at the level of press, radio, films.
12. Anonymity is the spiritual foundation of all our Traditions, ever reminding us to place principles before personalities.

AA is often described as a self-help group, but Grace disagreed with this label. "It is *group*-help," she explained, "You don't stay sober by helping yourself, you stay sober by helping other alcoholics. Besides, you depend on a Higher Power to get better. You can't do it yourself."

By the time Grace spoke before an audience, she had attended 15 neighborhood AA meetings. But this was just the beginning. Grace would go on to attend at least one meeting every day for over nine months, totalling more than 300 meetings, and she continued to attend meetings at least 3 times a week for the next few years. The content of the meetings varied somewhat, depending on what kind of meeting it was. Open meetings typically featured one, two, or three speakers who described their experiences. Other meetings involved discussions of the Twelve Steps, while some provided opportunities to work in pairs or small groups and practice the steps, a process called "Twelve Stepping." In addition to simply attending, Grace became involved in the actual running of the AA meetings. She started by offering to help set up, making sure the seats were arranged and the literature was stacked and available. Next she volunteered to make the coffee, an indispensable ingredient at any AA meeting. Next she became the anniversary person, who kept notes of the members' sobriety durations for small award ceremonies held during the meetings. Eventually she took on the task of arranging speakers, both within the group and from other groups, to present their stories. After three years she was asked to give inspirational speeches to other groups. With money provided by the

AA General Service Office, she toured the country delivering talks describing her own experiences, particularly to younger audiences. She also encouraged existing groups to be especially accepting to young alcoholics in their groups.

Contact with fellow AA members wasn't limited to the meetings. Grace has called members at their homes during particularly stressful occasions, especially in the early phases of her recovery. Although she felt vulnerable during periods of loneliness and depression, for Grace the hardest time to remain sober was when she felt good and wanted to have fun. This feeling of joy brought up many drinking cues, since many of her most joyful experiences involved alcohol and drugs. She also knows many fellow alcoholics who relapsed just when they were improving. She thinks that the satisfaction, joy, and relief from gaining control over one's life makes people want to celebrate, and for many people, as Pat described in her story, celebrating means drinking and using drugs, which starts the addiction cycle all over again.

In addition to AA, something that had been helpful for Grace was a local clubhouse. In Grace's case it was an apartment in a local building, but she knows of other clubhouses that are rented storefronts, separate houses, and other places. The clubhouse offers young people who want to abstain from drugs a place to go and hang out. Although it is not officially affiliated with any AA group, most of the people who go there are in AA or NA.

Grace's steady involvement in AA did not mean that she did not experience crises in her recovery. The first occurred right away, when she first learned about the Twelve Steps. At first Grace found the spiritual and religious overtones of AA difficult to accept. Her family had never been regular church attenders, and she had many personal doubts about the existence of a supreme being. This is a fundamental hurdle to overcome, since AA is based largely on submitting oneself to the will of God. Grace was able to reconcile this issue by seeing AA's meaning of God as metaphorical, referring to some generalized external, spiritual power. Gradually she came to accept this view and then to rely on it. "Although the AA meetings and sponsors help," she said, "sometimes there's only the Higher Power between you and that drink."

Another problem was that Grace's mother at first refused to let her go to AA meetings, basing most of her objections on Grace's renewed relationship with Conrad. After about two weeks, though, it became clear that Grace was seeing Conrad anyway, and she could detect a noticeable improvement in Grace's attitude. Convinced that AA was helping, her mother joined Al-Anon (an AA-type group for nonalcoholics who are affected by someone else's drinking) and met Grace for weekly family sessions with a counselor. Following the recommendations of the family counselor, the mother maintained a "dry house." Now she and her boyfriend drank only while out, and just this change cut their drinking significantly. Over the years Grace's relationship with her mother and (later) her stepfather steadily improved, though she was never as close with them as with her best friends at AA.

Conrad precipitated a crisis period when he began drinking and using drugs again after two months of being sober. Grace didn't want to stop seeing him, but it was too hard to be around him and his friends when they drank and used drugs, so she broke it off.

A final source of difficulty lay in the demographics of AA members. Grace described herself as having "three strikes against me" at the meetings: she was young, female, and Asian. *The Big Book* made it clear from its first printing in 1939 that AA should pose no racial, class, sex, religious, or any other barriers to potential members, and, at least in theory, AA welcomes everyone equally. This policy was remarkably progressive for its time. But the reality is that AA was developed by two white middle-class men in a time of relative social conservatism, and this beginning, combined with its puritanical tone, often led to members in some groups developing socially conservative attitudes. Although no one said anything openly derogatory to Grace, she often got the sense that older members just did not take her seriously. After all, how much life experience can a 13-year-old girl have? This same feeling of not fitting in has led to the formation of several organizations that cater to particular populations; those relevant to Grace include Women for Sobriety, National Asian Pacific Families Against Substance Abuse, and Narcotics Anonymous. Grace has spoken at meetings held by each of these groups, but she does so with mixed feelings. On the one hand, she wants to reach as many people as possible. On the other hand, though, she dislikes the idea of splintering AA into separate special interest groups. In the spirit of the Twelve Traditions, she thinks it is best to try to educate and broaden the views of all alcoholics instead of setting up demographic divisions.

Grace is now a junior at the University of Southern California, where she majors in psychology and works as a research assistant in the Institute for Health Promotion and Disease Prevention Research. She remains involved in two weekly groups and goes to an average of three meetings per week. She does not contemplate any end to these activities; as she told her mother, sobriety is a lifelong task for the alcoholic.

PROGNOSIS

In general, the prognosis for AA treatment is dismal. In their review on AA effectiveness, Galaif and Sussman (1995) estimate that only 5 to 13 percent of treated alcoholics will maintain a lasting AA membership; the reciprocal dropout rate is, of course, 87 to 95 percent. Another intervention study based on the Twelve Steps (Martin, Giannadrea, Rogers, & Johnson, 1996) reported that only 33 percent of their subjects completed the intervention, and only 6 percent remained in treatment 3 months after the intervention. These are bleak numbers, because most likely those who drop out have worse outcomes than those who remain in AA. For example, in a study of 299 adolescents attending an AA-based inpatient program, Stinchfield, Niforopulos, and Feder (1994) found that those who were difficult to contact at follow-up had worse outcomes than those who were contacted through routine means. Similarly, Watson et al. (1997) report that AA members who dropped out had higher rates of relapse and crime.

Another indicator of a poor prognosis is Grace's "three-strike" status, which would tend to make it more difficult for her to identify with AA groups. Although AA has become more accepting of younger members, female members, minority members, and drug-addicted members, still they can be fairly conservative in their approach. Knowing nothing else about the case, the prognosis would be poor indeed.

But more is known about this case: specifically, Grace's personal characteristics. Researchers (Galaif & Sussman, 1995; Kennedy & Minami, 1994; Sommer, 1997) estimate that the single most important factor in the success of AA groups is the personality of the individual, and they list personality characteristics most likely to lead to success in AA. Here is where Grace shines, for she possesses virtually every desired trait. For one thing, she voluntarily sought treatment long before she reached anything approaching "rock bottom." Although her drug use had resulted in some significant interpersonal problems and some frightening episodes, it never disrupted her schoolwork, nor had it ever caused any serious legal or health problems. Grace is flexible in her attitudes and tolerant of others. She is outgoing and willing to disclose her faults. She is intelligent, energetic, and organized. She is free from other psychopathology, such as depression or character disorders. She is goal-oriented and views helping others as her primary task. She takes responsibility for her actions and avoids blaming others. Finally, she is motivated by a personal spiritual revelation, which keeps her going in trying circumstances. In short, Grace has the personal characteristics tailor-made for successful AA experiences. As of this writing she has been sober for seven years, and she remains very active in the program. Grace is likely to become a star within AA, but of course she will remain anonymous.

DISCUSSION

Alcohol-related disorders are among the most common psychiatric disorders in the United States. *DSM-IV* reports a lifetime prevalence of alcohol dependence ranging between 8 and 14 percent of the general population; the ratio of men to women diagnosed with alcohol disorders (dependence or abuse) can be as high as 5:1. A recent study on the rate of substance use and dependence among adolescents (Warner et al., 1995) estimated that by age 14, 19 percent of boys and 13 percent of girls used drugs regularly, and of this combined group, 8 percent were considered clinically dependent. So Grace is certainly not alone as an adolescent with alcohol and drug problems. In addition, Grace's pattern of initiating drug use through older drug-using peers is typical. Webb, Baer, and McKelvey (1995) surveyed fifth- and sixth-graders as to their intention to drink in junior high school. The factor that best discriminated those who intended to drink from those who didn't was older peer use.

But in other ways, Grace's case is unique. Her status as a female Asian-American adolescent is unusual within the traditional AA framework. The underrepresentation of women and minorities results in large part from the assumptions of mainstream American culture in the 1930s, when AA was founded. This subtle discrimination should not be blamed on AA itself. As mentioned above, *The Big Book* was quite liberal in its social thinking. Though a chapter of the first edition, titled "To Wives," makes the assumption that most alcoholics are married men, the chapter nevertheless begins by saying that AA is as amenable for alcoholic women as men. By the third edition of *Alcoholics Anonymous* (1976), demographic expectations had changed. Of its 43 case histories (collected throughout the history of AA), 13 are female (1 adolescent), 2 African American, and 1 Native American.

The acceptance of younger members has not been so smooth. Younger members differ from typical adult AA members in many ways, such as limited life experience, greater likelihood of illegal drug use, and less mature self-evaluations. The most important difference, however, may be in morality. In a thoughtful article on the philosophy of AA, Delbanco and Delbanco (1995) argue that changing attitudes toward personal responsibility in the United States could be making AA obsolete. In the past, it was expected that one took personal responsibility for personal problems, regardless of who might have caused them. This willingness to confront and cope with one's own fate is central to AA philosophy. In contrast, the current trend of American society, as manifested by a proliferation of civil lawsuits and victims' groups, is to see oneself as a passive sufferer whose only recourse is to blame others. In addition, Americans have developed a me-first attitude, which breeds an expectation that AA is undertaken mainly for self-serving reasons—to end one's own addiction. The altruistic and evangelical components of AA—to seek out and serve other alcoholics—is being forgotten. Ironically, this self-focus makes self-improvement *less* likely; the interpersonal work is actually the basis of improvement. Grace agrees with Bob Smith and Bill Wilson, the two founders of AA, that reaching out to other alcoholics is the most effective aspect of her recovery.

Evaluating Alcoholics Anonymous

Alcoholics Anonymous is the most common treatment offered for alcohol-related disorders (McCrady & Miller, 1993) with a membership estimated to be well over 1 million (Berenson, 1987). Yet despite its popularity, until recently little controlled research has been done on the effectiveness of AA (Kassel & Wagner, 1993). Many factors underlie this difficulty, including the individually based spiritual approach (which devalues the empirical, nomothetic approach of controlled studies), the autonomy of individual groups, the voluntary and loosely structured meetings, and the anonymity of individual members. Despite these difficulties, some researchers have managed to conduct studies involving AA (or at least an AA-based treatment), and they have generally found AA to be effective, both in acute treatment and sustained maintenance.

Pisani, Fawcett, Clark, and McGuire (1993) assigned subjects to either AA treatment or pharmacotherapy with lithium and found AA to be more effective. Timko, Moos, Finney, and Moos (1994) assigned subjects to AA, outpatient counseling, inpatient counseling, or no treatment control. All three treatment groups showed significant and roughly equal gains over the control group. Other researchers have noted that regular AA attendance is correlated with higher rates of abstinence and lower rates of drinking and intoxication at 6-, 12-, and 18-month follow-up (Kennedy & Minami, 1994; McBride, 1991; Miller

& Verinis, 1995) and as long as a 3-year follow-up (Humphreys, Moos, & Finney, 1996).

But not all research reports are positive. Miller and Hester (1986) note that the high rate of attrition in the less controlled world of most AA groups makes the findings from controlled studies less generalizable to real-world treatments. Brandsma, Maultsby, and Welsh (1980) compared AA to rational behavior therapy and insight therapy. They found that the AA group had the highest dropout rate and the highest relapse rate. AA might not be suited to those who are forced to attend, as demonstrated in studies of criminal offenders (Ditman et al., 1967) and employees (Walsh et al., 1991).

A variety of other criticisms have been leveled at AA. One is that members are encouraged to become dependent on the program, in effect exchanging one addiction for another (Yoder, 1990), and that the closeness that often develops among members interferes with the alcoholic's outside relationships (Peele, 1992). Although group dependency and social disruptions indeed occur, they are almost always preferable to the alcoholic's pretreatment problems.

AA has also been criticized because it is not effective for those who do not want to abstain, for those who need other psychiatric treatment, for those who have difficulty speaking in groups or self-disclosing, and for those who object to its religious overtones. But this is to criticize AA for not being what it was never intended to be. Perhaps the fairest criticism of AA is that treatment is restricted to a single approach that does not work for everyone. Its greatest fault may be its assumption, which has become pervasive in American culture, that AA is the only viable treatment for alcohol problems (Bufe, 1991).

Abstinence versus Controlled Drinking.

There are other approaches. AA is an abstinence-based program; the goal is not simply to reduce drinking-related behaviors to subclinical levels, or even to prevent intoxication. The goal is to stop drinking completely. Period. Is this a realistic goal for most alcoholics?

Some would argue no. For example, Bandura (personal communication, May 1985), following the tenets of his social cognitive theory (Bandura, 1986), criticizes two aspects of the goal of abstinence. First, a goal of total, perpetual abstinence may be unrealistic, and self-esteem and motivation will be reduced after inevitable failures. Second, the complete subjugation to a Higher Power reduces self-efficacy, the sense of personal control over one's life. Instead, the alcoholic will develop a sense of dependency, which makes recovery more fragile. If faith is lost, all hope is lost with it.

In contrast, some successes have been found with controlled drinking programs, such as Rational Recovery, whereby the alcoholic is taught to recognize behavioral and physiological signs of their own developing inebriation so they can stop before becoming intoxicated (Sobell & Sobell, 1995; Schmidt, 1996). The alcoholic is also taught to avoid stressful situations or other occasions that might lead to uncon-trolled drinking (Marlatt, 1983; Sobell, Toneatto, & Sobell, 1990).

The answer to this controversy seems to lie in individual differences. Some alcoholics may indeed lack control over their drinking, and for them abstinence and dependence on a Higher Power may be the best alternative. Their lack of control could have genetic roots (Cloninger, Bohman, & Sigvardsson, 1981; Goodwin et al., 1973). Others, particularly younger alcoholics, might benefit from controlled drinking (Hester & Miller, 1989; Sobell et al., 1990). The best approach of all may be to match particular alcoholics to specific treatment goals, depending on their personal characteristics (Galaif & Sussman, 1995). Research has found support for this idea. Clinical trials that have allowed subjects to choose their own treatments have shown some positive results (Sanchez-Craig & Wilkinson, 1987; Walsh et al., 1991).

In the end, though, freedom to drink moderately could be too much for some alcoholics to handle. In recent comparisons of controlled drinking versus abstinence programs, abstinence was associated with better outcome (Humphreys et al., 1996; Watson et al., 1996). In a remarkable longitudinal study spanning several decades, George Valliant (1996) found that alcohol abusers were unlikely to ever return to a stable pattern of drinking, whereas after six years of absti-nence, it was very unlikely for abstainers to relapse.

OPIOID DEPENDENCE
Residential Treatment

PRESENTING COMPLAINT

John is a 30-year-old mechanic who lives in a middle-class neighborhood in Philadelphia. He has been married for nine years and has two daughters, ages 8 and 5. For the past seven years John has worked as a heating-ventilation-air conditioning (HVAC) mechanic at a large city hospital.

John demonstrated superior job performance when he first began working at the hospital. He was known for doing a thorough and conscientious job, and he had a knack for motivating others. After only two years on the job, the manager of the maintenance department had decided to promote John to supervisor at the first available opening. Over the last few years, however, John's performance has gradually deteriorated. Starting in his third year at the hospital, John began arriving late for work and leaving early, first only once or twice a month, but then once or twice a week. Verbal reminders went unheeded. Eventually John's supervisor filed a written reprimand. At this point John asked to work the night shift, and his supervisor agreed, glad to have John be someone else's problem. For a while John's punctuality improved somewhat, but gradually it deteriorated until he was rarely on time. Then John began to miss work altogether. His absentee rate was always a little higher than usual, but it was never really remarkable. After the move to the night shift, however, it began to climb. At first he missed work once or twice a month, but eventually it reached the point where he showed up for work less than half the time. His relationships with his coworkers were very strained. Surprisingly, the actual quality of his work, when he did it, had not suffered much over the years, though he was slower and more forgetful than before.

John's supervisor tried to be understanding. He asked John if he had any special health problems or personal issues going on, but John was vague and even evasive. Finally his supervisor became exasperated and instituted the formal three-step dismissal proceedings required by the union. First John was told verbally that his job would be terminated unless he showed marked improvement in his performance. He didn't. Two weeks later he received a written warning, and two weeks after that he was suspended from work. Knowing that the next step would be the actual firing, John consulted the coordinator of his union's employee assistance program (EAP) and described his heroin addiction. The EAP coordinator contacted a residential treatment center with a 28-day program (an arrangement rare in today's world of managed care, which limits most such programs to 7 days) and arranged to have John admitted the following Monday. He then called John's supervisor. Without any explanation, he said that John would be absent for one month and that his performance should be reevaluated one month after his return.

PERSONAL HISTORY

John grew up in a predominantly African American working-class neighborhood in Philadelphia. His father was a moderately successful electrician who maintained steady work through one or another of the many contractors he knew. He was a longtime member of the electricians' union and had become increasingly active in union politics over the years. He died suddenly of a massive heart attack a little more than two years ago. John's mother has never worked outside the home; she is supported by social security and a small monthly annuity from her husband's union death benefit. John is the oldest of three brothers. He attended vocational school, as did his youngest brother, who is now a plumbing contractor. The middle brother graduated from a local community college and now manages a retail clothing store in downtown Philadelphia.

John's father was a large man who was prone to alcoholic binges. Occasionally while drunk he would beat his wife or one of his sons, but usually he was good-natured and jovial. He rarely disciplined the boys for staying out late or drinking; in fact he seemed more amused than angry when one of his sons came home drunk. John's mother was a quiet, passive woman who abstained from alcohol and other drugs herself. She was often upset about her husband's drinking binges but never confronted him directly. She was alarmed when she began to notice signs of drug use in her children, but again she did little to intervene.

John began to experiment with alcohol and marijuana when he was 11 years old. These drugs were readily available at his middle school, and many of his friends were daily users. John gradually increased his use of alcohol and marijuana throughout middle school. By the time he entered high school, John drank to intoxication on most weekend nights and sometimes during the week, and he smoked marijuana an average of three or four days a week. Toward the end of middle school John and his friends began to experiment with other drugs, including amphetamines, cocaine, barbiturates, hallucinogens, and heroin. John continued to use all these substances off and on throughout high school; he most frequently abused alcohol, heroin, and, to a lesser extent, marijuana.

John remembers first trying heroin when he was 15. A friend brought a small amount to a party, and he and several other friends took turns snorting the white powder. The calm feeling of euphoria was similar to the effect of marijuana but more potent; he found that heroin combined with alcohol produced an especially intense high. Over the next few years John bought and snorted ever-increasing amounts of heroin until he found it difficult to find enough money to support his habit. He then began selling heroin and other drugs to fellow students.

During this period John spent a great deal of time buying, selling, and taking heroin and other illegal drugs. On many days it was difficult to get out of bed, and sometimes he didn't go to school at all. Even when he did go, he usually spent an hour or more in the school yard talking to dealers, pushers, addicts, and friends who had dropped out. His truancy rate increased year by year, and his schoolwork suffered accordingly. Fortunately for John, he had always been an above-average student, and although his grades were dropping, he still managed to graduate on time and enter a vocational school.

The vocational school was across town, and John spent much of each day either commuting to school or at the school itself, which cut down on the time available to socialize with his drug-using friends. After he completed his training, he got a job working for a heating contractor. About a year later John married Sharon, a woman he had met on the bus while he commuted to the vocational school; their first daughter, Natalie, was born about a year after that. Eighteen months later, John was hired in his current job, and soon afterward they bought a modest house in a quiet, residential neighborhood near the hospital. They had a second daughter, Cicely. During this period of time, John's heroin use remained steady at about three or four times per week, less for the high than to ward off the withdrawal effects. He still used alcohol and marijuana now and then, but for the most part he stopped taking other drugs. John felt in control of his life and his drug use.

Soon after John began at the hospital, his coworkers invited him to join them for a drink on the way home. At first he would stop for a drink once or twice a week, but this soon became a daily routine. John began to drink more and more and to linger at the bar later and later, eventually until long after his coworkers had gone home. John then began to frequent different bars. He made new friends who used marijuana, cocaine, and heroin in addition to alcohol. In this supportive atmosphere, his heroin use increased dramatically, to three, four, or more times a day. And for the first time in his life, John began to take heroin by injection.

John began injecting heroin subcutaneously (under the skin), but soon progressed to injecting it directly into a vein. With each step, from snorting to subcutaneous injection to intravenous injection, came a dramatic increase in the intensity of the euphoric experience. Sometimes John would combine the heroin with amphetamines or cocaine in an effort to heighten the euphoria and blunt the inevitable "crash" of the withdrawal, but he didn't really like the "edge" these stimulants put on the high.

An ever-increasing part of John's days was consumed by his drug use: obtaining drugs; recovering from highs, crashes, and binges; and actually taking the drugs. He couldn't come to work until he had an injection, and he had to have another during lunch break. If he didn't have any heroin, he had to find some. He had to shoot up again in the afternoon, and often left work early for this reason. John spent most evenings buying, selling, and taking drugs. This basic pattern continued after he changed to the night shift, except that now he had most of the day to sleep and engage in his drug activities. He began going to "shooting galleries," run-down apartments or abandoned buildings where ten or more heroin users would share their highs. Needle sharing was common, as was casual, unprotected sex. In his more sober moments John realized the dangers of this risky behavior, but all caution was lost during the high. On most mornings John came home to crash before going out in the afternoon. His new schedule worked out well; he came home after Sharon and the girls were gone, and he left again before the girls got home from school. Often he didn't come home at all.

Not surprisingly, John's drug use led to severe financial problems. Because he was on an hourly wage, his absentee rate resulted in his bringing home less and less money. As his habit became more and more expensive, more of what he made went to his drug habit. Soon the family's modest savings were gone. Then he began selling items in the house: the wedding silver, the family stereo, the VCR. When Sharon asked about these items, he said they had been stolen. Still bills went unpaid, and sometimes there wasn't enough money to buy groceries. Sharon demanded to know where all the money was going, but she never received an answer. Three years ago she had gotten a job as a secretary at the local school, but even so they couldn't keep up with their bills. They frequently borrowed money from both sets of parents, often saying that one of the girls was sick. After about a year Sharon's parents refused to lend them any more money. John then turned to his mother and siblings, and he continued to get money from his mother after she was widowed.

Eventually John began to sell drugs, mostly heroin but also some cocaine, marijuana, and amphetamine. Usually he acted as a lookout for a dealer, but sometimes he was involved in the actual buy. He bought a 9-mm automatic on the street, which he kept loaded and took almost everywhere. He was very careless with the gun; on several occasions he left it out within reach of the children. Fortunately he was rarely home when his children were awake.

Although it was John's declining work performance that directly precipitated his referral, his family had also suffered greatly over the past several years. It began gradually. John would stop off at the bar more often and come home later and later. He would miss dates he and Sharon made with friends, and he forgot promises he made to his children. Sharon became increasingly frustrated and depressed by his withdrawal from her and their children, and she wanted to know where he went all the time and where he spent all his money. She suspected that he had a problem with alcohol and perhaps other drugs. She was fairly sure that he was having sex with other women and figured that he was spending some of his money supporting one or more mistresses. She yelled, begged, threatened, pleaded, and cajoled him to tell her, but her efforts failed. John even managed to turn her accusations around and put the blame on her, accusing her of being needy, suspicious, and unattractive. Often their fights ended with violence. Her relationship with her own family had become strained because of their constant borrowing, and now she felt alone and helpless. On several occasions she threatened to leave him, and twice she and the girls even packed up some luggage, but she could never go through with it. Eventually she resigned herself to her existence and tried to take care of their daughters as best she could.

CONCEPTUALIZATION AND TREATMENT

DSM-IV lists several types of disorders associated with drug use: intoxication, withdrawal, abuse, and dependence. The first two involve acute responses to a psychoactive substance; the latter two involve established patterns of drug use. Although John suffered from repeated instances of heroin, alcohol, and cannabis intoxication and heroin and alcohol withdrawal, it was his long-term drug use that brought him in for therapy, and this became the focus of treatment.

Psychoactive substance dependence involves ongoing problems in controlling the use of a drug. The person exhibits cognitive, behavioral, and physiological symptoms related to drug use, and the person persists in using the drug despite the negative consequences associated with its use. *DSM-IV* outlines seven criteria for diagnosing psychoactive substance dependence; a person must meet at least three to warrant a diagnosis:

1. substance taken more than the person intended
2. persistent desire or unsuccessful attempts to control use
3. much time spent acquiring or recovering from the substance
4. social, occupational, and recreational activities are abandoned
5. continued use despite knowledge that use is harmful
6. marked tolerance
7. characteristic withdrawal symptoms

Substance dependence is categorized as having physiological dependence if either criterion 6 or 7 is met.

We see from John's history that he fulfills several of the criteria for alcohol dependence, cannabis dependence, and opioid dependence, and his treatment is aimed at these problems in combination. However, in the last few years John's heroin use has predominated and has led to extremely risky behavior. For these reasons, his therapy team decided to focus their initial work on John's heroin use.

John was admitted to a 28-day residential treatment program located in a newly remodeled 25-bed ward of a downtown hospital. For reasons of confidentiality, the program is located in a different hospital than where John works. The program is voluntary. Nevertheless, the program has some inviolate rules. Any instance of physical aggression or violence, sexual activity, or drug use (checked through periodic urine screens) results in immediate dismissal from the program. In addition, the program has a very structured daily routine, and the residents are expected to participate fully.

The staff consists of a treatment director, three full-time treatment counselors, clinical nurses, and two night staff. The staff is firm but friendly; they try to instill a sense of structure combined with an atmosphere of fairness and understanding. Staff and residents are on a first-name basis. Since about 80 percent of the staff members are in recovery themselves, they can well empathize with the residents. Still, every member of the staff is highly trained and holds a Chemical Dependence Counselor Certificate (CDCC).

The program begins with detoxification, which takes place during the first week or so. Yet even during the typically agonizing detox process, the residents are expected to participate in the highly structured treatment routine. The treatment approach is based on the Minnesota Model, so called because it was developed at St. Mary's Rehabilitation Center in Minnesota. This approach involves three aspects: changing drug behavior, tapping emotions, and restructuring living patterns. The goal of the program is not merely to end current drug use; it is also to make drug use less likely in the future. To achieve this goal, the addict must undergo a fundamental life change. Thus, the aim of the program is to restructure the habits, routines, cognitions, attitudes, and social environments of the addicts.

Many short-term changes can be accomplished on the ward, but lasting change after graduation requires an alteration in the person's social environment. For this reason the involvement of family members and intimate friends becomes an integral part of the treatment process, and the staff tries very hard to get the addict to sign a release that will allow these people to participate. Like most addicts, John was hesitant to get his family involved in his treatment. He felt embarrassed, ashamed, and guilty over how he had been mistreating his wife and daughters. His drug use had been the source of hostility between him and his family, and the program was likely to generate even more conflict as his wife learned the full extent of his drug use. This prediction proved to be accurate. Nevertheless, the staff strongly encouraged him to get his family involved, and he finally relented. Sharon was similarly hesitant, but the staff also convinced her that her participation would be beneficial, even crucial. Most residents of the treatment center eventually agree to involve their family, but despite the best efforts of the staff, some never do. Likewise, most family members do whatever they can to aid the recovery process, though some want nothing to do with the addict and flatly refuse.

For the first two weeks of treatment, John's daily routine was as follows:

 7:30 wake up, get dressed, make bed
 8:15 breakfast (All residents must sit in the cafeteria, including those who are not eating.)
 9:15 lecture
10:15 group therapy
12:00 lunch
 1:15 lecture
 2:15 group therapy
 4:00 supervised walk around the neighborhood
 5:15 dinner
 6:30 lecture
 8:00 Twelve-Step meeting, often with outside speakers
 9:00 homework assignments, free time (this is the only time TV is allowed)
11:00 bedtime

During the first week John missed some of the scheduled activities because he suffered symptoms of alcohol and heroin withdrawal: a craving for more heroin and alcohol, trembling, sweating, diarrhea, racing heart, fever, insomnia, running nose, watery eyes, weakness. In fact, aside from the drug craving, John's withdrawal symptoms felt like an incredibly severe case of the flu. Most of his withdrawal symptoms subsided within a week. Although John was expected to follow the daily routine despite his symptoms, the staff made allowances here and there. John's roommate, a crack addict, had a much sharper withdrawal course. Within a few days he became depressed, irritated, and agitated; his cravings for crack were obvious and desperate. However, the staff made few allowances for him and forced him to conform to the daily schedule right from the start. The staff had learned that instilling a sense of structure is paramount to treating cocaine dependency, and it must begin immediately, despite any withdrawal reactions.

John was assigned to a therapy group with seven other addicts, and each of them seemed to be as desperate as he was. Bill and José had just lost their jobs; Hector, Steve, and Curtiss were suspended or on probation. Maggie's husband threatened to file for divorce and seek custody of their son. Joe was referred by his psychotherapist. Bill and Curtiss were longtime alcoholics. Hector was a polyabuser who had a long history of taking heroin, amphetamines, cocaine, crack, alcohol, barbiturates, and marijuana, apparently with little particular preference. The rest had also abused a number of different drugs, but their predominant dependence was crack. During the first two weeks of treatment, the group members gradually revealed their secret stories of cruelty, violence, and prostitution. Most incredible of all, John realized that his story was just as horrific as theirs, and maybe even worse. Throughout his life John had always thought that he was in control of his drug use, even during the last few months. But now he could no longer deny his addiction. For him, this self-revelation was the most agonizing part of his treatment. But this was just a taste of things to come.

The third week of the program is known as "family week," when family members are asked to join the addicts in the treatment process. On Monday, Tuesday, and Wednesday, the morning activities are replaced by education classes that describe the disease model of addictions using lectures, guest speakers, and films. Instead of the usual afternoon activities, the addicts and their families engage in "fishbowl exercises." The fishbowl exercises are run like group sessions, but with two important differences. First, the families of the addicts are now in the group, along with the usual group members. To keep things down to a manageable size, usually no more than two families participate in any one exercise session. Second, the addict is placed in the center of the group, where he or she becomes the focus of the entire session (and is in the "fishbowl"). On Monday the addict must remain quiet while family members take turns describing how the addict had affected their lives. On Tuesday the family must remain quiet while the addict explains the drug use from his or her perspective.

On Monday morning John was surprised to see his mother and brothers accompany Sharon; she had not mentioned this at an earlier visit. Although everyone said they were happy to see him, their interactions were awkward and strained.

The session began with John in the fishbowl. Everyone was very hesitant at first, and their group counselor, Rick, had to do a lot of prodding. Sharon began by saying how much she had missed John these last few years. She saw him very little, but even then he seemed to be a different person. John's mother and brothers agreed that he had changed. Sharon continued that the girls missed their daddy. Natalie in particular wanted to know what she had done to make him not love them anymore. John felt a lump in his throat and tears well in his eyes, but Sharon was just starting. She said that John was a monster to live with; he always criticized, blamed, and belittled her. They never had any conversation that wasn't a fight, and they shared very few activities. When they had sex (she looked up at his mother but then continued), it was more of a punishment than anything else. He was so impossible to be with that Sharon was glad when he started working the night shift.

John was surprised at Sharon's hostility, and he was also surprised at how much she knew about his drug use. She saw the needle marks in his arms and knew that he used heroin or cocaine. She knew that he had sold their silver, stereo, and VCR for drug money. She knew that he carried a gun and probably sold drugs. She knew that he slept with other women and wondered if he supported any mistresses. Sharon then demanded to know what she didn't know already. "Who are those men I see you with in the morning?" "How much junk do you use?" "How many women are you screwing?" Although John was supposed to be quiet, he was allowed to answer direct questions. He didn't. The therapist marked down these questions to ask tomorrow. Finally, the session reached a crescendo.

> **Rick:** Sharon, tell John what makes you most angry about his behavior.
>
> **Sharon:** Angry? Angry? You know what this bastard did?
>
> **Rick:** Talk to John, Sharon.
>
> **Sharon:** You . . . I can't look at him. (She puts her face

in her hands and sobs openly. She continues, looking at the floor.) You know what the worst of it is? Do you? It's that you made me feel like this was all my fault. And the girls, too. You know, Cicely never really knew you; she thinks you were always like this. But Natalie's old enough. She remembers how you used to be, and she thinks it's all her fault that you treat her like that. I just can't believe how selfish you've been to treat us like this. I don't know why I care about you. I've asked myself a thousand times. I feel so weak and stupid. I hate my life; I hate *you* for making me so miserable.

Sharon sat with her face in her hands and sobbed for another few minutes. John noticed that his mother and brothers were also looking down and holding back tears. He couldn't hold back his own.

Rick helped John up, and Maggie replaced him in the fishbowl. John didn't notice much about what was said. He was too upset by the last half hour. He dreaded tomorrow; he knew that would be worse.

And he was right. This time Maggie was the first one in the fishbowl. John watched her husband sullenly look on as she described the history of her addiction to crack. The low point came when she described having sex with drug dealers in her own home while her husband was at work. This was more than her husband could bear; he simply got up and left the room.

On this glum note, John entered the fishbowl. The group members were there to provide encouragement, but also to correct any glossed-over accounts; there was no need for either. John simply and plainly narrated his long history of drug use, from middle school experimentation to his suspension from work. Sharon cried when he described his frequent casual sex, and a look of horror came over her when he described the shooting galleries. But the biggest shock of all came toward the end of his story.

Rick: John, what's the worst thing you did because of your heroin addiction?

John: I guess it was shooting that cop and the other guy. (At this, Sharon's jaw dropped.)

Rick: Did you kill them?

John: You just shoot, you know. You don't stick around to see what happens.

Rick: Is that what you feel worst about?

John: Not really, no. I never really thought about it much; I guess I never thought of much of anything except for myself. But sitting here thinking about it, I guess I feel worst about what I did to Sharon and Natalie, and Cicely too. I never thought they'd blame themselves. Hell, I never thought about them at all. I remember, after the drug bust, I came home and put the gun on the table. The girls were home from school, you know. And I just thought, "I hope one of them picks up the gun; they'll never trace *those* prints." Thank God they had enough sense not to get near it. But I mean, that's how I thought. I didn't think that they might get hurt or anything. God, how can anybody get like that? How did *I* get like that?

On Wednesday afternoon, the residents and their families made concrete plans for activities they could share that would replace the time spent in drug activities. Movies, trips to an amusement park, and other events were planned with the children, including a summer vacation. Two nights a month were set aside for a "date" with Sharon. John even agreed to attend church. And he consented to be tested for HIV. Finally, John enrolled in Alcoholics Anonymous (AA) and Narcotics Anonymous (NA). For her part, Sharon pledged to support John in these changes, and she enrolled in Al-Anon and Nar-Anon.

Thursday's time was devoted to a communication workshop based on the principles of Communication Theory outlined by Salvador Minuchin (1974). For most couples, the most crucial aspect of the workshop was the use of communication exercises aimed at promoting "fair fighting." John was pleased to see Maggie's husband at the workshop. Friday saw a summary of the week's events and a chance to solidify future plans. One important plan involved a future relapse. What would Sharon do if John began drinking or using any illegal drug? She was instructed to make a clear decision and to stick to it. She decided that her only choice would be a separation, and she vowed to actually go through with it.

The treatment program continued for one more week. At that point, every resident who had completed the program was given a medallion as a tangible sign of his or her effort and work. Each graduate was enrolled in a two-year aftercare "growth group," a weekly two-hour meeting that provides support to recovering addicts and their families. All graduates are invited to an annual banquet sponsored by the hospital. Most years between 600 and 800 people attend.

PROGNOSIS

It is difficult to provide a definite prognosis for John. His treatment program keeps no records on relapse rates, so it is impossible to estimate John's chances of remaining sober based on the performance of other graduates. The program does know that about 65 percent of its graduates remain in the growth group for the full two years. This does not necessarily mean that all 65 percent remain abstinent (in fact that is doubtful), nor does it necessarily mean that 35 percent have relapsed (some may have moved away, or even died). But it is a rough guess as to the number who have at least maintained the sense of responsibility required to keep up with the growth group.

Because most treatment programs are voluntary and dropout rates are so high, true relapse rates are difficult to determine. Most estimates place the one-year relapse rate at about 60 percent. Two

European studies corroborate this figure. Sanchez-Carbonell, Cami, and Brigos (1988) reported a 49 percent 12-month relapse rate in their sample of 311 addicts drawn from 16 drug-free outpatient clinics in Spain; and Nicolosi et al. (1991) report a 70 percent 11-month relapse rate in a sample of 460 Italian addicts. Both studies found that most addicts who relapsed at least decreased their drug use and needle sharing. Complete abstinence is far less common than a reduction in drug use, which is the outcome standard adopted by many recent research studies (e.g., Tuma, Siegel, Alexander, & Wanderling, 1993).

Given these outcomes, it is more likely than not that John will use heroin again within a year. Yet John has some advantages that work in his favor. He had the determination (or desperation) to attend drug treatment, and he was able to stay in treatment and graduate. Thus, John is one of the minority who saw the program through to completion, and this is a very good sign. John has a relatively stable and supportive family environment. John returned to work on a new shift and seems to be doing well. Most importantly, John no longer associates with his "drug friends"; instead he spends most of his free time with his family and attending meetings for AA, NA, and the growth group. Finally, John has entered his thirties, a time when most heroin users begin to reduce their drug use. Though one must always be cautious with cases of substance dependence, John seems to have a better chance than many at recovery.

DISCUSSION

Many Americans consider heroin addiction to be a problem of the 1970s, and indeed, surveys of drug use among American adolescents indicate that heroin use has decreased since 1975 (e.g., Johnston, O'Malley, & Bachman, 1987). However, Kozel and Adams (1986) found a cohort and aging effect for heroin use. That is, although fewer adolescents are trying heroin, those who become addicted tend to remain addicted. In the last few years, though, some urban treatment centers, including John's, have been seeing an increase in the rate of heroin use.

In contrast, the prevalence rate for heroin use in Europe has remained relatively stable over this period, and for this reason more research has been done there than in North America. Much work has been done in Great Britain. Some researchers reported a gradual increase in heroin use from 1975 to 1982 (Ghodse, Stapleton, Edwards, & Edeh, 1987), whereas others found little change over this period. A point prevalence rate of about 3.5 to 4.5 per thousand was consistently found in samples (e.g, Parker, Pool, Rawle, & Gay, 1988). That is, at any one time, between 0.35 and 0.45 percent of the population is addicted to heroin.

Heroin addicts show diverse treatment histories and patterns of use (Watters, Cheng, & Lorvick, 1991), but some generalizations can be made. Heroin use typically starts early. Parker et al. (1988) found that 92 percent of their sample was under 35 years old, with some addicts as young as 10. Another British study (Sheehan, Oppenheimer, & Taylor, 1988) found that the typical heroin user had a nine-year history of heroin use with a 4-year injection history. In the United States, the rate of heroin addiction among African Americans and Latinos is disproportionately high, making up about half of all heroin users. Desmond and Maddux (1984) uncovered differences that distinguish Chicano heroin users from Caucasian and African American addicts. For one thing, Chicanos are more likely to terminate treatment before completion. They are also more likely to get arrested and will spend more time being incarcerated. However, this group is also more likely to abstain from heroin voluntarily and will spend more time employed during their drug careers.

Medical and Behavioral Complications of Heroin Use

Prolonged use of most psychoactive substances entails some medical complication: cirrhosis of the liver for alcohol dependence, lung cancer for nicotine dependence, coronary arrest for cocaine dependence, and so on. In contrast, heroin use per se has few negative health consequences, and in fact many heroin addicts look young for their age. However, the behavioral consequences of heroin use can be devastating.

First, most heroin users develop incredible tolerance, and as a result, their dose increases dramatically; some addicts take a regular dose over 100 *times* their initial dose. This need for ever-increasing amounts of heroin is complicated by the fact that illegally obtained heroin is poorly regulated, resulting in wildly varying purities. These factors contribute to a high risk of overdose. An associated complication is poisoning from impure or harmful substances used to "cut" (dilute) the heroin sold on the street.

Second, the relatively short pharmacological effect of heroin (about four hours) requires the addict to take the drug three, four, or more times a day. As a consequence, much of each day becomes involved in drug activity.

Third, buying the frequent, large amounts of heroin needed to support a habit requires a great deal of money, sometimes more than $100 *per day*. Because so much time is spent in drug-related activities, methods of obtaining this money usually involve drug-related crime. The experience of John's treatment center is that virtually all female heroin addicts engage in prostitution in some form or another. The same is true for women addicted to other substances, especially crack. Most male addicts turn to various forms of crime to raise money, most often larceny, robbery, and drug dealing. In a study of 354 male narcotic (mostly heroin) addicts, Shaffer, Nurco, and Kinlock (1984) found that, on the average, 63 percent of their days included at least one crime aside from buying and taking the illegal drug. Johnson, Wish, Schmeider, and Huizinga (1991) interviewed 1,539 adolescents ranging in age from 14 to 20 years and found a high rate of felony crimes committed by heroin and cocaine addicts. Interestingly, many of these crimes seem to be committed for reasons other than a need to purchase drugs; according to the adolescents' reports, fewer than 25 percent were committed primarily to obtain money for drugs.

Finally, the drug culture poses increased risks for contracting life-threatening diseases such as hepatitis B, hepatitis delta, and HIV (O'Connor & Selwyn, 1997). Over half of all IV drug users share unsterilized needles (Hall, Darke, Ross, & Wodak, 1993) and many, probably most, engage in casual, unprotected sex. A study of 194

Swedish heroin users (Kall & Olin, 1990) found that 45 percent tested HIV positive. Rates of HIV infection among urban U.S. samples are generally higher; a recent survey of 687 female prostitutes who use IV drugs found an average infection rate of 74 percent across seven sites in the United States (Rosenblum et al., 1992). By 1988, HIV infection was more prevalent among IV drug users than all other risk categories combined (Centers for Disease Control, 1989). The rates of HIV and hepatitis infection among IV drug users continues to rise.

Professionals have noted several factors that contribute to this problem; Rick, John's group counselor, mentions three particular problems. Most IV drug users live in poor, violent neighborhoods where few opportunities for education exist. Prolonged drug use often leads to habitually poor judgment, resulting in risky behavior despite the known dangers. Finally, some IV drug users living a violent drug lifestyle have adopted a helpless, nihilistic attitude. Few expect to live past age 30 anyway, so they are unconcerned about contracting HIV.

As a final note, it should be emphasized that one's environment has much to do with one's drug use. People living in stressful situations where drugs are readily available are especially at risk. Indeed, numerous studies have shown that being undereducated, unemployed, and low in socioeconomic status, and having unstable family relationships are all risk factors for developing an addiction, and often a change in social environment will affect the course of the addiction. And yet a person's physical environment is not the whole story. John had an adequate income, a steady job, and a stable family life, and still he was unable to overcome the draw of heroin. A person's social acquaintances, self-esteem, and attitudes must all be considered.

Approaches to Treatment

Treatment for opioid dependence falls into three broad classes: dependence medication, maintenance medication, and drug-free treatment (abstinence). Dependence treatments attempt to reduce the anxiety, depression, and withdrawal-based problems associated with substance dependence. Maintenance programs ameliorate the constant cravings of physically dependent addicts by substituting a drug that relieves withdrawal symptoms without producing any significant euphoric effect. Abstinence programs are aimed at eliminating, or at least reducing, the drug-taking behavior itself.

A variety of medications are available for dependence treatment. Among these, clonidine (sometimes combined with naltrexone) and lofexidine have shown promising results (Best, Oliveto, & Kosten, 1996; Kosten, 1990; Ling & Shoptaw, 1997).

Most maintenance programs involve methadone (Kosten, 1990; Strain, Stitzer, Liebson, & Bigelow, 1993; Ward, Bell, Mattick, & Hall, 1996). The withdrawal symptoms of methadone are somewhat less severe than those for heroin, so there is a greater chance that the addict will eventually abstain completely. Perhaps the biggest advantage of methadone is that it is administered orally, thus obviating the behavioral complications arising out of using shared or otherwise unsterilized needles.

Unfortunately, methadone maintenance has several drawbacks. It requires a daily trip to a methadone clinic, and many addicts lack the self-discipline to keep coming. In addition, the side effects of methadone, including constipation, insomnia, and decreased sexual performance, further erode the addict's will to remain in treatment. Worst of all, when taken intravenously in relatively high doses, methadone will sometimes produce a high, and a black market has sprung up, allowing for the unregulated availability of the drug, which would seem to defeat its very purpose. Alternatives to methadone are being developed; the most promising of these are levacetylmethadol (LAAM) and buprenorphine (Best et al., 1996; Ling & Shoptaw, 1997). Strain et al. (1996) compared buprenorphine to methadone and found similar effects in the short term but greater efficacy for buprenorphine in continued improvement.

Drug-free programs attempt to eliminate drug use completely and rather abruptly ("cold turkey"). They almost always involve a highly structured setting that both supports an addict during the withdrawal and yet instills a sense of order and responsibility. Many programs try to break through the addict's characteristic denial by exposing the newly sober addict to critical and sometimes harsh

137

feedback from the counselor, fellow addicts, and even family members. Often this becomes too much for the addict to tolerate, and many programs experience high dropout rates. But often dropping out can be minimized by instituting a clear, categorical penalty (divorce, loss of job, and so on) for failure to complete the program. Some research has shown an increased efficacy of maintenance programs over drug-free programs (Strain et al., 1993), whereas others report no differences (Tuma et al., 1993).

Regardless of which approach is adopted, supportive therapy is a vital component. Typically this supportive therapy includes education regarding the course of drug use and its effects. Therapy often outlines a disease model of substance dependence. Most important, therapy encourages addicts to change their social environments. Often family members are involved in therapy so that they can understand the addict more fully and set up an environment that will serve as an alternative to the old drug lifestyle. Often specific activities are assigned to provide order in the addicts' lives. Finally, clear rules for behavior are set down, and equally clear responses and penalties are formulated. Take as an example an addict who habitually beats his wife. This couple might decide that physical abuse will no longer be tolerated in the home. At the first instance of violence, the husband must see a therapist. If he fails to do so or if he commits another violent act, the wife will file for divorce. Of course, the wife must be prepared to carry through should the need arise. Although these firm rules often seem impersonal and harsh, they are just the sort of structure addicts need to help maintain a sense of order in their new lives.

How successful are these programs? As was discussed in John's prognosis, the best evidence available indicates that fewer than half of those with successful therapy experiences remain abstinent for one year. And this figure doesn't include the majority of addicts who drop out! Clearly, substance dependence is a very persistent problem. Professionals are making progress, but there is a long way to go.

MALE ERECTILE DISORDER
Eclectic Therapy

PRESENTING COMPLAINT

Jim is a 29-year-old actor living in Santa Monica, California, a suburb of Los Angeles. He has a day job as a salesman in an electronics store. He frequently auditions for various roles in television shows and commercials, and he has had what he described as "bit parts" in two movies. On the whole, though, he assesses his acting career as "struggling."

For the past few years, Jim has experienced intermittent sexual problems, and once in a while this has come up in conversations with other actors while waiting for auditions. Last week a fellow actor he had known for some time suggested that he see a therapist for his problems and provided him with a recommendation.

At his first session Jim appeared to be somewhat hesitant and awkward. He looked off in the distance when he described himself, and he occasionally stammered and giggled nervously. After several minutes, though, he became a little more relaxed and described the precise nature of his sexual problems.

For the past three or four years, Jim suffered from what he terms "off-and-on impotence problems." Sometimes he had trouble maintaining an erection during intercourse, and he estimated that he successfully achieved orgasm "only about half the time, maybe less." Sometimes he achieved penetration but then lost the erection soon after. Often he lost tumescence upon attempting penetration, thus being unable to complete intercourse. Occasionally he failed to achieve an erection altogether. These difficulties seemed to be limited to intercourse; masturbation, performed either by himself or by his sexual partner, almost always resulted in orgasm.

Jim stated that his sexual problem was compounded by what he perceives to be an overemphasis in the African American culture on masculinity and sexual prowess. He said that the women he dates, both black and white, expect him to be a "terrific lover." He felt that his behavior was inadequate in comparison to this relatively strict standard, both in his own eyes as well as in the eyes of his partners. His partners usually felt frustrated and hurt when he lost his erection. Most blamed themselves and wondered whether they were not "exciting enough" or "couldn't do it right." One partner felt so upset that she locked herself in his bathroom and cried for several hours. Most of his partners have not expressed their frustrations directly, although two or three have said that their evening with him was "a disappointment." This problem had been a considerable source of anxiety for him over the past few years.

Jim was also concerned about the effects of these problems on his sexual relationships. Because of the embarrassment and anxiety he felt as a result of his disorder, he often felt ambivalent about initiating sexual encounters for fear that he would not be able to "perform." Jim was convinced that his disorder was the primary cause of his inability to form lasting romantic relationships, and this realization made him anxious and depressed.

PERSONAL HISTORY

Jim grew up in a working-class household in Los Angeles. He has two older brothers and a younger sister. His parents, neither of whom had finished high school, held a number of different unskilled jobs while Jim was growing up. For the past 15 years his father has been employed with the U.S. Postal Service. His mother has worked as a waitress, a store clerk, and most recently as a beautician. His brothers both work "in the neighborhood"; his sister moved to San Jose after she married. Jim could not think of anything unusual about his childhood. He summed it up by saying that his parents were "good people; they worked hard and always had food on the table."

Jim described himself as having been a mediocre student who "barely finished" high school. For the past several years he had held various day jobs while auditioning for acting parts and taking an occasional acting class. Because of his unstable financial situation, he had lived with a variety of people in various places in and around Los Angeles. Usually he would move in with someone out of economic necessity. Sometimes, though, he would move in with a woman he was dating, in some cases after dating for only a few weeks. But in these cases the motivation was mostly financial, not romantic. He shares his present apartment in Santa Monica with a couple he met at a recent audition. He is not sexually involved with either member of the couple.

Jim's sexual history also shows instability. He became sexually active at age 14 and described his sex life in high school as "successful." He has had many female sexual partners since then; he estimates the total number at "around ten or twelve a year." For the most part he met his sexual partners while auditioning for acting parts. He described his partners as "people in the business" (actresses, script prompters, makeup and wardrobe personnel, etc.). He and his partners typically engaged in sex very early in the relationship, usually in the course of their initial encounter. Some of these became one-night stands, but usually he attempted to establish relationships with his sexual partners. In most cases, though, the relationship ended abruptly after only a few weeks. He guessed that the number of times he ended the relationship is about equal to the number of times his partner did. He is not now in a steady relationship.

When asked if he practices safe sex, he took on a guilty, defensive tone. "No, not really. You know, it's tough enough for me without those things (condoms) making me numb." Despite the relatively heightened awareness of HIV infection within the entertainment industry, rarely did a partner mention safe sex; no partner had ever refused an encounter on these grounds.

CONCEPTUALIZATION AND TREATMENT

According to *DSM-IV*, male erectile disorder is a sexual dysfunction characterized by a persistent or recurrent failure to attain or maintain erection until the satisfactory completion of the sexual activity that results in distress and/or interpersonal problems. This diagnosis is not warranted if the dysfunction occurs only during the presence of some other disorder, such as a major depressive episode. In addition, *DSM-IV* asks clinicians to specify whether the disorder has been lifelong or was acquired after a period of normal sexual functioning; and whether the disorder is generalized to all situations or is specific in nature; and whether the disorder is the result of psychological causes or a combination of psychological and physiological causes. (Erectile dysfunctions with a clear physiological cause, usually a medical condition or substance use, warrant diagnoses of sexual dysfunction due to a general medical condition and/or substance-induced sexual dysfunction, respectively.)

Jim's primary complaint was that he lost his erection, and in some cases his sexual interest, during intercourse. This had been a cause of much anxiety and frustration for him as well as his sexual partners. He has no identifiable illness or pattern of drug use that would explain his problems. Thus, his complaints match the criteria for male erectile disorder very well. Clearly his dysfunction was acquired, since he had been having sex for 15 years and his symptoms began only a few years ago. His problem appeared to be situational, that is, specific to intercourse; Jim was able to complete the sexual act approximately half the time and was consistently able to masturbate to ejaculation. Given these characteristics, it was very likely that his disorder is psychogenic, that is, due to psychological factors.

Jim's diagnosis addressed only the objective manifestations of his disorder, and Jim himself seemed to focus only on this superficial level. However, several aspects of his complaints suggested that the picture was more complex. The underlying cause of his dysfunction seemed to be that he was a disorganized, impulsive, and anxious young man who lacked self-understanding and self-discipline. These characteristics would negatively affect both his sexual performance and his sexual relationships. On a performance level, self-discipline and self-confidence are needed to carry through the sexual act, especially to the point where the partner is satisfied. Lacking this, subtle signs of a performance deficit can erode the person's sexual behavior. On an interpersonal level, a certain amount of steadfastness and trust is required to develop an awareness of the partner's wants and needs and to work through the problems that inevitably occur in relationships.

Jim appeared to be a good candidate for therapy. He was young and open in his descriptions of his actions and his feelings. Although he described his problem almost completely in behavioral terms, he was nevertheless responsive to the suggestions and dynamic interpretations of the therapist. Finally, he was not resistant to the notion of behavioral exercises, many of which involve masturbation.

The overall goal of Jim's therapy was for the therapist to act as an objective facilitator, a separate, "objective" person who would "spark," or regenerate, his sexual behavior. Her eclectic background was useful in providing Jim with a foundation of explicit behavioral training combined with dynamic analysis. Following eclectic principles, the therapeutic plan for Jim operated at two levels. On a cognitive and behavioral level, Jim received information about his anatomical functioning and his disorder. He also was given instruction in different practical exercises to increase his control over his sexual performance. On an emotional level, the therapist treated Jim through psychoanalysis. This analysis was aimed at increasing his psychological awareness of himself and others and putting him back in touch with repressed aspects of his personality.

Because Jim initially sought a rather short-term, limited treatment for his sexual problems, therapy at first involved specific behavioral techniques and recommendations. Jim was taught the basic physiology of human sexual behavior, including a brief discussion of the four phases of the sexual response cycle: desire, excitement, orgasm, resolution. The primary value of this education was to eliminate any myths Jim may have had. For example, most men are physiologically incapable of attaining an erection for a certain period immediately after ejaculation (the resolution phase). Unaware of this, many men become anxious because they are "impotent" after having sex. Simple information describing the physiology of the male sexual cycle will often dispel the anxieties associated with this myth.

Another topic of education involved the risk of contracting sexually transmitted diseases (STDs) and HIV, which was of particular concern given Jim's high-risk sexual behavior. Jim was urged to practice using a condom, which the therapist described as "an acquired taste." She reassured him that although condoms were often distracting when first tried, their use quickly becomes routine.

Next, Jim was taught two specific techniques to improve his control over his erection (and thereby to improve his confidence in his sexual performance). Instructions for these techniques were given during early therapy sessions; he practiced these exercises at home.

The first of these is Seeman's exercise, also called "The Start and Stop Technique." First, Jim was instructed to masturbate to orgasm quickly to reduce tension about achieving orgasm. The next time he masturbated, however, he was to gradually build up an erection and try to maintain it before ejaculating. Eventually Jim was able to attain an erection, maintain it for at least 3 minutes, let the erection slowly subside, and then to repeat the excitement, maintenance, and relaxation stages several times before finally reaching orgasm. The goals of this exercise are fourfold (1) to develop control in attaining and maintaining an erection, (2) to increase the quality of the erection (i.e., its tumescence and duration), (3) to gain control over the timing of orgasm, and (4) to increase the patient's confidence in his sexual capabilities.

The second technique is known as the Kegel Exercise. In this exercise Jim was taught to tighten and loosen the pubococcygeal muscle (the muscle in the pelvis that restricts the flow of urine, sometimes called the "love muscle"). Jim flexed this muscle in two ways: by tightening and relaxing it for long durations and by rapidly flexing it for many repetitions. There were three general goals to this technique (1) to increase muscle tone, (2) to stimulate the genital region, and (3) to increase the engorgement of blood into erectile tissue.

In addition to these physical exercises, Jim was also given specific instructions pertaining to his sexual activity. Most importantly, he was told to restrict the frequency of penetration so that he can concentrate his strength and thus make intercourse more exciting. In the therapist's words, "Intercourse is exhausting. You may want to think of other ways to have sex with your partner and save intercourse for the weekends." The therapist's second piece of advice was to delay penetration until both partners were ready. Often penetration will fail simply because the penis has not been sufficiently stimulated. Similarly, intercourse can be painful and/or uncomfortable for the partner if she is not sufficiently aroused. Intercourse is more pleasurable for both partners after sufficient foreplay.

Jim was very responsive to these suggestions. He came to therapy regularly and reported that he performed the exercises as instructed. As therapy progressed, the focus of the sessions gradually widened from his specific sexual problems to more introspective topics. A particularly important topic of discussion revolved around Jim's perceptions of the expectations of his partners. He stated that most of his partners seemed to focus almost exclusively on orgasm and that he felt a strong pressure to perform. He also complained that the majority of his sexual partners lacked any deep emotional involvement, which he felt diminished the quality of his sexual relationships with them. In general, he felt that sex was too "rushed and selfish." He suggested that the stereotype of African American men as uncaring and macho may have contributed to this problem.

The therapist responded that if any broad generalizations were to be made, strong demands for sexual performance and a callous, uncaring attitude seemed more descriptive of the entertainment industry than of African American men. In actuality, Jim's complaints seemed to reveal more about himself than about these groups. For example, if Jim had a strong need for intimacy, why did he choose to earn his living and meet sexual partners in an industry notorious for its shallowness and insensitivity? Thus the focus of therapy gradually shifted from others' expectations to his own attitudes and beliefs.

Once Jim felt comfortable discussing his psychological themes, the therapist widened the focus of therapy to deal with issues that did not relate directly to sex. They discussed his feelings about his acting career, his anxieties about his chances of forming satisfying romantic relationships, and his needs for intimacy, among other topics. Gradually the therapist raised issues that she felt were particularly significant for him, such as his disorganized nature, his impulsiveness, and his anxieties over becoming intimate with women. They discussed the importance of these characteristics for his sexual behavior and for his life in general. As he gained a better understanding of himself and his shortcomings, he slowly began to understand that he had walled off many aspects of his personality. For example, it was possible that his impulsive and nomadic living habits were manifestations of his refusal to acknowledge his need for intimacy and commitment, perhaps because of a deep anxiety that he would be let down. As he tackled these important issues, he very gradually uncovered these repressed parts of his personality. As he became more emotionally mature, he developed a better sense of what was missing in his life. Acknowledging these underlying needs made him more confident in his relationships and more secure in his own worth.

Jim has been in therapy for slightly over three years, and he seems to have made significant behavioral and emotional progress. After about two months of therapy Jim no longer complained about his "impotence," and the behavioral aspects of his problem were for the most part resolved. His first dynamic breakthrough came after about six months of therapy. He told the therapist that he found himself being less impulsive and casual about his sexual partners. By limiting his relationships to only those women in whom he had an emotional interest, he greatly increased his chances of developing an intimate and lasting relationship. It seems that this process paid off; for the past 15 months he has been in a steady relationship. He has also made a great many other self-discoveries; in general, his emotional awareness is at a much more sophisticated level than it was when therapy began, and he is better able to assess his sexual and emotional needs and those of his partner. He also feels ready to commit to a long-standing, intimate relationship.

PROGNOSIS

The prognosis for Jim is good. He quickly eliminated his sexual symptoms and has continued to grow emotionally. He has reduced many of his impulsive behaviors, such as moving in with casual sexual partners, and his level of anxiety about his career and his relationships has decreased. He has developed greater awareness of the needs of his sexual partners, and he appears to have the ability to maintain a more mature, intimate relationship. Jim is very satisfied with the gains he has made in therapy.

In general, a patient's prognosis in these sorts of cases is based on two factors: his responsiveness to therapy and his underlying emotional stability. To a large extent, patients who are willing to accept the therapist's suggestions and to perform the behavioral exercises generally show noticeable behavioral improvement after only one or two sessions. When therapy does not prove to be effective, often it is because the patient is not in touch with his repressed feelings. Unless the patient is willing to first acknowledge these underlying issues, the chances for lasting behavioral changes are relatively low. Furthermore, patients who are less emotionally stable are generally less amenable to therapy, particularly that which involves a great deal of introspection and self-discovery.

DISCUSSION

Male erectile disorder (MED) is not uncommon. Community surveys have reported rates between 3 and 9 percent of all adult men (Ard, 1977; Frank, Anderson, & Rubenstein, 1978). MED is the most common problem of men seeking treatment for sexual problems, accounting for between 36 and 53 percent of initial complaints (Bancroft & Coles, 1976; Frank et al., 1978). Furthermore, the incidence of MED appears to be increasing (Spector & Carey, 1990). Rosen (1996; Rosen & Lieblum, 1993) suggests that this recent increase may be due in part to a greater awareness of the condition, new treatment options, and reduced stigma through "medicalization" of the disorder, where it is considered an illness rather than a personal weakness. Indeed, pharmacotherapy using vasoactive agents such as yohimbine or are now the most common treatment for MED (Virag,

147

1997). These are generally effective and well tolerated, but their use is limited by the need to administer them by injection as well as other side effects. Sildenafil (Viagra), which is available in pill form, was first described by Boolell and his colleagues (Boolell et al., 1996; Boolell, Gepi-Attee, Gingell, & Allen, 1997). Immediately upon its approval by the FDA, Viagra became a media sensation, which did much to medicalize MED and thus increase the public acceptance of treatment for this disorder. As had happened with Prozac a decade before, questions about Viagra's safety have made it something of a media controversy, and it will take a few years before controlled research can clarify this issue.

Jim's specific pattern of complaints is typical. In a survey of 258 men with erectile disorder, 78 percent reported difficulties in both attaining and maintaining erections, while 20 percent had diminished sex drives severe enough to warrant diagnoses of hypoactive sexual desire (Segraves & Segraves, 1990).

An initial consideration in conducting psychologically based therapy for MED is to establish clearly that the problem is truly psychogenic. One indication is a prior history of normal sexual performance. Masters and Johnson (1970) distinguished two types of erectile difficulties based on sexual histories. Males who were previously able to achieve erections were considered to have a secondary difficulty (a condition frequently termed "secondary impo-tence"). It is likely that these men suffer from a psychogenic disorder. On the other hand, men who had never achieved a satisfactory erection are considered to have a primary difficulty ("primary impotence") and most likely suffer from a biological condition. A more reliable indication is the Nocturnal Penile Tumescence Test, or NPT Test. All normal-functioning males have erections during REM (rapid eye movement) sleep. In the NPT Test, the circumferences of the base and tip of the penis are measured. If the patient shows no sign of an erection during REM sleep, he most likely has a biogenic erectile dysfunction. If the patient does have erections, however, it is probable that his erectile dysfunction is psychogenic. Secondary erectile difficulties are much more common. Masters and Johnson report that

50 percent of men seeking treatment suffer from secondary dysfunction, whereas only 8 percent experience primary dysfunction. A study by Renshaw (1988) yielded similar rates: 48 percent and 3.5 percent, respectively. This is fortunate, for many therapies are ineffective for primary dysfunctions. For example, Mann et al. (1996) found yohimbine to be effective for patients with nonorganic erectile dysfunction but not effective for those with organic dysfuction.

In the past, most therapies for sexual dysfunctions employed traditional psychodynamic analysis consisting of a series of interviews with the patient conducted in the therapist's office. Specific behavioral "exercises" were not used; in fact, the patient's specific sexual complaints were seen as merely a manifestation of underlying neuroses and were dealt with only tangentially. After the rise in popularity of behavioral sex therapists (e.g., Kaplan, 1974; Masters & Johnson, 1970), sexual dysfunctions began to be treated almost exclusively with direct behavioral techniques. Currently most sex clinics offer some sort of behavioral sex therapy such as Masters and Johnson's sensate focus program combined with psychotherapy to address interpersonal issues such as psychoeducation, performance anxiety, and relationship enhancement (Rosen, Lieblum, & Spector, 1994).

An important aspect of these behavioral exercises is that they rely heavily on the cooperation of a supportive partner (Wylie, 1997). One shortcoming of this type of treatment is that an uncooperative or unsympathetic partner can hinder or completely obstruct therapy. Some patients lack a partner with the required emotional maturity to carry out the program; other patients, like Jim, seek therapy without any steady partner whatsoever. Efforts are being made to make cognitive-behavioral-interpersonal treatment programs beneficial for singles (Rosen et al., 1994).

The eclectic therapy presented in this case combines behavioral treatments with dynamic therapy. Specific exercises are seen as very useful in surmounting particular problems, especially during the early stages of therapy. Providing the patient with dynamic analysis is seen as crucial in bringing about lasting behavioral and emotional changes.

Like Jim, many patients seeking therapy for sexual dysfunctions expect a direct, short-term behavioral therapy. When therapy begins to include broader dynamic issues, some become uncomfortable and either quit or switch to a more purely behavioral approach. Others, though, believe they can make gains from analysis and stay in therapy long after their behavioral symptoms disappear. The prevalence of MED increases dramatically with age, but ironically, older men are generally more resistant to therapy. Perhaps because of their more traditional sexual upbringing, they are less willing to perform the different exercises, especially those involving masturbation. As a group, they also seem to be less self-aware and less amenable to self-discovery. It is possible that as sexual attitudes in society become more accepting, a growing cohort of men will be better able to face their sexual problems.

SCHIZOPHRENIA, RESIDUAL TYPE
Pharmacotherapy with
Residential Treatment

PRESENTING COMPLAINT

Jerry was detained by U.S. Army MPs when he attempted to walk through a U.S. Army checkpoint on the East German border, ignoring the commands of several border guards. In their report the border guards stated that Jerry said "something about pursuing freedom and living off the land," but for the most part what he said was vague and incoherent. During his detention Jerry was interrogated by officers at the checkpoint. He was calm, even passive, but he seemed to be completely unaware of where he was and the situation he had gotten himself into. He appeared to be an American around 50 years old, but this could not be confirmed because he carried no passport, travel visa, or any other identifying papers. In addition, he did not tell the Army interrogators anything specific about who he was or where he was from, saying only his name and that he was from "different places over there." He reported having no present address in West Germany, no steady means of support, and no means of travel. Somewhat stupefied, the officers asked him just what he planned to do in East Germany. Jerry replied, "Oh, just wander around, here and there. Nothing much, just see stuff, you know?" Jerry was then admitted to the camp infirmary for psychiatric observation. Here he was first diagnosed as schizophrenic and admitted to a U.S. Army hospital in Coburg, West Germany, where he was given chlorpromazine (Thorazine), an antipsychotic medication, which had little effect. Gradually he was now able to tell the hospital staff some details about his identity and background, and the staff eventually tracked down Jerry's parents in Munich, about 140 miles to the south. After five weeks on the ward Jerry seemed to be under control and was discharged to the custody of his parents, who reported that this was the third time Jerry had "wandered off" since he had moved to Munich the previous year. For a month Jerry's parents agonized over what to do with him. They realized they could not control him, but they refused to commit him to an institution. Finally Jerry was sent to live near an aunt in Salt Lake City.

Jerry's aunt rented a small studio apartment for him and set him up with a job at a local supermarket. On his third day at the market, he walked off the job in the middle of his shift. Jerry returned to his apartment and did not go outside for several weeks; his aunt then became responsible for doing his laundry and shopping for his groceries. One morning at two o'clock, Jerry somehow became locked out of his apartment. He began yelling and banging at the door, and after about 20 minutes he finally broke it down and went inside. After this incident (which followed numerous other complaints by neighbors), Jerry's landlord began proceedings to evict him. Jerry's aunt promised to keep a closer eye on him and persuaded the landlord to hold off on the eviction. She then found him a part-time job as a church custodian. However, after two weeks of spotty attendance, Jerry again wandered off the job. This time, however, Jerry did not return to his apartment. After three days Jerry's aunt contacted the police and reported him missing.

Seven months later Jerry was arrested for vagrancy in a small town outside Bakersfield, California. In the meantime, his parents had returned from Europe to the Los Angeles area. The police contacted his parents, who then drove out to Bakersfield to be present at his court hearing. A court-ordered psychiatric evaluation suggested that Jerry was not competent to stand trial. After consulting with his parents, the judge committed Jerry to a psychiatric ward in a Veteran's Administration hospital located in a suburb of Los Angeles.

PERSONAL HISTORY

Jerry's descriptions of his past are for the most part extremely vague and lacking in content. He is unable to specify any dates, places, or events in his life. Occasionally he does provide some information, but most often this is inaccurate. For example, Jerry once reported to a hospital staff psychiatrist that he was an only child, when in fact he has an older brother. As a result, the hospital staff is forced to rely on other sources of information (his parents; his brother; his aunt; various medical, school, and military records) to provide the bulk of his background data. Although these secondary sources provided most of the basic information on the important events in Jerry's life, they could not describe his perceptions of these events or his emotional reactions to them. This subjective information is irretrievable.

Jerry is the younger of two sons in an upper-middle-class family. His father is a successful executive for a German automobile manufacturer; his mother has never been employed outside the home. According to his family and the available records, his childhood was unremarkable. He seemed to have had a happy childhood and got along well with his family. He received good grades throughout school, mostly A's and B's. According to his parents, Jerry seemed to have had a successful social life in high school; he dated often and participated in football and track. After high school he enrolled at a large state university to study mechanical engineering. It is in college that his odd behavior first appeared.

Jerry's grades for his freshman year were considerably below his usual performance, averaging in the low C range. His professors, his roommate, and his neighbors in the dormitory confirmed that he was not working up to his potential; they reported that he would frequently miss lectures and assignments. He seemed unconcerned about making friends or becoming active in campus activities, and his phone calls home became more infrequent as the year progressed. During his summer break he refused to work at a job set up by his father and spent most of his time either alone in his room or wandering aimlessly around the neighborhood. When he first returned home from college, Jerry's high school friends frequently came by to see him, but he seemed uninterested in them and made no effort to maintain their friendship. Although Jerry returned to college for the fall semester, it appears that he stayed in his dormitory room for most of the term. His academic work continued to deteriorate, and he wound up failing every course. In addition to having academic difficulties, Jerry was beginning to cause serious problems in his dormitory. His roommate complained that he would spend almost all of his time in his room either sleeping or mumbling to himself. He did not do his laundry the entire semester, and he often went without bathing for stretches of up to 10 days. After eight weeks his roommate demanded to be transferred to another room. Over the winter break Jerry was informed that he would not be allowed to continue at the university because of his academic and social difficulties. After his expulsion he was no longer eligible for a student deferment from military service.

Four months after he left the university Jerry was drafted into the Army. According to his evaluation during basic training, Jerry was found to be of above-average intelligence. However, his records also show that he lacked motivation and paid poor attention to instructions. He was described as a recruit who understood orders and instructions but followed them without any particular concern over what they were or if he would execute them properly. After completing basic training, Jerry was assigned to an ambulance unit in Vietnam. Jerry's combat record was similar to his record as a recruit. He never resisted orders, but he had to be supervised constantly to ensure that he actually carried them out. He was involved in combat on several occasions and once received superficial wounds to both legs. After his combat tour Jerry was assigned to work in the motor pool of an army camp in northern Texas. His stay at this camp was unremarkable aside from the fact that he again was quite indifferent about his assignments and required constant supervision to carry them out. Finally he was discharged from the Army after his two-year hitch was completed.

After his discharge Jerry got a job working at a fast-food restaurant near Wichita Falls, Texas, but he left this job after about a month. Two weeks later he was arrested for shoplifting in Norman, Oklahoma. Apparently Jerry had attempted to walk off with several items from a grocery store. In light of his veteran status and his clean record, however, the store owner decided not to press charges. For the next several years little was heard of Jerry, and his own accounts of this time are not particularly informative. Finally he was arrested for vagrancy and disorderly conduct in Omaha, Nebraska, after he repeatedly harassed passersby in a park, asking strange and incoherent questions on the order of "Where's the freedom land?" and "I want to hear freedom ring!"

During Jerry's tour of duty in Vietnam, his father was transferred to the corporate headquarters in Munich, West Germany. While in the Army Jerry corresponded with his family only rarely, and they heard nothing from him for the next three years. Through Jerry's military records, the Omaha police managed to identify him and contact his parents in West Germany. The court agreed to release Jerry to the care of his parents, and they took him to live with them in Munich.

CONCEPTUALIZATION AND TREATMENT

The term *schizophrenia* refers to a collection of diagnostic categories characterized by the presence of severe disturbances in thought, behavior, and interpersonal relationships. Researchers have organized schizophrenic behaviors into positive and negative symptoms (Andreasen & Olsen, 1982; T. Crow, 1980) that can be reliably distinguished (Kay, Fiszbein, & Opler, 1987). Positive symptoms are behaviors that most people do not express but schizophrenics do, such as hallucinations, delusions, and disorganized speech and behavior; negative symptoms refer to qualities most of us have that schizophrenics lack, such as emotional feeling, motivation, planning, and personal hygiene. Although the terms *positive symptom* and *negative symptom* are relatively new, the distinction between these behaviors among schizophrenics is not, having been described by Kraeplin in the nineteenth Century (Carpenter, 1992).

When positive symptoms occur, they are usually expressed in episodes characterized by three distinct phases. During the *prodromal phase*, schizophrenics will show a significant deterioration of their social and cognitive functioning from a premorbid level, showing negative symptoms, mild positive symptoms, or most often both. For example, a schizophrenic might withdraw from social situations, neglect personal duties and hygiene, have strange thoughts and emotions, and lose energy and initiative. This deterioration in functioning, called "decompensation," is usually the first visible sign that a serious disorder is present. During the prodromal phase, other people generally describe schizophrenics as "acting differently from their usual selves."

During the *active phase*, florid positive symptoms emerge. These include delusions (organized thought systems that are based on clearly false or bizarre ideas), hallucinations (vivid but illusory perceptions, most commonly auditory), disorganized thought patterns, odd speech, gross incoherence, inappropriate or restricted emotional reactions, and severe abnormalities of motor movement. *DSM-IV* categorizes schizophrenics into five subtypes based on the constellation of symptoms they exhibit during this active phase of their disorder. These subtypes are described below.

As the positive symptoms recede, schizophrenics enter a *residual phase*. The symptoms of this phase are very similar to those in the prodromal phase with the exception that emotional blunting (lack of emotional reactivity) and a neglect for one's duties are particularly pronounced in the residual phase. Other signs that could linger from the active phase are illogical thinking and some relatively mild delusions and hallucinations. The majority of schizophrenics display some symptoms for the rest of their lives; a complete absence of symptoms, known as *remission*, occurs in only about one third of the cases.

As noted above, *DSM-IV* distinguishes five subtypes of schizophrenia based on the particular pattern of positive symptoms exhibited during the active phase of the disorder. These five subtypes are labeled the catatonic type, disorganized type, paranoid type, undifferentiated type, and residual type.

Catatonic schizophrenia is characterized by severe disturbances in psychomotor behavior. Catatonics are frequently mute and unresponsive to the behavior of other people. They might assume rigid, passive, or otherwise bizarre postures. In some cases catatonics also show brief periods of wild, excited, and purposeless activity. One unifying quality of virtually all catatonics is that they are almost completely unresponsive to their environment.

Disorganized schizophrenics are also characterized by strange, incoherent, and often silly behavior. However, their symptoms reflect gross disturbances in their thought processes as opposed to their psychomotor processes. Their speech tends to be characterized by loose associations (unpredictably drifting from one topic to another), neologisms (made-up words others do not understand), and clanging (silly, rhyming sounds). Disorganized schizophrenics also tend to show emotions that are utterly inappropriate for their current situation, such as crying when hearing a joke. In contrast to catatonics, most disorganized schizophrenics appear to be somewhat responsive to their environment. They will answer questions, notice objects, and recall events. For most people, however, these responses are bizarre, incomprehensible, and unpredictable.

Paranoid schizophrenics are preoccupied with elaborate delusional systems, usually relating to themes of grandiosity, persecution, jealousy, and/or suspiciousness. The cast of these delusional systems typically involves divine or supernatural beings, important figures from the schizophrenic's life, or images from history or the media. Unless they are in the process of acting on their delusions, paranoid schizophrenics usually appear to act fairly normally, at least at a superficial level. As they become more involved in their strange ideation, however, the full extent of their delusional thinking becomes apparent.

Undifferentiated schizophrenics either display prominent psychotic symptoms from more than one of the above categories or show symptoms that do not fit easily into any of the above categories. Thus, schizophrenia, undifferentiated type, is a "garbage can" label for schizophrenics who exhibit the psychotic symptoms of an active phase but cannot be described by any of the three subtypes just described.

Schizophrenics categorized as *residual type* have not shown a clear history of the bizarre positive symptoms of an active phase. However, their behavior is characterized by negative symptoms such as disrupted daily functioning, social withdrawal, blunted affect, and illogical thinking. Most residual schizophrenics have a long-standing history of more or less continuous negative symptoms. In most cases there is evidence of a past active phase, but the details of this behavior are not sufficiently clear to allow a diagnosis of any particular subtype. Residual schizophrenics show no noticably strange characteristics, but their lives taken as a whole generally lack meaning and coherence. They seem to have a severe deficit in many of the higher-order abilities most people take for granted, such as setting life goals, making plans, and taking on and fulfilling responsibilities.

Jerry was 37 years old at admission, though he appreared to be 10 to 15 years older. His IQ was above average. His life seems to have had little meaning or coherence. He appeared to be unconcerned about the events of his life, and he showed little emotion in his day-to-day existence. He was not at all concerned by his lack of a permanent home, a steady job, companionship, or even a reasonably consistent source of food. He habitually withdrew from social situations, frequently wandering off from his home or job without any perceptible purpose. When he did engage in conversation, his speech was vague and lacking in content, as illustrated by his intake interview at the VA hospital:

> **Therapist:** Jerry, you left Salt Lake City about seven months ago, right?
>
> **Jerry:** Yeah, I guess.
>
> **Therapist:** So, what did you do during that time?
>
> **Jerry:** Oh, I don't know. Different things I guess.
>
> **Therapist:** Like what?
>
> **Jerry:** You know, this and that. Nothing special.
>
> **Therapist:** Well, like what? What did you do? Did you work?
>
> **Jerry:** Oh, well, I did odd jobs. You know.
>
> **Therapist:** What kind of odd jobs?
>
> **Jerry:** Little things here and there.
>
> **Therapist:** Like what? Can you think of any particular one?
>
> **Jerry:** Um, yeah. I was a janitor for a while.
>
> **Therapist:** How long did you do that?

Therapist: Like what?

Jerry: You know, this and that. Nothing special.

Therapist: Well, like what? What did you do?
Did you work?

Jerry: Oh, well, I did odd jobs. You know.

Therapist: What kind of odd jobs?

Jerry: Little things here and there.

Therapist: Like what? Can you think of any particular
one?

Jerry: Um, yeah. I was a janitor for a while.

Therapist: How long did you do that?

Jerry: Not long.

Therapist: What's "not long"? A few days, weeks,
months?

Jerry: A few days, I guess.

Therapist: Did you get paid for that?

Jerry: No, I don't think so.

Therapist: Well, how did you get money?

Jerry: Different ways.

Therapist: What kind of different ways?

Jerry: You know, odd jobs and stuff.

Therapist: Well, tell me this. How did you eat?

Jerry: You know, garbage.

(Later)

Therapist: Of all the places you were, where did you
like it best?

Jerry: Arizona, I guess.

Therapist: Why Arizona?

Jerry: Oh, different reasons.

Therapist: Could you name one?

Jerry: Well, it's drier there.

Therapist: Do you mean it's less humid?

Jerry: No, not really.

Case 10

Therapist: Well, what then?
Jerry: The ground's drier.
Therapist: What do you mean, "The ground is drier"?
Jerry: Well, there's less dew when you wake up.
Therapist: Oh, I see.

It is important to note that Jerry was not being secretive or evasive; he answered the questions as best he could, but his answers were strangely vague and distant.

Jerry also showed emotional blunting, an almost complete absence of any emotional reaction. His blunted affect is illustrated by the following excerpt from the same interview:

Therapist: So, you were in an ambulance unit in Vietnam?
Jerry: Uh huh.
Therapist: Did you see any combat.
Jerry: Some.
Therapist: How often?
Jerry: A couple of times.
Therapist: How many times? Once, twice?
Jerry: I don't know. Ten or twelve, maybe.
Therapist: Could you describe what it was like?
Jerry: Oh, well, you know, lots of blood and stuff. Smoke. People yelling a lot. You know.
Therapist: Were you frightened?
Jerry: I guess so.
Therapist: What did you think about?
Jerry: Different things, nothing really. I just did my job.

Recollections of combat are very traumatic for most veterans.

Either they are frightened and disturbed by the memories themselves, or they are bothered by the fact that these horrible memories do *not* disturb them. Jerry did not appear to have any kind of a reaction to these memories whatsoever.

Jerry's collection of social withdrawal, his blunted affect, his peculiar lack of motivation or initiative, his vague uninformative speech, his lack of any sense of planning or purpose, especially in the absence of any full-blown psychotic symptoms, characterizes someone suffering from schizophrenia, residual type with prominent negative symptoms. Because his symptoms had existed consistently for more than two years, his residual schizophrenia was categorized as continuous.

Jerry's history also included references to occasional agitated outbursts, such as beating down his door and harassing people in a park. These outbursts seemed to indicate the emergence of active phases of Jerry's schizophrenic disorder. By the general descriptions of these outbursts, Jerry probably would have been characterized as a disorganized or paranoid schizophrenic. Unfortunately, the information available from Jerry's records was not detailed enough to determine which of these labels was most appropriate, or even if the outbursts indicated an active phase at all. The active phases of Jerry's illness could not be classified reliably, and so the appropriate diagnosis for Jerry at his most recent hospitalization was schizophrenia, residual type, continuous with prominent negative symptoms.

As is the case for most schizophrenics, Jerry's treatment was primarily pharmacological. Upon admission to the VA hospital, he was given chlorpromazine at a standard maintenance dosage of 100 milligrams four times a day. The primary purpose of this treatment was prophylactic: it was aimed at preventing a recurrence of an active phase of his disorder. Because Jerry's history included only isolated instances of psychotic behavior, his therapists were confident that this relatively low maintenance dose would be effective in warding off the reemergence of any future active phase. Patients who are presently in an active phase or who have a history of frequent decompensations generally are given higher doses.

In addition to taking medication, Jerry also participated in various therapeutic activities designed to improve his social and occupational skills. On Tuesdays and Fridays, the patients and the therapeutic staff (therapists, interns, and nurses) of Jerry's ward gathered together for community meetings. To promote their sense of control and responsibility, the patients were put in charge of these meetings. One patient was chosen to be the discussion leader, and another was chosen as the secretary who organized the proceedings and took minutes. These biweekly community meetings allowed the patients to raise issues and concerns in the presence of the entire ward and were intended to facilitate direct discussions among the patients and between the patients and staff. The primary focus of these discussions usually concerned practical issues on the ward (e.g., who was leaving or joining the ward, the policy on issuing day passes, information on field trips and events). The patients also participated in group therapy sessions. These sessions involved only a few patients at a time and were led by a single staff member. The object of these groups was to discuss interpersonal issues that are of concern to individual patients. The smaller size of these groups made it possible for an individual patient's problems to be addressed more thoroughly and in an open and frank manner.

Like most of the patients, Jerry was not particularly interested in participating in either group activity. After a few weeks on the ward, however, he was elected as the group secretary, an activity that had several positive, though indirect, effects. Mostly it forced him to interact with other patients just to organize the meetings. He also had to review the minutes of the last session prior to reading them, and he had to pay close attention during each meeting. Jerry's acceptance of these responsibilities was a positive sign.

A prime topic in group therapy was Jerry's indifference to social relationships. Jerry and his group leader set up a behavioral contract that reinforced him (through public recognition and added ward privileges) for spending time interacting with other patients and staff members. Jerry responded to this contingency almost immediately. Instead of spending most of his recreation time alone, he began to take long walks around the hospital grounds with other patients. He also became much more involved in ward outings and other special events. For example, during an observation visit by a group of graduate students, Jerry approached several students to strike up conversations. Although he had a friendly attitude and was responsive to their questions, the students found the actual content of his speech to be rambling and rather uninformative. Nevertheless, even this limited approach behavior represented a big advance for Jerry.

Another aspect of Jerry's treatment program involved limited vocational training. As patients' symptoms begin to recede and become more manageable, they are enrolled in supervised workshops run by the hospital. Here they are trained to perform unskilled tasks (washing dishes, sorting cartons, etc.). Some patients are placed into semiskilled workshops. The therapeutic importance of this training is not in learning the vocational skills per se but rather in developing the discipline needed to hold a steady job. Jerry received carpentry training and presently works in the hospital's wood finishing shop, where patients refurbish used or abandoned furniture. This furniture is then used by the hospital or sold to the public.

The next step in the program is to discharge the patients from the ward and set them up in semi-independent apartments, which are located in a complex about three miles from the hospital. Patients live in individual studio apartments and are responsible for their own food, laundry, transportation, and entertainment. The rent of the apartments is controlled, and the hospital can arrange to pay a patient's rent directly from his or her disability check if he or she proves to be incapable of doing so. In addition, the patients are supervised by a staff member who lives in the complex.

After six weeks on the ward, Jerry moved into his apartment. He works at the wood finishing shop three days a week and attends group therapy once a week. He has had no problems taking public buses to the hospital, and his attendance at work and at group therapy has remained around 90 percent. He seems to have no problem in performing his personal errands, such as shopping and doing his laundry. One month after moving into his apartment, Jerry's medication was reduced to 200 milligrams per day; for the past eight months he has been maintained on this relatively low dose and appears to be doing well. Jerry's only particularly noticeable symptom is his persistent disinterest in forming interpersonal relationships.

PROGNOSIS

On the whole, Jerry seemed to be functioning well in his structured job and sheltered living situation. Many of his more pronounced residual symptoms, such as his inability to feed and clothe himself and his unwillingness to stay at a job, had decreased as he developed a more steady, normal routine. In all likelihood, though, Jerry will need to continue living in a fairly sheltered environment and taking his medication to maintain these therapeutic gains and prevent a recurrence of his more serious psychotic symptoms. As is the case with most chronic schizophrenics, getting Jerry to continue taking his medication is the key to his prognosis. Provided he remains in his supervised apartment and continues to take his antipsychotic medication, there is little reason to believe that Jerry's level of functioning will change significantly in the foreseeable future. Although his treatment had enabled him to live somewhat independently and even to be productive, there is little chance that Jerry will ever become truly autonomous. Thus, his prognosis is poor, and the goal of treatment, like that of most schizophrenics, is continued maintenance, not cure.

DISCUSSION

The schizophrenias constitute a diverse class of disorders that progress through distinct phases and manifest themselves in a variety of ways. To make matters even more complex, schizophrenics show great individual differences in their behavior patterns. Some will show residual symptoms almost continuously and will decompensate into an active phase only rarely, if ever. Some will display a single acute, psychotic episode without a recurrence. Still others will cycle between episodes of negative and positive symptoms. Furthermore, psychiatric professionals have found it very difficult, if not impossible, to predict when a particular patient will enter an active phase. Thus, estimates of the percentage of schizophrenics who fall into each of these groups at any given time vary widely, although it is generally agreed that about 1 percent of the population will suffer some form of schizophrenia during their lifetimes (Regier et al., 1988; Robins et al., 1984).

The majority of schizophrenics exhibit some residual symptoms most of the time, and these negative symptoms are the most commonly observed signs of the disorder. Interestingly, research findings and public perception take virtually opposite tacks on schizophrenia. Researchers agree that the presence of negative symptoms is more predictive of the severity of the disorder. Buchanan, Kirkpatrick, Heinrichs, and Carpenter (1990) found that negative syptoms, but not positive symptoms, were related to poorer premorbid adjustment. Similarly, Hwu, Tan, Chen, and Yeh (1995) report that the severity of negative symptoms at release is the best predictor of future relapse; in fact, in both studies the severity of positive symptoms at release showed no correlation with prognosis. In contrast, public perceptions focus almost exclusively on the bizarre, "crazy" positive symptoms that emerge during the active phase of the disorder.

Although it is clear that schizophrenia has a genetic component (Gottesman, McGuffin, & Farmer, 1987), at the present time little is known about the causes of schizophrenia (Landrine, 1989). So far, therapists have not been successful in bringing about a cure for this disorder. However, a number of antipsychotic drugs are available to control the symptoms of schizophrenia. The initial wave of neuroleptics, first prescribed in the 1950s, have proven to be very effective in reducing the overt, positive symptoms of the active phase.

Today chlorpromazine (Thorazine) and haloperidol (Haldol) are commonly prescribed. Recently a variety of so-called novel, or atypical, antipsychotics such as clozapine (Clozaril) and resperidone (Risperdal), have been developed (Arnt & Skarsfeldt, 1998; King, 1998), and these appear to be effective in treating negative symptoms, at least to some extent (Al-Semaan, 1996; Carpenter et al., 1995; Paillère-Martinot, Lecrubier, Martinot, & Aubin, 1995; Trappler, Kwong, & Leeman, 1996), often in combination with antidepressants or other medications (e.g., Szegedi, Wiesner, & Hiemke, 1995). Because these medications offer no cure but merely control schizophrenic symptoms, they generally must be taken indefinitely (Gilbert, Harris, McAdams, & Jeste, 1995).

When prescribing antipsychotic medication, psychiatrists must keep several issues in mind. First, the dosage must be carefully monitored to correspond to the patients' needs. Patients in the midst of an active phase are given a relatively large "loading" dose (up to 1200 milligrams per day of Thorazine, for example) to counteract their florid positive symptoms. As these symptoms subside, their medication is gradually reduced to a maintenance level. Some patients will show notable improvement in their negative symptoms while at a maintenance level, and their dosage may be further reduced.

Occasionally a patient will not show residual signs following the abatement of the psychotic symptoms. In these cases the patient is not likely to suffer a psychotic break in the near future and may be withdrawn from medication entirely. It is possible that the person suffers from another disorder with psychotic features, such as bipolar disorder or organic delusional syndrome.

A second consideration in prescribing antipsychotic medication is patient compliance; making sure the patients actually take their medication. Most patients who take antipsychotic medication suffer some side effects such as nausea, grogginess, and irritability. Without supervision, most schizophrenics discontinue their medication soon after release. Subsequently they slowly decompensate to an active phase, and at this point they are readmitted for treatment and again given antipsychotic medication. This cycle of treatment and decompensation has become known as the "revolving door syndrome." This problem has become more widespread as the number of available psychiatric beds declines, limiting most facilities to short-term pharmacological treatment.

Sometimes the patients' odd cognitions in and of themselves can interfere with pharmacological treatment. One case, for example, involved a paranoid schizophrenic's delusions concerning thioridazine (Mellaril) tablets, which are either green, yellow, or pink, depending on the dosage. This patient refused to take any green pills, saying they were poisoned. As a result the staff had to make sure to keep a supply of pink Mellaril tablets available.

A third consideration is for therapists to be aware of other medications and/or drugs the patient is taking. The home environments of many patients, especially those in poor urban areas, commonly include alcohol and illicit drugs. Sometimes friends or family members even attempt to smuggle drugs into the psychiatric wards. As much as possible, the staff must avoid prescribing medication that can have an adverse, or even lethal, interaction with other substances.

Finally, therapists must be wary of the possible long-term side effects of medication, particularly a condition known as tardive dyskensia, a condition of impaired motor movements and shakiness resulting from prolonged pharmacological treatment. This condition has long been associated with more traditional antipsychotics such as thorazine, but cases have been reported which involve newer medications, such as risperidone (Woerner, Sheitman, Lieberman, & Kane, 1996). Rittmannsberger and Schony (1986) recommend frequent reviews of medication dosages. A common practice was the "drug holiday," a temporary withdrawal from a neuroleptic in an attempt to avoid tolerance. Lengthy treatment, particularly with large dosages, has been linked to a variety of permanent side effects, most notably tardive dyskensia. Though it is important to gradually taper medications to their lowest effective doses, it appears that drug holidays are ineffective in preventing tardive dyskensia and might even be harmful (Gilbert et al., 1995).

Despite these limitations, pharmacological therapy remains the most effective treatment for the schizophrenias. Residential programs that provide schizophrenics with a sheltered environment, psychosocial interventions (Penn & Mueser, 1996), and family behavioral treatments that teach symptom management (Terrier, 1991) seem to provide some gains over pharmacological therapy alone. Thus, a combination of antipsychotic medication and a sheltered environment appears to be the best method now available for fostering at least a minimal level of functioning and preventing the onset of future active phases.

Jerry received a comprehensive treatment that effectively combined pharmacological therapy and residential therapy. Jerry's treatment took place in the early 1980s, when more money was available for comprehensive treatment at VA hospitals (and when East Germany and West Germany were separate countries). The vast majority of current treatment programs for schizophrenics cannot offer such facilities; most are short-term programs that can afford to treat only the most severely psychotic schizophrenics on a "crisis management" basis. Because of a lack of sheltered housing, patients whose overtly psychotic symptoms have subsided after a brief period, sometimes as short as a few days, are simply released. In many cases these schizophrenics have no steady home or family, and they just wander the streets until their next active phase emerges. For most schizophrenics, this revolving door syndrome will be a behavior pattern that will predominate the rest of their lives.

DEMENTIA OF THE ALZHEIMER TYPE
WITH LATE ONSET
Supportive Therapy

PRESENTING COMPLAINT

Emma is a 74-year-old woman who lives alone in a small town in central Indiana. She has been widowed for six years. Her daughter and son-in-law, Susan and Bill, also live in this town and visit her several times a week.

Approximately two months ago Emma and Susan went on a shopping trip to Indianapolis. Emma seemed to enjoy the ride to the city, and she and Susan engaged in friendly, although somewhat vacuous and disorganized, conversation. When they arrived downtown, Emma became very confused. She did not know where she was or why she was there. She asked several odd questions, such as "What's the name of this place?" and "Why are you taking me here?" She became very upset and asked her daughter to take her home again. Susan was used to her mother being confused now and then, but she had never seen her this disoriented. When she tried to explain where they were and the purpose of the trip, Emma continued to be confused and agitated. Seeing little use in continuing the outing, Susan drove home.

When they returned to Emma's house, Susan noticed other signs that something was wrong with her mother. Emma had left her stove on, and she had also left a pan with scrambled eggs in the refrigerator. Emma could not say how long the stove had been on or when she had put the pan in the refrigerator; in fact, she had no memory of having made scrambled eggs at all. She soon became very upset, refused to answer any more questions, and asked Susan to leave.

169

That evening Susan called to check up on her mother and ask if she were feeling ill. Emma denied having any problems and asked Susan why in the world she might have thought so. Emma had only a vague memory of their trip that morning and no recollection whatsoever of their argument.

The next day Susan took Emma to see their family physician. He found nothing wrong with her physically, but he did notice that she was vague, even evasive, about recent events. Alerted by Susan's concerns, he found that Emma suffered mild memory loss and seemed mildly disoriented during the examination. He then referred her for a more detailed neuropsychological examination at the neurology clinic of a nearby hospital. Emma was given a battery of diagnostic tests, including a CT (computed axial tomography) scan, an EEG (electro-encephalogram), and various blood tests. After analyzing the results of these tests, the neurologist found what he expected: evidence of cortical atrophy and nonspecific, bilateral brain-wave slowing. He was noncommittal about his diagnosis, but he mentioned the possibility of Alzheimer's disease. Susan and Bill were dissatisfied with this diagnosis and sought a second opinion. They were referred to the neurology clinic of a major teaching hospital in Indianapolis.

PERSONAL HISTORY

Susan and Bill drove Emma to the neurology clinic in Indianapolis. Emma appeared nervous, confused, and disoriented during the initial interview with the neurology resident; Susan provided the bulk of Emma's history.

Emma was born in Chicago, the daughter of Swedish immigrants who came to Illinois at the turn of the century. She was the second child of six: two boys and four girls. She had an eighth-grade education and worked as a store clerk in Chicago until her marriage at age 22. Susan was born two years later; medical complications during the birth prevented her from having any more children. Soon afterward Emma's husband bought a hardware store in central Indiana and moved the family. When Emma was 40 years old, she took a job as a teller at a local bank. In accordance with company policy, she retired when she was 65. This policy has since been revoked.

Emma's medical history is unremarkable. She is described by her daughter as a "light social drinker." When she was first married, she smoked tobacco occasionally, but she then quit and has not smoked in over 40 years. She has no history of any head injury, thyroid disease, or any other serious medical problem. Fifteen years ago she had cataract surgery without any complications.

The medical history of Emma's family of origin is somewhat unclear. Her mother died about 20 years ago at the age of 81, and her father died over 50 years ago when Emma was still a teenager. Susan cannot state the cause of their deaths other than saying that Emma's mother died of "old age." Emma's husband had a history of coronary disease and died six years ago from cardiac arrest. One of Emma's brothers was diagnosed as having Alzheimer's disease before he passed away four years ago; her other siblings are still alive and in reasonably good health.

According to Susan, Emma suffers from "minor mood problems" involving occasional feelings of anxiety and depression. Fifteen months ago Emma was prescribed the tricyclic antidepressant doxepin (Sinequan), and she continues to take a very small maintenance dose of 30 milligrams per day. (Today she would probably be prescribed an SSRI such as paroxetine [Paxil] due to its lowered risk of side effects.) Other than this, Emma has no history of any psychiatric disorder. She takes no other medication.

When the neurologist asked Susan to describe Emma's "minor mood problems" in more detail, she replied:

> Mom was fine until a couple of years ago. She had been living alone for about four years. About this time she started staying home a lot. She didn't seem to want to go out much, even to visit friends, and she started calling us less often. She seemed to get angry and irritable with other people much easier than she used to. She also starting

getting confused about things—where she kept different
things around the house and who she talked to, that sort of
thing. This was all pretty gradual. Lately she's been very
hesitant to do things on her own. It seems that I take her
just about everywhere now: shopping, to the beauty parlor,
to the bank. And you know about the trip to Indianapolis.

About a year ago we took her to a gerontology specialist. We told him what we had been noticing, but he didn't
seem to think that she was unusual. He gave her medication
for her anxiety, though. She still takes it, but it doesn't seem
to help much; actually she seems to be getting worse. As
you know, we saw another neurologist two weeks ago, but
he also didn't seem to know what was wrong.

CONCEPTUALIZATION AND TREATMENT

Emma's worsening memory and increasingly frequent periods of
disorientation suggest that she is suffering from a progressive dementia.
According to *DSM-IV*, dementia is a condition marked by a significant
impairment in higher cortical function. Characteristic symptoms include
feelings of confusion and disorientation in familiar settings, memory
loss, difficulty in maintaining concentration, impairment in one's ability
to exercise good judgment and think abstractly, and an increase in
irritability and aggression. In many cases there may be evidence of
paranoid delusions and hallucinations, aphasia (disruptions in the ability
to use or understand language), agnosia (inability to recognize familiar
objects or events), and apraxia (difficulty in carrying out coordinated
actions).

Several neuropsychological tests have been developed to
measure the extent of a person's dementia. One is the Blessed Test
(Blessed, Tomlinson, & Roth, 1968). The Blessed Test is a 33-item
questionnaire that assesses the patient's functioning in the following
areas: orientation (the patient's name, the time and date, the present
location), memory (place of birth, names of family members), and

concentration (adding two numbers, counting backward). The patient scores one point for every incorrect answer. Thus, the higher the score on this test, the more extensive the cortical impairment.

Emma scored 24 on the Blessed Test. She was able to state her name and her place of birth, and she knew the names of close family members. However, she failed at tasks that made use of less personal information. She did not know the correct date, the day of the week, or the month. She could not say where she was, or even that she was in a hospital. She could not recall an address or a series of numbers given to her five minutes before, or even that they had been given to her at all. She was also unable to count backward. When she was asked to add 8 and 5, she appeared confused and copied these numbers over and over.

Emma's responses on this test indicate moderate to severe impairment in her cognitive abilities. This finding is not wholly surprising, considering Susan's description of her odd behavior. Another factor consistent with this result is her age. Whereas dementia is rare for persons under 50, the prevalence of this disorder increases greatly with age.

About half of all cases of dementia are of the Alzheimer type, commonly referred to as "Alzheimer's disease." This form of dementia is marked by an insidious onset and a gradual but inexorable deterioration in a multitude of intellectual abilities (Grady et al., 1988). Memory, judgment, and decision-making processes are affected, and personality changes might be noticed. Agitation and irritability are common, and paranoid delusions and hallucinations could be present. Patients experience difficulty in comprehending complex and abstract problems, but in time the ability to perform even simple tasks is impaired. Eventually the patients are no longer able to care for themselves.

There is no practical test to provide a definite diagnosis of Alzheimer's disease; the only conclusive evidence is the existence of senile plaques and neurofibrillary bundles in brain tissue. Unfortunately, these can be detected only by brain biopsy, which is usually conducted at autopsy. (Brain biopsy has been used for premorbid diagnosis of Alzheimer's disease, but only in extraordinary cases where there is a good possibility of finding another potentially treatable cause of dementia, such as brain tumor or stroke). Without a reliable positive indicator, diagnosticians are left to rely on negative indicators; that is, they must rule out other known causes of dementia. At this point a tentative but more or less reliable *DSM-IV* diagnosis of dementia of the Alzheimer type is made. When symptoms manifest themselves before age 65, the disorder is said to have an early onset; symptoms that emerge after age 65 indicate a late onset. Some researchers (Barclay, Zemcov, Blass, & McDowell, 1985; Silverman et al., 1994) argue that a presenile onset marks a more severe form of the disorder with a more malignant course, but others (Grady et al., 1987) have found no differences between patients with early and late onset.

The neurology resident who interviewed Emma could not identify any known cause of her symptoms. The failure to identify a specific cause of her disorder, combined with the insidious onset and the gradual but steady progression of her symptoms, led him to conclude that the chances were about 90 percent that she suffered from Alzheimer's disease. The attending neurologist, a specialist in research on dementia, concurred with this assessment.

At the time of Emma's diagnosis, there was no known treatment for the cognitive decline of Alzheimer's disease. In the past few years, though, two medications have been approved by the FDA to treat this sort of progressive dementia: tacrine (Cognex) and more recently donepezil (Aricept). The introduction of donepezil was particularly exciting because it has a milder side effect profile and thus can be prescribed much more widely in the frail elderly population (Geldmacher, 1997; Rogers et al., 1998). These drugs work to increase the availability of acetylcholine (Ach), a neurotransmitter involved in memory and cognition. In the short term these drugs improve cognitive functioning to some degree, but they do not improve long-term cognitive function; rather, they work to retard the progression of decline (Kumar & Cantillon, 1996; Rogers & Friedhof, 1998). Nevertheless, this provides significant lifestyle benefits.

Even with the advent of these medications, the bulk of therapy typically focuses not on the demented patients themselves but on the families who must now deal with the profound burden of caring for them (Long, 1997; Pruchno, Michaels, & Potashnik, 1990). The need for this therapy should not be underestimated. Small et al. (1997), for example, found that about half of the caregivers became depressed. This therapy has several purposes. First, it can inform the patients and their families what the disease is and what they can expect in terms of functioning. Second, this therapy can suggest several strategies to aid patients' memory and concentration, thus prolonging their ability to function independently. Third, this therapy gives both the patients and their families a place to air frustrations and complaints. Last, and perhaps most important, this therapy helps the patients, and especially the families, to cope with the relentless progression of this disorder.

Immediately after Emma's diagnosis, she and Susan began meeting with a counselor from the hospital once a week. Gradually these meetings became less frequent until they were held approximately once a month. These sessions provided Emma with an empathic listener with whom she could share her doubts, fears, and frustrations. Emma also found her counselor to be a useful sounding board for her complaints, especially those concerning Susan.

The counselor also provided Emma and Susan with some specific strategies, or tricks, to help them cope with Emma's impaired memory and judgment. First, the counselor suggested that when other people ask Emma questions, they should phrase the question to provide her with a choice of possible reponses. The counselor explained that often memory is aided when a person is asked to decide whether a given event had happened or not (recognition) rather than having to generate the event from memory (recall). For example, Emma found it easier to answer a question such as "Did you have eggs or cereal for breakfast?" instead of "What did you have for breakfast?" Similarly, "Was that Gladys on the phone?" was easier to answer than "Who was that on the phone?"

A second set of tricks was designed to reduce Emma's increasing confusion about her household routine. To help Emma remember to perform these minor chores, Susan put labels around the house. Thus, a label on Emma's nightstand reading "Take your pill" reminded her to take her medication at bedtime. Labels near the door also reminded her to lock the door and to turn off the stove. Because Emma forgot which light switches controlled which lights, Susan labeled each switch with its corresponding fixture: "Hall Light," "Kitchen Light," "Porch Light," and so on. As Emma's aphasia worsened, she gradually lost her ability to recognize the words on these labels. At this point Susan, with a fair amount of ingenuity, added pictures to many of the labels.

Third, because Emma often lost her place in the middle of doing her chores or errands, Susan wrote out directions for various everyday tasks. For instance, the particular steps involved in doing the laundry were written out in detail and attached to the washing machine. Emma found it easier to complete these tasks if she had some concrete set of directions to refer to when she forgot her place in the sequence of steps.

An important aspect of counseling is to provide reassurance and encouragement to the families of Alzheimer patients, who often need this help as much as the patients themselves. One issue that emerges early is simply trying to accept the disease. Susan was particularly resistent to the idea that her mother had a progressive, terminal disease. One indication of her denial was the great discrepancy between her description of her mother's behaviors and Emma's performance on neuropsychological tests. Susan reported' that Emma suffered from "getting confused" and had "minor mood problems." In contrast, Emma's Blessed Test score of 24 provides evidence of considerable cognitive impairment. Another indication of Susan's denial was her rejection of the findings of Emma's first neurological examination. As the neurologist stated, "I get the distinct impression that Susan just refuses to believe that her mother has Alzheimer's disease." Ronald Reagan's public announcement of his own diagnosis of Alzheimer's disease has served as a model for openness and allowed many patients and family members overcome their own resistances.

Once she finally accepted the diagnosis of Alzheimer's disease, Susan was able to care for her mother in a more constructive way. Much of her frustration at Emma's seemingly illogical behaviors evaporated. She became more aware of the many signs of her mother's dementia, and she became more patient and caring. She was eager to set up the various memory "tricks" around Emma's home. She also made an effort to explain Emma's condition to friends, who had been surprised by the mother's apathetic and sometimes hostile attitude. She decided to take over Emma's financial affairs as well.

PROGNOSIS

Six months after her visit to the clinic in Indianapolis, Emma was unable to recall the majority of recent events, most noticeably conversations she had had with her family or friends. She was frequently disoriented and increasingly had great difficulty linking individual actions into purposeful behaviors. One by one she gave up her friendships (usually because she failed to recognize her friends and acquaintances), and she became more irritable around her daughter.

After a year she was brought back to the specialist in Indianapolis and given a follow-up examination. As he predicted, her deterioration was marked. She now scored 31 on the Blessed Test. She was able to provide only her name and place of birth, and she did not appear to understand most other questions.

After another year her cognitive functioning had deteriorated to the point where she was unable to care for herself. She could no longer dress or wash herself and was frequently incontinent. At this point, Susan was spending virtually all her time at her mother's home. With the encouragement of her husband and her counselor, Susan finally decided to place Emma in a nursing home. There Emma's cognitive abilities continued to deteriorate, and she died of pneumonia approximately 18 months later.

DISCUSSION

Studies conducted in various countries report that roughly 5 percent of the population over 65 years of age suffers from some form of dementia and that about half of the dementia cases are of the Alzheimer type (Martin, 1989; Shibayama, Kasahara, & Kobayashi, 1986). In the United States, this translates to approximately 4 million sufferers, and this figure is expected to triple in the next 50 years (Geldmacher, 1997). Women are roughly twice as likely as men to suffer from the disease (Henderson, 1990; McGuffey, 1997). The prevalence of Alzheimer's disease increases exponentially with age. For example, a Canadian study (Gautrin, Froda, Tetreault, & Gauvreau, 1990) found Alzheimer type dementia in 1 percent of those aged 65 to 74, 4 percent in those aged 75 to 84, and 10.5 percent in those aged 85 or older.

Alzheimer type dementia is more common among first-degree relatives, particularly early-onset dementia (Silverman et al., 1994). African Americans and Hispanics are two to four times more likely to develop the disease (Tang et al., 1998). Patients with little or no education tend to be diagnosed earlier (Katzman, 1993), though it remains to be demonstrated whether this reflects a difference in the diagnostic procedure (less educated patients interview and test more poorly) or in the incidence of the disease itself (lifelong "mental exercise" delays dementia).

Like many other forms of dementia, Alzheimer's disease is characterized by a general cerebral atrophy (wasting away), which can be identified by CT and MRI (magnetic resonance imaging) brain scans as an enlargement of the lateral ventricles, particularly the third (right) ventricle (Luxenberg et al., 1987). Another indication is lowered cortical metabolism as shown on PET (positive emission tomography) scans. However, these neurological tests are not precise indicators of the disease. Cerebral atrophy can also occur in patients with other forms of dementia as well as in cognitively normal subjects, and many Alzheimer patients do not show these neuroanatomical abnormalities. Another nonspecific finding in dementia is an EEG showing slow, diffuse patterns, but again, this can occur in subjects without Alzheimer's disease.

Many neuropsychological tests to measure dementia are also available. In addition to the Blessed Test, researchers and physicians often use the Alzheimer's Disease Assessment Scale (ADAS) (Rosen, Mohs, & Davis, 1984) and the Mini Mental State Exam (MMSE) (Folstein, Folstein, & McHugh, 1975). These two measures are relatively quick and easy to administer, albeit at a cost of diagnosic precision. Others use the Wechsler Adult Intelligence Scale, Third Edition (WAIS-III) (Wechsler, 1997), often administered by utilizing separate subscales. Generally, abnormalities appear earlier in neurological scans than they do in neuropsychological tests (Haxby et al., 1990).

The course of Alzheimer's disease is one of gradual, progressive cortical deterioration through the stages of cognitive loss to functional impairment to behavioral disinhibition/apathy (Gauthier, Panisset, Nalbantoglu, & Poirier, 1997). Cognitive impairments such as memory loss and disorientation become increasingly pervasive. Typically the patient also experiences increased agitation and apathy as the disorder worsens. The patient might withdraw almost completely from social interactions. In severe cases the patient will experience difficulties in mobility and become bedridden. Eventually the patient could lose his or her ability to perform even the most routine task, such as eating a meal, and may require constant supervision. Only a minority of the patients with Alzheimer's disease die as a direct result of their dementia; however, their prolonged illness makes them especially vulnerable to opportunistic diseases such as pneumonia that ordinarily would not be fatal. The duration of Alzheimer's disease varies widely among individuals, though there is some evidence that men succumb somewhat more quickly than women (Barclay, Zemcov, Blass, & McDowell, 1985). For any particular case, the duration of the illness depends in large measure on how alert the patient's family is to his or her condition and how quick they are to respond when medical problems arise. Generally, though, the outlook is rather bleak; Belloni-Sonzogni et al. (1989) followed a group of Alzheimer's patients in an Italian geriatric institution over four years and observed a mortality rate of 86.9 percent.

Emma's case is typical. The insidious onset of her cognitive impairment, the gradual progression of her symptoms, her deepening social withdrawal, her loss of self-care skills, and her final submission to an opportunistic disease are all sadly common.

Another typical aspect of this case was Susan's denial of her mother's disorder. Because of the insidious onset of Alzheimer's disease, at first few family members notice any behavioral changes. Although most detect memory impairment and disorientation, these symptoms are frequently dismissed as part of "growing old."

As a result of the obvious physiological base of the patients' symptoms and the need to rule out competing diagnoses, the diagnostic focus in these cases is almost exclusively on the medical and neurological aspects of the patients' histories. Factors that would be ignored in most psychiatric evaluations are of vital importance, and patient histories tend to be limited to past diseases, surgeries, physical traumas, medication, and psychiatric disorders. In particular, factors that support a competing diagnosis (high blood pressure, hypothyroidism, a history of depression, impairment of localized cognitive or physical function) are investigated closely. Little weight is given to subjective experiences; in fact, most case histories are provided by family members and not by the patients themselves. Attention is paid to personal feelings, concerns, or memories only to the extent that they may provide information about the existence or extent of the patients' dementia.

Alzheimer's disease is a profoundly disturbing and frightening experience for the patient, and taking care of someone with Alzheimer's disease is an emotionally and physically taxing responsibility, particularly if the patient is a close relative (Pruchno et al., 1990). For these reasons, supportive therapy is very important, perhaps more so for the families of these patients than for the patients themselves. For many family members, the information about the nature and progression of the disease and reassurance that the patient's behavior is largely involuntary are the most valuable aspects of therapy. This knowledge often helps the family members remain patient and calm in particularly trying situations.

Another common problem involves the level of commitment and responsibility family members often take on (Pruchno et al., 1990). Some report feeling a great sense of duty to the patient (who is usually a spouse or parent) and avoid being away from him or her, even briefly, lest some unfortunate accident or mishap should occur. As the patient becomes more impaired, the caretaker finds it increasingly difficult to meet the demands of his or her own life while looking after the constant needs of the patient. Feelings of frustration and resentment are common, as are pangs of guilt. Typically the central focus of counseling at this stage of the disorder is to address these very issues. Family members are told not to let the patient's needs disrupt their own lives. If the patient degenerates to the point where constant care is necessary, they are encouraged to accept this fact and either hire a private nurse or companion, or place the patient in a nursing home. Institutionalizing a patient, particularly a spouse or parent, is a very difficult decision, and supportive therapy aids the caretakers in coming to grips with this painful issue.

BULIMIA NERVOSA
Cognitive-Behavioral Therapy

PRESENTING COMPLAINT

Jill is a 25-year-old single woman who works as a flight attendant for a major airline. After getting home late at night after a particularly difficult flight, Jill went out to a local convenience store and bought a half gallon of chocolate ice cream, a 1-pound box of cookies, a medium-sized frozen pizza, a loaf of French bread, and a quart of milk. When she got home, she put the pizza in the oven and waited impatiently for it to cook; everything else stayed on the table. When the pizza was just edible, she brought it out and placed it with the other food. She then lunged into the food and ate everything she bought as quickly as she could, stuffing in huge mouthfuls and dribbling milk, crumbs, and pizza sauce down her chin and onto her blouse. When she finished, she ran to the bathroom, knelt in front of the toilet, thrust her hand down her throat, and vomited everything she had just eaten.

The next day Jill consulted an internist for help concerning recent periods of weakness and dizziness, the most recent of which occurred on yesterday's flight. After performing a routine examination, he asked her about her eating habits. Jill was extremely embarrassed and guilty about describing these to him, but she felt that if she wanted to get well, she had to tell the truth. She confessed to a long-standing pattern of uncontrollably consuming extremely large quantities of food (known as binge eating) and then vomiting this food (purging). This binge-purge pattern began years ago, but it has become more severe and more frequent since Jill began working as a flight attendant. When he asked her to describe her eating pattern in more detail, she awkwardly described last night's binge and purge. According to Jill, this was a fairly typical amount of food for a binge, which she usually finishes within 20 minutes. She almost always induces vomiting right after binge eating. At first she stuck her finger down her throat, but gradually that became less effective. Now she usually purges by sticking her hand down her throat, though on occasion she has used other objects, including a popcicle stick, a spoon, and a folded electric cord.

Jill admitted that her eating behavior must appear very strange and repulsive to him; it was certainly disgusting to her. She promised herself a thousand times that she'd stop, but she couldn't. She goes through this binge-purge cycle once or twice a day when she is at home; she can control herself to some extent "on the road" and only rarely binges when she is traveling. She estimates that she binges an average of six times per week. She also swallows a "handful" of laxatives, perhaps 12 to 15, once or twice a week after binge eating. In addition she takes Lasix (a diuretic) and diet pills in an effort to lose weight.

Although it was very difficult for Jill to tell her doctor about her strange eating patterns, she felt relieved once she did. Her doctor reassured her that she wasn't disgusting. Instead he sympathetically explained that it sounded like she had bulimia nervosa, which is not so uncommon in young women, and referred her to an eating disorders clinic. Before her appointment at the clinic, Jill read several articles about this disorder and was very relieved to find out that, as her internist had said, many other women suffered from these same odd symptoms. When her therapist first met her and asked her what brought her to the eating disorders clinic, she looked down and replied, "I have bulimia."

In the course of her initial interview, Jill admitted that she felt very depressed following a breakup with her boyfriend. During this depression she felt so despondent and weak that she occasionally missed work. Although she frequently had suicidal thoughts during this time and had even formulated several suicide plans, she did not make any actual suicide attempts. The episode lasted about a month and then seemed to lift by itself. She had a similar bout with depression about two years earlier, following her withdrawal from college. She did not seek treatment for either of these episodes.

PERSONAL HISTORY

Jill is the youngest of three daughters in what she considers to be a fairly average middle-class family. When asked if her parents had any psychological or medical problems, she described her father as having a "some problems with alcohol, but I wouldn't call him an alcoholic." Her mother seemed to have had occasional bouts of depression. Like Jill, neither parent ever sought professional help. Jill was aware of some degree of conflict between her parents, but she did not feel they were unusual in this regard. There is no childhood history of abuse or neglect.

Jill described herself as having been preoccupied with her weight since she was 13 years old and having been constantly concerned about being thin ever since. At age 14 she reached her adult height of 5 feet 6 inches and weighed 130 pounds, which she considered to be very overweight. She dieted on and off for the next two years, but without any lasting success. When she was 16, a friend told her about self-induced vomiting. Initially she was horrified at this idea, but nevertheless she tried this method after she overate one night. She found that the vomiting was tolerable, and she quickly adopted this method as a clever trick to diet without being hungry. In her words, "Throwing up wasn't so bad; it sure beat trying so hard not to eat." During the next year she lost over 20 pounds.

When Jill was 17, she weighed 105 pounds and felt more or less satisfied with her weight. She decided to apply for a job as a model. The modeling agency did not hire her, saying that she should try to lose more weight. Discouraged, Jill gave up on modeling and, with the encouragement of her parents, enrolled in a local private university.

In college Jill had more freedom to experiment with her eating habits. She discovered that by vomiting she could eat rather large amounts of food and still maintain her weight. Gradually her binge eating became more severe and more frequent until she was eating huge amounts of food twice daily. It was now becoming more and more difficult to hide her odd eating behavior from her roommates, and she even stole food from them. Jill recalled one particularly embarrassing incident:

Shelley had bought a bunch of ice cream and potato chips for a party for a club she was in. Well, I couldn't stand

185

having all that stuff around, so I just went at it. Of course I had planned to replace it all, but I didn't get around to it before she got back. Boy, was she shocked to find all that stuff gone! I felt really bad and apologized. I made up a story about how some of my friends came over and we all couldn't resist it. She didn't say anything, but I think she knew what really happened.

At this time Jill also began abusing laxatives and diuretics. As her control over her eating weakened, she also began abusing alcohol. She said that she became intoxicated and vomited at almost every party she attended. By her junior year she began to feel weak and ill for long stretches, and she started missing assignments. She also began staying away from her friends on campus, partly because she felt so embarrassed and ashamed about her eating. During her junior year Jill dropped out of college and worked as a receptionist. Relieved of the social pressures of campus life, she gradually decreased her binge eating to an average of twice a week over the next few years, and gradually her weight increased to 135 pounds. Jill felt totally dissatisfied with herself at this time of her life. Upon the recommendation of a friend, she enrolled in flight attendant school.

Jill was surprised to find that the airline had a strict weight limit for their flight attendants. Trainees who were overweight were dropped from the program, and attendants who did not make their weight target were grounded. Worried that she would be cut from the program, Jill now became more weight-conscious than ever. She frantically sought ways to lose weight, and she began binge eating and purging two or three times daily. She eliminated alcohol from her diet and ate only dietary foods (vegetables, diet soda, and so forth) when she was not binge eating. After two months she had lost 20 pounds. She was now within the airline's weight guidelines, and she also felt much better about her appearance. However, she had begun to feel weak and dizzy and was concerned that she was losing control over her eating. At this point she consulted her doctor.

CONCEPTUALIZATION AND TREATMENT

Jill herself recognized the clear indications of bulimia nervosa in her behavior: her frequent binge eating and purging; abuse of laxative and diuretics as purging agents, her fluctuating body weight, and her constant concern with her body image. Most bulimics are fully aware of the unusual nature of their behavior; many even know the formal diagnostic label of their disorder. Nevertheless they report feeling unable to control their odd binge-purge cycles. Not all bulimics purge themselves, however. Some compensate for their binge eating by fasting, severe dieting, or excessive exercise.

Jill's history contains many social and occupational pressures that induced her to focus on her weight and appearance, particularly her job as a flight attendant. For the past 10 years bulimic eating has been an effective way for Jill to control her weight, and it seems reasonable to conclude that these factors may have contributed to her development of bulimia nervosa.

After her evaluation interview, Jill was admitted as an outpatient in the eating disorders clinic. The initial focus of therapy was to alter Jill's bulimic eating pattern. Jill's cognitive-behavioral therapy incorporated three general goals: (1) to identify the circumstances that surround her binge eating, (2) to restructure her thoughts about herself and her eating, and (3) to educate her on the risks of bulimic behavior, on meal planning and nutrition, and on an awareness of cultural standards that may contribute to her bulimic behavior.

First, Jill was instructed to keep a detailed record (which she called her "eating diary") of where, when, and what she ate so that she and her therapist could examine the exact conditions that were associated with her binge eating. Jill was also told to note her moods in this record to see how her emotions were associated with her bulimic behavior. Jill's record showed that she frequently binged in the late afternoon and early evening, often after a particularly long or stressful flight. Her emotional entries in her record also showed that she felt a sense of relief following her binge-purge episodes. By analyzing this record, it was evident that Jill's bulimic behavior was often used as a way to cope with stressful events in her life.

Second, Jill's distorted and illogical self-cognitions regarding her body image and self-worth were addressed using a cognitive restructuring procedure. Through confrontational, Socratic dialogues in individual therapy, Jill was taught to review her thoughts and feelings, to identify her distorted or illogical thoughts, and to adjust them. Some of these disordered cognitions emerged in the the course of therapy, others were taken from her record.

Jill: Well, here's one from my diary. When I tried on a pair of slacks, they were too tight. I felt really fat, and I was miserable for the rest of the day. I just felt worthless.

Therapist: Did you consider other possibilities?

Jill: Like what?

Therapist: Maybe the slacks shrank in the laundry. Maybe it was humid and sticky, and they just felt tight. Or maybe they were just too small to begin with.

Jill: Sure, I guess it's possible, but I don't know. I mean, they fit before. I thought it meant that I was getting really fat.

Therapist: OK. Let's say that you really did gain a few pounds. So what?

Jill: So what!? It shows that I have to diet even harder because I'm getting obese.

Therapist: Let's look at some of your assumptions. It sounds to me like you have no middle ground; gaining a few pounds means being obese. Do you think that's really an indication of obesity?

Jill: Well, no, I guess not. But you know what I mean.

Therapist: It sounds to me like you have a lot of assumptions about gaining weight. For instance, you feel that gaining a few pounds will make you a failure, and no one will love you or accept you if you do. Is that true?

Jill: Yeah, but some of it's true. The airline might ground me if I get too fat. I mean, it's a real worry.

Therapist: Then maybe being a flight attendant is not the right career for you.

Jill: But I like it. I don't want to quit.

Therapist: I'm not saying you have to. All I'm saying is that you should look at what it's doing to you and maybe consider other possibilities. OK?

Jill: OK.

In addition to her individual therapy, Jill attended group sessions. Mostly these group sessions focused on sharing experiences with other bulimics and fostering a sense of mutual support. In particular, the group members discussed the difficulty they had in controlling their binge eating, and they offered to be available should any member of the group need support or encouragement.

The third goal of therapy was to provide Jill with information regarding various aspects of her eating disorder. First, her therapist described the emotional and physical risks inherent in the binge-purge cycle, such as social isolation, dizziness, electrolyte imbalances, gastrointestinal irritations, and tooth decay. Second, Jill was taught to plan reasonable meals for herself. She was given homework assignments that required her to research the nutritional value of various foods and formulate healthy meal plans. Most importantly, she was to actually eat these meals. Third, Jill was taught to recognize our culture's expectations and norms regarding appearances and weight. In Jill's case, the norms of her airline were clear and explicit. For most bulimics, however, the expectations of our society (often conveyed through the entertainment and advertisement industries) are more subtle and difficult to identify.

Jill was treated for a total of 10 weeks. For the first two weeks her meals were planned for her. She found it difficult to follow these plans without bingeing now and then; she vomiting eight times after meals during the two weeks. Still, Jill was making progress over her pretreatment rate. For the next several weeks Jill devised her own meal plans with the help of the staff. She found that having planned her own meals made it a little easier to stick to the diet. Gradually she reduced the frequency of her vomiting until went through the seventh week without vomiting. After three weeks of relatively normal eating behavior free of purges, Jill discontinued treatment. She was encouraged to follow her meal plan and to contact her therapist or a therapy group member if she felt that she was having trouble controlling her eating behavior.

PROGNOSIS

Jill's treatment appears to have been effective in altering her bulimic eating patterns. In a letter she wrote to her therapist approximately two months after she ended therapy, Jill stated that she had only binged and vomited twice since ending her treatment. She ate healthier and more balanced meals, both at home and during her layovers, and she felt more energetic and active. Jill also said felt better about herself and her appearance, and she did not feel as "stressed" after difficult flights as she used to. In short, therapy seems to have greatly reduced the frequency of Jill's bingeing and purging, and it seems to have created enhanced feelings of self-worth that may help prevent these symptoms from reappearing in the future.

Despite Jill's obvious improvement, however, her prognosis must remain guarded. Bulimia nervosa is a persistent eating disorder, and it has proved to be difficult to effect lasting behavioral changes.
Research on treatment for bulimics is mixed. According to a review by Mitchell, Raymond, and Spector (1993), about 50 percent of the bulimics who improve in therapy relapse within 12 months, and the majority of these relapses occur within 3 months. Cooper, Soker, and

Fleming (1996) report that 39 percent of their sample of bulimics abstained from binge eating and purging for the first year post treatment. However, although bulimic behavior is often not eliminated entirely, still significant improvements are made. In one study of 196 bulimic females (Fichter & Quadflieg, 1997), when assessed at a 6-year follow-up, 71.1 percent did not meet *DSM-IV* criteria for any eating disorder, and 90.4 percent described themselves as having a good or fair therapeutic outcome.

DISCUSSION

The specific causes of bulimia nervosa are not yet known, and there are great variations from case to case in the presenting complaints and personal histories (Martin, 1990). However, it is generally agreed that bulimics put an inordinate amount of importance on their physical appearance as a way of determining their self-esteem (e.g., Johnson, Tobin, & Lipkin, 1989), and this preoccupation probably contributes to their development of the disorder. For most bulimics, these cognitions usually have been evident for years. There is some evidence that certain cultural and/or occupational demands might exacerbate this behavior. Mitchell, Hatsukami, Pyle, and Eckert (1986) report that the majority of bulimics feel pressure to lose weight. Other researchers (V. Schmidt, Sloane, Tiller, & Treasure, 1993; Sykes, Leuser, Melia, & Gross, 1988) found the instance of bulimia to be higher in Catholic and Jewish women and in homes where there was long-standing parental conflict. Bulimics are also noted for their relatively ineffective coping styles, which tend to focus on their emotional problems rather than practical solutions (Yager, Rorty, & Rossotto, 1995). A physiological theory of bulimia involves the satiety mechanism. Leitenberg et al. (1988) suggest that persistent vomiting can disrupt normal satiety cues, thus perpetuating the binge-purge cycle. Although these factors may not necessarily have caused bulimics to develop their odd eating patterns, they do appear to be involved in maintaining the disorder.

Bulimia is 10 to 20 (or more) times as common in females than in males (Gross & Rosen, 1988). Generally bulimia first emerges in junior high and becomes most prevalent in high school and college. Stein and Brinza (1988) diagnosed 2 percent of their female junior high sample and 4 percent of their female high school sample as bulimic. Other surveys of high school girls average around 4 to 5 percent (Gross & Rosen, 1988; Hart & Ollendick, 1985; Mintz & Betz, 1988). Hart and Ollendick also surveyed working women, and they found a rate of 1 percent among this sample. There is evidence that the rate of bulimia may be dropping, though many young women remain vulnerable. Johnson et al. (1989) surveyed girls in one high school in 1981 and repeated the survey in 1986. They discovered a 50 percent drop in the rate of bulimia. They also found decreases in the girls' preoccupation with thinness and their dieting behavior. However, the proportion of subjects who reported poor body image remained constant. Bulimia nervosa also occurs in foreign samples in roughly the same age proportions as in U.S. samples, though the overall rates are somewhat lower (Dolan, 1991).

However, disturbed eating patterns could be much more prevalent than these figures suggest. In a sample of 682 college women surveyed by Mintz and Betz (1988), 61 percent showed some form of eating behavior problem, though only 3 percent could be classified as bulimic according to *DSM-III* criteria. Martin and Wollitzer (1988) studied 277 women in a family practice setting and surveyed them regarding instances of purging (self-induced vomiting, use of laxatives, and/or fasting). They found that 21 percent engaged in some form of purging, but less than 20 percent of these purgers, or about 4 percent of their sample, met *DSM-III* criteria for bulimia nervosa.

In a discussion of bulimia nervosa, it is important to distinguish this disorder from anorexia nervosa, another serious eating disorder. These two disorders do share many common features: their victims are primarily young females who are preoccupied with food, overly concerned with maintaining a slim figure, and have a rather distorted view of their own bodies. Despite these similarities, bulimia nervosa and anorexia nervosa are distinct disorders. Anorexia nervosa is much more rare; for example, Whitaker et al. (1990) report a rate of 0.2 percent among their sample of high school students, compared to a rate of 2.5 percent for bulimia nervosa. Anorexia nervosa is characterized by maintenance of a dangerously low body weight (at least 15 percent below the minimum normal weight), usually by a severe restriction of food intake. Anorexics are consequently jeopardized by medical complications including malnutrition, metabolic changes, and amenorrhea (a cessation of menstruation). Most anorexics deny their disorder and refuse to enter treatment except by force.

In contrast, the majority of bulimics recognize that their eating behavior is abnormal. Whereas anorexics rigidly restrict their food intake, most bulimics are unable to control their binge eating and purging. The majority of bulimics are of approximately normal weight and only rarely are they in any serious medical jeopardy, though they may suffer from the physical side effects of their purging: gastrointestinal difficulties, eroded tooth enamel, electrolyte imbalances, and so forth. The primary concern for bulimics involves the social and/or psychological complications that arise from their disordered eating patterns. Their attempts to hide their disorder and their feelings of guilt and shame about their binges and purges lead many bulimics to isolate themselves from friends and family members. In Martin and Wollizer's (1988) sample of 58 purgers, only 2 percent had ever mentioned their purging to a physician, and 58 percent had never told anyone at all.

The binges described by Jill are typical of most bulimics (Hadigan, Kissileff, & Walsh, 1989; Rosen et al., 1986). Binges usually involve high-caloric foods rich in complex carbohydrates (sugars and starches) and fat, which in most cases are eaten very quickly. Binges are most often followed almost immediately by purging, usually self-induced vomiting. According to Jill's therapist, in many cases it seems that the purpose of binge eating is to bring on the purge; the binge food itself is relatively unimportant. For nonpurging bulimics, binge eating is usually followed by excessive exercise or prolonged fasting.

The psychological reactions that Jill had to her eating behavior are also typical (Weiss & Ebert, 1983). Many bulimics feel guilt and shame over their uncontrolled eating behavior. Others report a feeling of "psychological numbing" or relief following the binge-purge cycle. This relief does not seem to be specific to any particular mood; bulimics have reported that their binges reduce their level of anxiety, depression, anger, and even elation. Thus, for some bulimics, their binge eating serves as a buffer that insulates them from extreme emotional states.

Bulimia nervosa is associated with a number of other psychiatric problems, including substance abuse, personality disorders, depression, and suicide (Fichter, Leibl, Kruger, & Rief, 1997; Mitchell et al., 1986; Sykes et al., 1988; Weiss & Ebert, 1983). Because of this comorbidity, a combination of therapy and medication, usually antidepressants, is efficacious (Crow & Mitchell, 1996; Walsh et al., 1997). Thus, it is important to assess a bulimic's level of psychiatric functioning on a number of measures at the initiation of treatment.

As was the case with Jill, cognitive-behavioral therapy for bulimia nervosa is usually brief, in most cases lasting less than six months. Because the primary goal of treatment is to regularize the patients' eating patterns, some treatment programs hospitalize bulimics to more closely monitor and control their eating behavior. With the limits imposed by managed care, this it becoming quite rare. Most programs begin treatment on an outpatient basis. When these patients end therapy, they are encouraged to attempt to follow a regular eating routine that includes healthy, nutritious food and a strict avoidance of any dieting. Bulimics have been found to be more susceptible to relapse if they deviate from a regularized eating schedule. Follow-up studies indicate that 65 to 75 percent of the bulimics treated with cognitive-behavioral therapy show some improvement, and about half of these patients maintain these therapy gains for at least 18 months (Fichter & Quadflieg, 1997; Keller et al., 1989). Group therapy has been found to be helpful for this population (McKisack & Waller, 1997; Olmsted, Kaplan, Rockert, & Jacobsen, 1996). Traditional psychodynamic therapy has also been utilized with this population, but with less success (Martin, 1990; Walsh et al., 1997). However, many behavior therapists concede that bulimics with particularly chronic or persistent symptoms, especially those who are also depressed, may derive some benefit from traditional, long-term psychotherapy.

SEPARATION ANXIETY
DISORDER
Psychodynamic Therapy

PRESENTING COMPLAINT

Eva is a 10-year-old fifth-grader in a middle-class suburb of Chicago. In February Eva contracted a mild case of pneumonia, which kept her home for two weeks. During this time she had the undivided attention of her mother. On the day before Eva was scheduled to return to school, she complained of severe abdominal pain. This pain was so severe that she could barely walk, let alone go to school. Eva was taken to the emergency room of the local hospital, but the physician on call could find nothing wrong with her. Still, she complained of fever (though her temperature was normal), headaches, and diarrhea. She was allowed to stay home one week longer. Throughout the week Eva's complaints persisted, and her parents took her to her pediatrician three times. However, neither the parents nor the pediatrician could find any objective evidence of any physical illness; her temperature was normal, she did not cough or have any difficulty breathing, she did not go to the bathroom more than usual, and her appetite and sleep seemed good. With the recommendation of Eva's pediatrician, her parents now insisted that she return to school. Eva flatly refused. She began throwing tantrums and having "yelling matches" with her mother. She carried on for hours, complaining that she still was not feeling well and that she should not be forced to go back to school when she was so sick. She accused her mother of being cruel and neglectful and of wanting to get rid of her. In the mother's own words, "It's been pure bedlam ever since she got over her pneumonia and wouldn't go back to school."

Eva had always been a somewhat dependent and demanding child, but she had never acted out to any extent before. Her mother became increasingly alarmed at and frustrated with Eva's uncharacteristic behavior. Although Eva did not carry on in front of her father like she did with her mother, he nevertheless became very concerned about her refusal to go to school. After another week of refusing to go to school (now making a total of five weeks of staying home), Eva's parents decided to contact a local psychiatrist who specialized in childhood disorders.

Eva's mother took her to her initial interview at the psychiatrist's office. When the mother came in and sat down next to Eva, she was asked to remain in the waiting room. She left after some hesitation and obvious concern. Eva then described how she felt about the events of the last few weeks. She was unusually articulate and self-disclosing for a girl her age; she began by saying, "OK. Let's start at the beginning."

From Eva's viewpoint her problem was much more involved than just refusing to go to school. At first she complained that she was still sick with a fever of "almost 100" and diarrhea that would strike twice a day. (The psychiatrist guessed that her mild diarrhea was most likely a side effect of the medication she was still taking for her pneumonia.) She was very angry with both her mother and her pediatrician for expecting her to go back to school. They did not appreciate how sick she felt and did not take her complaints seriously. "They just don't understand me. Whatever I say is a joke. I mean, what would happen if I got *really* sick?" Her psychiatrist then asked her for more detail, but Eva interrupted him, saying, "I'm not done yet!" She then described a second problem:

> My mind thinks ahead. It's like my mind gets ahead of me. Every time something good happens to me, I think ahead to the bad things that may happen afterwards. It's like a state of shock or fright. Sometimes I'm afraid my mom will get killed or the house will burn down or something. This happens at school a lot. I wish I could jump out the window and run home to help. I call it The Fright. When it

happens, I mostly want to be at home where someone can take care of me.

Eva was obviously very upset by The Fright, which primarily involved her morbid preoccupations of her own safety and the safety of her family. Eva could not specify any particular cause for her anticipatory anxiety. She denied that anything or anyone bothers her at school; she said that she has several good friends and that her schoolwork is very easy. The only really consistent aspect of The Fright is her strong desire to be home, a place she described as "secure and protecting," until the last few weeks, that is.

Eva also explained that she feels "sadness and madness" most of the time. She described this feeling as "crying inside" and said that she cries frequently, usually for no reason. She also said that The Fright sometimes wakes her up in the middle of the night, and she has trouble getting back to sleep.

Suicidal ideation is fairly rare in children Eva's age, and usually this topic is not discussed in therapy. However, Eva's psychiatrist thought it prudent to ask her if she had ever thought of killing herself. She said that she had wished to be dead on many occasions, and she would often tell her mother that she was going to commit suicide. She would even feign suicide attempts. For example, two days before her interview she emptied a bottle of aspirin and left it where her mother would find it. She then locked herself in the bathroom with the faucet running, having flushed the aspirin down the toilet. She said that her mother was very frightened and pounded on the bathroom door for several minutes before Eva finally opened it. She claimed that she would never actually go through with a suicide attempt; she just wants to know that her mother cares.

Eva also reported hearing voices, which usually said terrible things. She remembers that one time the voices said that she was a very bad girl and needed to die. She said that some voices seemed to be coming from inside her head while others seemed to come from outside. Occasionally there would be an argument between the inside and outside voices. Eva was very frightened by these voices and wanted them to go away. When the therapist asked if she thought these voices were unusual, she replied, "Don't you? I think they're really weird! You know, I get nervous just talking about them."

Finally, the psychiatrist asked her if she had any problems getting along with her friends, with the other children at school, or with her family. Eva denied any serious interpersonal problems. She apparently got along well with her friends at school, and she seemed to have fairly normal relationships with her two sisters. She said she respected and admired her father, and aside from disliking the fact that he wanted her to go back to school, they had a good relationship. She did, however, complain of problems with her mother. Interestingly, these problems stemmed from the fact that she and her mother were too much *alike*.

Therapist:	So, Eva, can you tell me about the troubles you have with your mother?
Eva:	She's just like me; we're exactly alike. We're both yellers and screamers, and we have screaming matches all the time.
Therapist:	Do you like your mom or do you dislike her?
Eva:	Oh, I really like her.
Therapist:	Eva, let's pretend you were giving your mom a grade on a pretend report card, OK? What grade would you give her?
Eva:	B. No, B+.
Therapist:	B+, OK. Why B+?
Eva:	Well, she helps me most of the time, and she's good to me, so I gave her a good grade.
Therapist:	Why not an A?
Eva:	Because she yells at me and jumps to too many conclusions.

PERSONAL HISTORY

Eva is part of a Protestant middle-class family. Her father is a middle-level business executive, and he appears to be responsible and concerned about Eva. He spends time with his children on weekends, but because of his busy work schedule, including frequent business trips, his interactions with them during the week are limited. Her mother has never been employed outside the home; as she put it, "My job is to take care of my girls and worry about their welfare." Eva has two sisters, one older and one younger. Their relationships with each other seem to be fairly normal for children their age; they get into occasional arguments and shouting matches, but on the whole they get along well.

Eva's early childhood was unremarkable. Her mother could think of nothing unusual about it, and her medical records show no indication of any serious or unusual injuries or illnesses. Eva's school history was also unremarkable. At age 4 Eva enrolled in nursery school held for half a day, three days a week. Transportation to and from the nursery school was provided by a carpool organized by some of the parents. Eva's mother remembers that Eva was very reluctant to go into other parents' cars in the carpool. In kindergarten the next year, Eva took a bus to school. She apparently loved the bus rides, and until now she has had no other school-related problems.

Eva's relationships with her peers do contain some early signs of her separation anxiety, however. Since kindergarten, Eva has attended a summer day camp. Although she has always enjoyed these experiences, she has steadfastly refused to attend an overnight summer camp, which her older sister has done for several summers. Similarly, Eva avoids any overnight stays with friends. Once, in second grade, she was invited to a slumber party for one of her close friends. According to Eva, all of her friends were invited the party, and she "just had to go." But on the afternoon of the slumber party she complained of leg pains so severe that she could not walk. Her mother took her to an orthopedist that afternoon. The orthopedist could find nothing wrong with her legs, but to be cautious he recommended that she not attend the party. This leg pain has reemerged off and on ever since.

199

The psychiatrist also interviewed Eva's parents to identify any significant aspects of their histories. Her mother reported a particularly noteworthy event that occurred when she was 19. She was found to be at fault in a boating accident that nearly killed her mother. She admitted to feeling guilty and responsible for her mother's welfare ever since. She also has been quite worried about her father, who has had a heart condition for many years. "He could go at any time. I'm constantly waiting for the phone call."

Although Eva's father at first appeared to be very responsible and concerned for his daughter's welfare, he was personally resistant to the idea of therapy for her, and psychotherapy in general. He met with the psychiatrist only once and was very reluctant to disclose personal information. Eva's mother confided that there is a long history of depression in his family. When asked about this, he flatly denied any history of mental illness in any relative. He made it clear that although he would go along with Eva's treatment, he wanted no part in it personally.

CONCEPTUALIZATION AND TREATMENT

DSM-IV defines separation anxiety disorder as a child's excessive and unwarranted fear about being apart from one or more important attachment figures, usually the mother. This anxiety must have existed for at least four weeks. This disorder can be manifested through a number of symptoms, including unrealistic worries about the welfare of the attachment figures' or one's own health, complaints of medical symptoms, persistent refusals to be separated from the attachment figures, and a need to be in constant contact with the attachment figures.

Eva clearly fit the *DSM-IV* criteria for separation anxiety disorder. For five weeks she refused to go to school and instead expressed a strong need to stay home. She exhibited excessive anxiety about being apart from her mother, which is probably a long-standing concern. She complained of numerous physical ailments (headaches, abdominal pains, leg aches) and showed excessive distress when she was separated, or even anticipated being separated, from her mother. She persistently worried about her own health should she become separated from her mother ("What if I got *really* sick?"), and she had excessive worries that some terrible fate will befall the people close to her. As is the case with most children her age, Eva's separation anxiety disorder was manifested primarily in her refusal to go to school.

Eva also showed symptoms of a major depressive episode. She complained of depressed mood and a lack of interest in her usual activities. She also complained of feelings of sadness and frustration, frequent crying, early morning awakening, various somatic complaints, mood-congruent hallucinations, and suicidal ideation. Although it is not uncommon for separation anxiety disorder to co-occur with a major depressive episode, the severity of Eva's mood disorder is somewhat unusual for a child her age. The extent of her mood disturbance and her apparent family history of affective disorders suggested the possibility that Eva may be genetically predisposed to depression.

Eva was seen for therapy once a week at the psychiatrist's office. Her therapist formulated a relatively straightforward conceptualization of her case. Her symptoms resulted from her neurotic fear that she would be abandoned and left alone. She feared that some catastrophic event would befall her parents because this would leave them unable to care for her. As Eva grew, she was confronted with an increasing number of subtle demands of independence, such as slumber parties and summer camp. It was apparent that she was unable to cope with these demands.

The primary aim of Eva's treatment was to reduce the neurotic defenses that have thus far inhibited her psychosocial development. The first stage of therapy consisted of three broad, progressive steps. First, Eva's pervasive anxieties, depressed mood, hallucinations, and suicidal ideation were brought under control, in part through medication. Second, her relationship with her mother was stabilized. Third, the psychiatrist worked with Eva's mother to get her to return to school.

The second stage focused on dynamic psychotherapy, which explored her unconscious thoughts and feelings. As these were uncovered and discussed, the therapist provided her with clarifications, reinterpretations, and occasional confrontations. Throughout treatment the psychiatrist provided Eva with emotional support, primarily by reassuring her that she was loved by her parents and that their frustrations and expectations were intended to be for her own good.

The first concrete action taken by Eva's psychiatrist was to put her on a small initial dose of the tricyclic antidepressant imipramine (Tofranil). This dose was gradually increased until an appropriate blood level was achieved. This procedure provides the best chance of finding an efficacious and long-lasting dosage of medication while minimizing negative side effects. Because Eva was only 10 years old, it was essential to monitor her medication and her reactions to it. After two and a half weeks on Tofranil, Eva's hallucinations and suicidal ideation ceased, her anxiety lessened, and her depressive symptoms began to remit. Eva was maintained on Tofranil throughout therapy. Had her therapy happened today, the most likely first try at a medication would be an SSRI antidepressant such as fluoxetine (Prozac) (Birmaher et al., 1994).

Another aspect of Eva's therapy involved several sessions with her mother. Typically, both parents are seen, but Eva's father was unwilling to participate. One goal of the sessions with Eva's mother was to inform her of how she might have been unwittingly exacerbating Eva's symptoms. In particular, she was told to avoid screaming matches with Eva. "How?" she asked incredulously. "Just walk away," was the therapist's response.

A second purpose of therapy with Eva's mother was to emphasize that Eva's fears were very sincere and were not consciously intended to punish or irritate her parents. Eva's morbid preoccupations were not simply attempts to manipulate her parents; Eva actually feared for her own safety and for the safety of her family. These fears might not have had a logical basis, but they were real to Eva. To emphasize this point, the psychiatrist informed Eva's mother of Eva's suicidal ideation and hallucinations. Her mother quickly came to realize that Eva's anxieties were more serious and painful than she had ever imagined. Similarly, Eva's frequent somatic complaints were seen not simply as childish attempts at avoiding things, although of course they often did produce this effect; Eva really did feel pain.

Four weeks after she began therapy, Eva returned to school. Despite her 9-week absence, she had no trouble catching up on her missed schoolwork. Gradually her relationship with her mother improved; they argued less and Eva became much more obedient. With Eva's return to school, therapy now focused on more underlying dynamic issues. At this point Eva's psychotherapy was increased to twice a week.

First, Eva's fears were addressed. She was reassured that neither she nor her parents were in any actual serious danger, and that they would be available when she needed them. Eva's perceptions of her parents' demands on her, such as their insisting that she go to school and their suggesting that she attend summer camp, were also discussed. She was told to think of these expectations not as their wish to get rid of her but rather as signs that they really did care for her. They wanted to give her opportunities. They expected her to be a "big girl" who could take care of herself, and they wanted her to grow up and be successful. By and large Eva reacted favorably when her parents' behavior was explained in this light.

Second, the therapist attempted to uncover Eva's latent feelings. Like most children, Eva found it difficult to express these ideas directly, especially those that involved hostility or anxiety. As a result, dynamic therapy with Eva was conducted in a subtle and indirect manner. As the first step in this process, the therapist attempted to foster a close therapeutic alliance with her through the establishment of a nonerotic transference. As the therapeutic alliance developed, Eva's unconscious perceptions of the people in her life began to be expressed in her current perceptions of the therapist. By listening to her carefully and observing her closely, the therapist helped Eva understand her perceptions of her world and clarify her real experiences from her imagined ones. In the course of therapy, the therapist often attempted to have Eva "slip into" a discussion of her unconscious feelings through expressive play, where her feelings were projected onto the play situation. For example, Eva occasionally played with a dollhouse during the therapy sessions.

During one session she placed a small doll next to a larger one and labeled the small one "Baby" and the larger one "Mommy." The therapist asked her what the baby was thinking. Eva replied, "The baby is very sad. She thinks that her mother is dying and that she'll be all alone." Eva's underlying cognitions were also expressed through art. During a later session Eva drew a picture of a sea star. This creature had a broken arm that appeared to be dangling from its body. In the course of describing this picture to the therapist, Eva commented that her family was like the sea star and that she was the broken appendage that was not really a part of the whole. By paying close attention to this sort of simple play example, the therapist was able to assess many of her unconscious fears and motives. As therapy progressed, the therapist was able to uncover and reinterpret many of the direct, core issues of Eva's problem, primarily her strong fears of abandonment. Because Eva's behavioral symptoms were thought to be merely a superficial manifestation of these underlying cognitions, therapy remained focused on these central issues and made no attempt to address her school avoidance or her somatization directly.

An important aspect of conducting psychotherapy with children is to relate to them from their own frame of reference. Therapists attempt to match their techniques to the cognitive level of the children they treat and to discuss issues that are important to these children. For example, when Eva's psychiatrist discussed the process of growing up, he made sure to put this concept in terms that she would be able to understand. Whereas for older patients "growing up" may mean learning to handle interpersonal situations, choosing a career, or making life goals, for Eva "growing up" was much more circumscribed and meant going to different rooms for different school subjects (instead of staying with the same teacher all day) and having a locker of her own. As a second example of bringing therapy to the child's maturity level, Eva's general desires and goals were given a concrete form by phrasing them as birthday wishes. So, to tap Eva's hopes for the future, her psychiatrist asked, "What would you wish for on your next birthday?" As mentioned above, abstract ratings of other people are put in the context of pretend report cards. Generally speaking, discussing topics at an abstract level usually surpasses a child's cognitive development and is less effective therapeutically.

After about six months, Eva's father suggested that her antidepressant medication be discontinued. Her depressive symptoms had long since remitted, and she appeared to be making slow but steady progress in overcoming her anxiety. Moreover, the process involved in monitoring her medication was very time-consuming and expensive. To comply with her father's request, Eva was gradually withdrawn from Tofranil, but within two weeks her depressive symptoms began to reappear. Eva was then put back on a maintenance dose of Tofranil, and she continued to take this medication for over a year.

Over the next 15 months of therapy, Eva's fears of separation gradually diminished. Her morbid preoccupations were rare, and her anxieties no longer interfered with her behavior. At this point Eva discontinued therapy. She still exhibited some mild residual signs of her disorder, such as a refusal to sleep over at friends' houses and a resistance to attending a full-time summer camp. However, most of her more incapacitating anxieties had long since remitted. Although her psychiatrist felt that Eva could have benefited from an additional year or so of therapy, the family's finances were such that continuing therapy was considered impractical, especially considering that only relatively small gains in functioning were anticipated.

PROGNOSIS

Eva made good progress in her 15 months of therapy; nevertheless, there are reasons to classify her prognosis as guarded. First, she has an apparent family history of depression and has shown a reasonably full major depressive episode by age 10. Although she responded well to imipramine, a brief interruption in her medication resulted in a rapid reemergence of her symptoms. Taken together, this information indicates that Eva might have a genetic predisposition toward depression. She will likely remain vulnerable to depression throughout her life, and her medication must be monitored carefully.

A second cause for concern is that Eva's symptoms have not remitted completely; she continues to show subtle signs that her disorder is persisting. In particular she continues to be apprehensive about being away from home for more than a few hours at a time; overnight outings are still out of the question. Researchers (Flakierska-Praquin, Lindstroem, & Gillberg, 1997) report that a history of separation anxiety disorder can be a risk factor for developing multiple anxiety disorders in adulthood. It remains to be seen whether these symptoms will fade gradually or whether they will develop into a life-long pattern of dependency.

In short, the combination of antidepressant medication and dynamic psychotherapy appears to have been very effective in lessening Eva's anxious behaviors and reducing her defensive anxieties. However, some anxious symptoms persist, and she can be expected to have some mild symptoms for many years.

DISCUSSION

Eva's diagnosis was straightforward. Her pervasive fears clearly indicated a childhood anxiety disorder. Eva's symptomatology was very typical; school refusal, a fear of leaving loved ones for any extended period, morbid preoccupations, and somatic complaints are very common among children with separation anxiety disorder (Bell-Dolan, 1995; Last, 1991). Other children with this diagnosis show symptoms that were not manifested by Eva. Some have great difficulty in falling asleep without the major attachment figures. They might demand to sleep in their parents' bed, or if this is not allowed, they might sleep by their parents' door. Many complain of frequent nightmares involving their morbid ideation. Some cannot stand to be separated from their attachment figures for even small periods of time. They either cling to them most of the day or constantly follow them, a behavior pattern known as "shadowing."

Separation anxiety disorder is relatively common, affecting an estimated 2.4 percent of the childhood population (Bowen, Offord, &

Boyle, 1990). In formulating Eva's diagnosis, it is important to consider the possibility that her refusal to attend school could indicate a school phobia (Last et al., 1987). Her therapist was careful to probe her attitudes regarding school. Her lack of academic problems and her generally good relationships with her peers are indications that school is not a negative experience for her. Thus, her school avoidance appears to be only a by-product of her separation anxiety and not a problem in and of itself.

An interesting aspect of this case is that Eva also suffered from a major depressive episode. Her sadness, suicidal ideation, sleep disturbance (especially the early morning awakening, of which her parents were apparently unaware), and frequent somatic complaints all support this additional diagnosis. The fact that she described hearing voices may be taken by some as evidence of a psychotic disorder such as childhood schizophrenia. However, these auditory hallucinations were wholly consistent with her depressed mood and did not exist in the absence of other depressive symptoms. In general, mood-congruent hallucinations that occur within the context of a mood disorder are usually taken to be secondary to the mood disorder and not an indication of a psychotic disorder. Furthermore, Eva reported feeling frightened by these voices, and she realized that they were very odd. The fact that her hallucinations were not ego-syntonic (that is, they were not liked or accepted by Eva) or taken as normal provides further evidence that her psychotic behavior is probably secondary to her mood disorder. Nonpsychotic hallucinations in children with separation problems have been reported by other investigators (Balon, 1994).

Early Signs of Separation Anxiety Disorder

Many parents report some sort of subtle cues that foreshadow their children's separation anxiety disorder. Some children seem shy with strangers, and some seem hesitant about leaving their parents. Other children are afraid of the dark, monsters, odd creatures, or large, fierce animals. Some children are very demanding, whereas others are overly compliant and obedient. The majority of these signs are not very useful predictors because they are common for all children, regardless of whether they will develop separation anxiety disorder, another anxiety disorder, a mood disorder, or no disorder at all. For example, in Eva's case it was significant to her mother that Eva was leery of other drivers in her nursery school carpool. However, at that age most children are afraid of entering other people's cars (and rightly so). Thus, it is difficult to use parents' observations to predict which children may develop this disorder.

Another difficulty in predicting separation anxiety disorder is that its onset varies widely among different children. Patients generally begin to show symptoms fairly early in childhood (Last et al., 1987), but others show no signs of the disorder until adolescence. Many children, like Eva, first develop their symptoms after coming down with a serious illness that forces them to rely on someone else (usually one or both parents). Many other children develop their symptoms after the death of a family member or after some other catastrophe such as a car accident or severe damage to the home. Yet for others no such instigating event can be identified.

The course of this disorder also varies widely. Whereas some children will never show any evidence of a separation anxiety after their symptoms recede, others will show subtle residual signs for many years. Many seem to recover completely and function perfectly well throughout high school, but then they begin to show symptoms when they are about to separate from their parents (e.g., when they accept a job or go off to college). Other children manage to separate, but they still feel a strong need to keep in contact. These children will either come home almost every weekend or call their parents frequently, some up to several times every day. In a few cases the disorder takes a chronic course. These children never move far away from the family home. For them, continual contact with their parents, either by living with them, visiting them frequently, or calling them several times a day, becomes a lifelong pattern.

Because the symptoms of these children often emerge as a result of their subjective fears and not as a result of any observable trauma, it is frequently difficult for other people to recognize or understand the gravity of their anxiety. In particular, parents often have great difficulty determining just what is making their children so fearful. Many parents simply think that their children have overactive imaginations; others may accuse their children of being lazy or manipulative. Not surprisingly, as in the case of Eva, these attitudes are construed by the child as evidence of rejection, thus ironically exacerbating the anxieties. For this reason it is important for the parents to realize that their children's anxieties are unconsciously motivated. Children with somatic complaints really *do* feel pain; those with morbid preoccupations really *do* fear that their family will be harmed. Though these anxieties may not be logical or reasonable, they are nevertheless real to the child.

Children who develop a separation anxiety often have parents who have difficulties with separation themselves; they might be overly involved with their children, overprotective, or just overly worried, or there could be continuing conflict in the home (Hamilton, 1994). For example, during her recovery from pneumonia, Eva received her mother's "undivided attention," and each of Eva's many somatic complaints precipitated a trip to her pediatrician or the emergency room. During a session with the psychiatrist, Eva's mother admitted that she has never spent a night away from her children. From this information it seems clear that Eva's mother is overprotective and cautious. It is likely that she has some unresolved separation issues of her own. Indeed, the mother's constant guilt and fear concerning her parents' health provides evidence of her own separation anxieties. Generally speaking, children—especially girls—with one or both parents who display some form of anxiety disorder are at greater risk for developing separation anxiety disorder themselves (Shader, 1984; Silove, Manicavasagar, O'Connell, & Morris-Yates, 1995). In particular, parents who have had difficulties in establishing boundaries with their own parents are more apt to have children with anxiety disorders than are parents who have not.

One interesting aspect of this disorder is the parents' decision of when to seek help for their child. Some parents describe feeling "choked" or "smothered" by the excessive demands of their children. Others become embarrassed when their children act out excessively in public or refuse to go to school or on extended outings. Of course, what constitutes "excessive" anxiety will vary from parent to parent. Although many parents tolerate or even promote a sense of anxious dependency on the part of their children, it often comes to a point where they decide that the child has become *too* anxious. Most children with this disorder have a long history of dependent behavior, and it is often unclear to therapists why parents bring their child to therapy when they do and not sooner. This ambiguity can be especially confusing for the child, who must decide how much dependency is appropriate and how much is "too much."

Psychodynamic Treatment for Separation Anxiety Disorder

Traditionally, psychodynamic therapists hold the achievement of insight as an ultimate goal; however, the immature cognitive development of children Eva's age calls for a different objective (Chethik, 1989; Freud, 1926/1946). Here the aim of therapy is to free her from her defensive inhibition and facilitate future development; there is a relatively greater focus on support and encouragement. This is also the case for many adults who lack the cognitive maturity to truly achieve insight into their disorders.

Psychodynamic interpretations of separation anxiety focus on the morbid preoccupations of these children. Traditional psychodynamic theory has interpreted these anxieties as the children's projection of their unconscious hostile impulses against one or both parents. After the Oedipal drama these children are left with strong feelings of need and resentment toward their parents, particularly their mothers, engendering pathological mother-child relationships based on mutual hostile dependency. Because hostility toward attachment figures is unacceptable to the ego, these feelings are consequently projected onto other, less specific forces that might harm the parents (illnesses, accidents, storms, and so on). As these children mature, their hostile dependence on their mothers will interfere with their ability to cope with the increased demands of independence.

More recent psychodynamic formulations have focused on the fact that many of the parents of the children with this disorder are themselves neurotically needy and dependent. By identifying with their neurotic parents, these children may have developed particularly weak conceptions of them. Since the children's conception of their parents is so fragile, they feel especially at risk of being abandoned and left alone.

Most controlled research on treatment for separation anxiety disorder involves brief cognitive behavioral therapy or pharmacotherapy. Researchers (Hamilton, 1994; Kendall & Treadwell, 1996; Klein, Koplewicz, & Kanner, 1992) report some success with intensive cognitive behavioral therapy, especially when combined with family therapy (Barrett, Dadds, & Rapee, 1996). In contrast, pharmacotherapy trials involving clonazepam (Klonopin) (Graae, Milner, Rizzotto, & Klein, 1994) and imipramine (Tofranil) (Klein et al., 1992) have failed to show significant effects on separation anxiety symptoms.

AUTISTIC DISORDER
Behavior Modification

PRESENTING COMPLAINT

Tommy is a cute 5-year-old boy with straight brown hair and bright blue eyes. Except for his slightly crooked teeth and a somewhat blank expression on his face, he looks just like any other boy his age. But after watching Tommy for just a short time, it becomes apparent that he suffers from severe abnormalities that affect almost every aspect of his life: his speech, his thinking, his actions, and his relationships with others.

The first obvious sign of Tommy's psychological impairment is his speech. Except for occasional incoherent groans, Tommy is virtually mute. In the first five years of his life he has learned only a few signed words using American Sign Language (ASL). He can gesture for "more," "eat," and "toilet," the latter by signing the letter "T." He also tries to communicate by pointing at people, places, and objects, but most often the intent of these nonspecific gestures is unclear. Other than these rudimentary sounds and gestures, Tommy has no real linguistic ability.

Tommy's IQ is 48, as measured on the Wechsler Preschool and Primary Scale of Intelligence (WPPSI-III) (Wechsler, 1991). This score would categorize him as moderately retarded. Realistically, though, this score is only a rough estimate. Because of his pervasive lack of communication skills and his lack of interest in testing procedures, it is difficult to assess accurately the actual extent of his cognitive impairment.

What is easier to assess is Tommy's odd behavior. Frequently Tommy will sit with his arms grasping his chest or knees and slowly rock back and forth, all the while staring straight ahead. Tommy also engages in other forms of repetitive behavior such as pushing a toy car back and forth (often not on its wheels) and drawing page after page of parallel straight lines. It is not uncommon for these seemingly meaningless behaviors to last for four or five hours without interruption.

At these times Tommy shows little emotion and seems totally engrossed in his ritualistic behavior. In the past few months, Tommy's hand has become the central focus for many of his strange behaviors. He will suddenly stop what he is doing, hold his hand directly in front of his face, and intensely stare at it while rotating it slowly. As he examines his hand, he sometimes emits a high-pitched squealing tone; occasionally he smiles and giggles. Usually, though, he simply stares at it. He seems to be especially interested if his hand is wet and dripping or covered with food, which is often the case at mealtimes.

In addition to these strange, repetitive behaviors, Tommy also has bursts of wild, uncontrolled activity, usually when he is upset. Sometimes he will run around the perimeter of the room with his legs pumping and his arms flailing, screaming incessantly. At other times he pounds his hands against the floor or wall in an angry, frustrated tantrum. Often when he is examining his hand he will shake it so violently that it appears that he is trying to separate it from his arm. (This sort of flailing is termed "hand flapping.") On rare occasions Tommy manages to bite his hand while flapping, usually hard enough to break the skin. In the midst of these wild behaviors Tommy appears to be genuinely upset; his face takes on a grimace and grows red, and his whole body seems tense. When he is restrained during these uncontrolled actions, he usually struggles for a few moments and then inexplicably goes about his business as if nothing ever happened, seemingly oblivious of the person who restrained him.

By far the most salient aspect of Tommy's disorder, especially to his family, is his complete inability (or unwillingness) to form interpersonal relationships. During his short life Tommy has never engaged in any meaningful interpersonal communication, not even at the level of establishing sustained eye contact. He seems to understand that people exist, and he even reacts to them occasionally; however, he does not seem to attach any special significance to other people as fellow human beings. For the most part he treats other people like inanimate objects to be noticed, ignored, or avoided, much like most people treat large animals or pieces of furniture. Tommy appears to attach some special significance to his parents—he will look at them when they address him and will pay attention to their actions. Even this relationship is very distant, though. Perhaps the best description for his relationship with his parents is that he treats them like two strangers on a busy city street; he seems to understand that they are fellow humans and may even be temporarily interested in what they are doing, but he seems to have no particular interest in establishing any sort of meaningful relationship with them.

Tommy's parents attempted to care for him at home, but his disruptive behavior became increasingly more unmanageable. At this point that he was evaluated at a special school for autistic and emotionally disturbed children.

PERSONAL HISTORY

Tommy is the younger child of two in an upper-middle-class family living in a prestigious suburb of Milwaukee. Tommy's father is a senior vice president of a medium-size manufacturing firm, and his mother is an associate professor at a large university. Tommy's brother, who is four years older, is successful in school and popular with his friends.

During his infancy, Tommy's mother described him as a "model baby." He was always quiet and hardly ever cried or fussed. Throughout the first two years of his life, Tommy was usually quiet and independent. However, from early on it was difficult for Tommy's parents to get his attention or make eye contact. He was unresponsive to games such as peekaboo, and he did not demonstrate any need to be held or comforted; in fact, he completely ignored his parents, his brother, and other relatives who came to visit. Although his parents thought these traits were somewhat peculiar, they did not worry about them at first.

When he was about six months old Tommy was enrolled in day-care. At first he was considered a quiet, cooperative child, but before long his utter failure to interact socially became obvious. He spent the majority of his day silently staring off into the distance. He began to show odd repetitive behavior and to throw angry tantrums. These odd behaviors seriously disrupted the day care routine, and Tommy was required to leave. The day care staff suggested that Tommy should see a specialist, but Tommy's parents were convinced that his odd behavior was something that he would eventually outgrow. They hired a private sitter to stay with him during the day, but after only eight months three sitters had already quit.

By this time Tommy's parents began to worry seriously about his intellectual abilities. He was taken to numerous pediatric and neurology specialists, who said that Tommy suffered from childhood autism. Tommy's parents realized that he needed special care, so they hired a private pediatric nurse to stay with him. Over the next year, Tommy's disruptive behavior became more frequent and more severe. In addition, he began to flap and bite his hand. His parents and the nurse had to monitor his behavior constantly to make sure he did not injure himself. After about a year the private nurse quit, and Tommy's mother was forced to take a semester off to look after him herself. Finally she contacted a school for autistic and emotionally disturbed children. After being on the waiting list for approximately four months, Tommy was enrolled when a space became available.

CONCEPTUALIZATION AND TREATMENT

The staff at the special school had no difficulty diagnosing him as having autistic disorder. Autistic disorder, commonly referred to simply as "autism," is a pervasive developmental disorder that affects almost every aspect of a child's life. The primary feature of autism, which literally means "self-ism," is the child's inability to form meaningful interpersonal relationships and a more or less complete withdrawal into a private world. This profound social withdrawal is usually accompanied by severe disturbances in the child's intellectual and linguistic abilities; most autistic children are mentally retarded and have very limited communication skills. In addition, autistic children are characterized by odd behaviors, typically consisting of meaningless repetitious behaviors and bursts of wild activity. Many autistic children also engage in self-mutilating behaviors, including hand biting, scratching and gouging, head banging, and pica, eating nonnutritive substances such as paste or feces.

Tommy clearly fits this category. Throughout his short life he has been unable to form any adequate relationship with any other person, including the other children at his day care, his sitters, or even own family members. His intellectual skills are severely impaired, and his communication skills are virtually nonexistent. His meaningless rocking, playing, and drawing; his wild fits, his hand flapping; and his frequent tantrums all provide additional behavioral evidence of his autistic disorder.

Tommy was enrolled in the school for autistic and emotionally disturbed children in November. During the academic year, the school runs from 8:30 to 4:30 on weekdays. The staff consists of nonmedical personnel with doctorates or master's degrees in clinical psychology and special education. There are five full-time therapists, three part-time therapists (one occupational therapist and two speech therapists), and several volunteers from local colleges and high schools. The pupils range from 5 to 25 years of age and are drawn from the entire Milwaukee metropolitan area. The number of pupils varies; presently the school is full with 18. Fourteen of the children are autistic. The other four are diagnosed as having Asperger's disorder. Like autistic children, Asperger children exhibit extreme shyness, withdrawal, and anxiety that seriously impair their social development. These children are so intimidated by interpersonal situations that their scholastic performance also suffers. They also engage in stereotyped or restricted activities, though these are usually not as florid as in autistic disorder. However, emotionally disturbed children differ from autistic children in that they show no delay in cognitive or verbal development.

Tommy's school also runs an eight-week live-in summer camp where the students are supervised for 24 hours a day. The staff at the camp consists of one staff member from the school who acts as a supervisor and six trained undergraduate counselors. The number of students who may attend camp at any one time is limited to seven. Because there is a long waiting list for this camp, the younger and more disturbed children are limited to two weeks at the camp. The older and more capable students are allowed to stay the entire eight weeks. Being the youngest and most severely disturbed child in the school, Tommy was limited to two weeks during his first two summers.

Tommy's school employs a model of treatment based on behavior modification. The primary focus of the staff is not to "cure" the students but rather to teach them some basic skills that may help them to lead more independent lives. The therapists attempt to achieve this goal by carefully controlling the children's environment, particularly the level of reinforcement (and occasionally punishment) the children receive. The more formal classroom therapy, conducted in both group and individual instruction, concentrates on providing the children with opportunities to develop social and cognitive skills. Lessons in social interaction and basic hygiene are taught through less formal instruction, which is conducted just about anywhere: on the playground, in the cafeteria, and even in the bathrooms. Because therapy relies to such a great extent on controlling the children's social environments, parents are encouraged to adopt behavioral techniques at home to help maintain the changes made at school. Researchers (Howlin & Rutter, 1978) have found that instructing the parents in behavior modification techniques leads to more widespread and lasting improvements.

Group lessons take several forms; their general aim is to teach these self-absorbed students to cooperate with each other. For example, in a shared finger painting task, each child starts a picture and then exchanges pictures with another student. The children are reinforced for allowing another student to work on "their" project, and they are given special rewards for working on a project together. In another group activity, this time conducted on the playground, students are assigned to either ride on a swing or to push another student. Again, the children are reinforced for displaying cooperation and reciprocity. During these sessions the therapists have to be careful to notice whenever a student behaves appropriately and to reinforce that student as soon as possible through encouragement, hugs, and occasionally, snacks. Just as important, inappropriate or injurious behavior must be stopped immediately.

Individual therapy focuses on developing the children's cognitive and linguistic skills. For example, the therapist might employ flash cards and practice booklets to work on a student's vocabulary or basic math skills. In addition, each child meets with a speech therapist for 50 minutes every other day to practice his or her diction or, in the case of more severely disturbed children, signing. Every student is also instructed in basic vocational skills (e.g., matching wires by colors, sorting various nuts and bolts, sweeping the work area). Getting a job in a sheltered workshop is probably the only employment opportunity most of these children will ever have.

In addition to these relatively formal lessons, the staff takes every opportunity to teach the students basic life skills. During lunch the staff attempts to monitor closely the students' behavior, and students are reinforced for such things as waiting in line cooperatively, eating with others, not playing with their food, chewing their food sufficiently before swallowing, and not causing disturbances (throwing their food, taking other students' food, running or screaming). Similar practical training takes place in the bathrooms. Although being toilet trained is a requirement for admission to the school, accidents are not uncommon among the younger and more disturbed children. The students have to be carefully monitored to ensure that they perform the common steps of toileting that most people take for granted (putting the toilet seat up or down, making sure to urinate or defecate *in* the toilet and not on or around it, wiping themselves adequately, flushing the toilet, washing afterwards). The staff regards teaching the students these basic life skills as a vital step in developing a greater degree of independence.

Teaching basic life skills is the primary focus of the summer camp. Students, who are called "campers," are taught to perform a variety of everyday tasks that include cleaning their room, doing their laundry, taking a shower, and preparing for bed. Each of these basic tasks is broken up into smaller, more manageable subtasks. For example, getting the campers ready for bed involves several individual components: picking up their toys and clothes, changing into their pajamas, brushing their teeth, and so forth. The other focus of the summer camp is to develop the campers' social skills by providing opportunities for interaction and reinforcing prosocial behavior. This training occurs primarily during recreational activities and at mealtimes.

The school uses a variety of reinforcers to reward appropriate behavior. First and foremost, secondary reinforcement in the form of attention, praise, encouragement, and hugs is given to every student whenever appropriate.   However, because one of the primary characteristics of autistic children is a marked disinterest in interpersonal relationships, this social reinforcement is usually supplemented by more tangible rewards such as candy and snacks. As the students become accustomed to the structure of the program, their privileges (recess time, dessert at lunch) become used as reinforcements with increasing frequency.   This is especially true at the summer camp, where the students' recreational activities (swimming, hiking, playing games), their participation on field trips, and even their choice of food are contingent on their behavior.

Eliminating inappropriate behavior is more difficult. Because the staff's attention and concern may serve as secondary reinforcers for inappropriate actions, these behaviors are ignored whenever possible. In this way the staff attempts to extinguish the inappropriate behaviors. Negative behavior can be very disrupting to the other students, especially during group lessons, so often this extinction process is carried out by placing the child in a separate room, which is commonly referred to as a time-out room. Occasionally the children are punished by scolding them or withdrawing their privileges. On some occasions they must be physically restrained by the staff to prevent injury or damage. Such an occasion arose when Tommy suddenly ran off the playground and began beating on the back of an elderly man who was walking down the sidewalk.

Occasionally a child exhibits odd behavior that demands close supervision. For example, one autistic girl had a persistent habit involving pica. She would hide in a bathroom stall until no one was around. Then she would defecate, reach down and grab her own feces, and quickly begin eating. The staff learned to keep a close eye on her.

When they noticed that she was not with the other students, they would immediately run to the nearest bathroom and most often catch her in the act. Her habit took on the air of an addiction; when she ate her own excrement, she smiled, giggled, and became very upset when she was interrupted. The staff was careful to prevent this behavior and reinforce her for flushing her feces. Over the course of four months, her pica was eliminated.

Tommy was extremely upset when he first came to the school. He threw frequent tantrums, about four or five per day, and spent most of his time flapping his hand or rocking quietly in a corner. Soon he became accustomed to the school routine, though, and it became possible to engage him in the daily lessons. By the holiday break in December, Tommy had grown to expect the daily routine of the school and had in fact become very distressed when it was interrupted by the vacation.

Initially the staff concentrated on eliminating Tommy's disruptive behaviors. When he threw a tantrum, the staff was careful to ignore him. If the tantrum persisted, or if it was interrupting a group lesson, Tommy was placed in the time-out room for 10 minutes or until his tantrum ended. During the next few weeks Tommy's tantrums became less and less frequent, and by the first vacation break they had virtually ceased. Tommy's parents were also instructed to use this extinction procedure.

The staff employed a behavioral shaping technique to control Tommy's hand flapping and uncontrolled running around. When Tommy first began these actions, he was physically restrained by a staff member. Usually he would resist this restraint by squirming or shouting. If he started to calm down, however, he was given a reward. Effective reinforcements for him were apple slices, peanuts, and fruit juice. After several incidents Tommy learned to calm down merely in response to the staff's commands and requests. Now he was reinforced for stopping his disruptive behavior only if he did not need to be restrained. Later, as Tommy learned to remain quiet after calming down, his reinforcement became contingent on remaining in control for a set period of time, first 10 minutes, then 15, then 30, and so on.

Tommy was gradually shifted from primary reinforcers (snacks) to secondary reinforcers such as hugs and praise. After six months, Tommy's hand flapping and uncontrolled running was reduced to its present level. Although he still performs these disruptive actions on occasion, he does so much less frequently than he used to, and he usually stops this behavior after a short warning from a staff member.

The next focus of therapy was to increase Tommy's level of social interaction. By selectively reinforcing his cooperative play and recreation behaviors, the staff gradually got Tommy to participate with them and with the other students in group recreation projects and unstructured play activities. Tommy's change was very slow, and even after two years he still gives little indication of empathy or interpersonal understanding.

The overriding goal of Tommy's speech therapy is to increase his vocabulary. After more than two years of intensive individual and group therapy, Tommy's vocabulary has increased from 2 words to slightly over 100. Throughout the first year, Tommy refused to make any attempt at verbal communication. As a result, most of his speech training consisted of teaching him the ASL sign for various objects and concepts in his world (e.g., "teacher," "hungry," "outside"). During the training sessions, Tommy was asked to make various signs demonstrated by the speech therapist or shown on cue cards and was given primary reinforcers for doing so. During his second year, Tommy began to verbalize the words he was learning. As was the case with his other training, Tommy was selectively reinforced for making closer and closer approximations to the words' actual sounds. Although his articulation is very poor and the majority of his speech is incomprehensible to most people, his willingness to verbalize at least some of this thoughts represents a great advancement in his communication skills.

During summer camp Tommy's training concentrated on more basic life skills, particularly his eating behavior and his personal hygiene. By using his dessert or favorite foods as rewards, Tommy was taught to eat with utensils and to keep the majority of his food on his tray. After two weeks of having his eating carefully monitored, Tommy by and large stopped throwing food and began to use a spoon; after a month he began to use a fork, albeit sporadically. His eating habits were not otherwise affected by his camp experiences.

Another aspect of Tommy's disorder was his need to have order, predictability, and routine in his everyday life. For example, part of Tommy's hygiene training took place in the shower, where he was taught to wash himself thoroughly. It soon became clear that Tommy had a set ritual when he washed himself: left foot first, then left leg, then left side, then left arm, and so on. If he performed this washing ritual out of sequence or forgot a step, he would become very upset and would insist on repeating the entire ritual. It was not uncommon for Tommy to spend over two hours in the shower, with the counselor standing with him in the shower the entire time. In an attempt to get Tommy to give up this ritual, the counselors scheduled his showers directly before his most preferred activities, swimming and hiking. Although his showers became somewhat shorter, his shower ritual did not change significantly. On several occasions he forsook his favorite activities. Tommy's second stay as a camper also had little effect on his shower ritual. Apparently, it was more important for Tommy to complete his ritualistic behavior than to participate in his favorite recreation events.

PROGNOSIS

After more than two years at the school (including two camp sessions), Tommy has made limited improvement. His vocabulary has increased to over 100 words, and he is beginning to develop his speech skills. Tommy is also capable of performing some simple addition problems. For the most part, though, the progress in his communication and academic skills has been very slow, and his IQ has not changed significantly. Tommy's most noticeable change is a reduction in his disruptive behaviors. The amount of time he spends flapping his hand and running around wildly has been greatly reduced. In general, he is calmer in most situations and much easier to control. In addition, he is more cooperative during games and when working on recreation projects. Still, the staff and Tommy's parents get the impression that his cooperation is merely in response to their expectations; he doesn't seem to be particularly interested in pleasing others, or even forming relationships with others. Tommy still spends the majority of his free time absently playing with his favorite toys, staring at his hand, or just rocking quietly. The overall prognosis for Tommy is poor. It is unlikely that he will ever be able to establish anything resembling a normal interpersonal relationship, nor will he be able to live with any degree of independence.

This discouraging prognosis is true for most children with autistic disorder (Kanner, 1971). Some of the less disturbed children may eventually be able to live relatively independently in a supervised apartment or halfway house and may hold down steady jobs in a sheltered work environment. A rare few will recover completely. A rough, though fairly reliable, indicator of a child's prognosis is his or her attainment of speech skills. By and large, children who have developed recognizable speech by the age of 5 will be able to benefit most from therapy and have the greatest chance of eventually living on their own (Gillberg, 1990). Most of the more severely disturbed children, however, will probably require professional care for the rest of their lives.

DISCUSSION

The prevalence of autism is a subject of some controversy. Some epidemiologic studies (e.g., Burd, Fisher, & Kerbeshian, 1987; Ritvo et al., 1989) report a very low prevalence rate, ranging from 0.012 to 0.04 percent. Others, however, have reported rates around 0.10 percent (e.g., Bryson, Clark, & Smith, 1988), and others double this latter figure to a rate of 0.21 percent (e.g., Suriyama & Abe, 1986). This last figure is 17 *times* higher than the figure provided by Burd et al. (1987).

Many factors contribute to this confusing situation, including demographic differences and unusual immigration patterns (Gillberg,

1990) and methodological differences (Ritvo et al., 1989; Gillberg, 1990). However, the greatest contributor seems to be inconsistencies in defining autism (Szatami, 1992). Before *DSM-III* was published in 1980, researchers' conceptions of autism were to some extent idiosyncratic. The *DSM-III* definition was fairly narrow and restricted the diagnosis to children who exhibited most of the classical symptoms of autism. This strict definition of autism is sometimes known as Kanner's syndrome. In addition to using the Kanner definition, *DSM-III* required onset to be before the age of 30 months. *DSM-III-R* (1987) did away with the age restriction, which may have inflated rates in some surveys. A more important factor is that some European researchers (Ehlers & Gillberg, 1993; Wing, 1981) have begun to adopt a more broadly defined notion of autism that includes less severe symptomatology, known as Asperger's disorder, which has been included in *DSM-IV*. Ehlers and Gillberg (1993) estimated the minimum prevalence of Asperger's disorder in a Swedish community sample as 0.36 percent.

Researchers tend to show more agreement on the demographic characteristics of autistic children. Boys tend to outnumber girls roughly 3 to 1 (Ehlers & Gillberg, 1993; Lord, Schlopler, & Revicki, 1982; Ritvo et al., 1989). Interestingly, autistic girls score lower on IQ tests than do autistic boys (Lord et al., 1982; Ritvo et al., 1989). In other words, girls are less likely to develop autism, but when they do, it is accompanied by more profound intellectual impairment. Overall, between 65 and 85 percent of autistic children have an IQ below 70 (Rutter, 1983; Gillberg, 1990).

Researchers have associated autism with a wide variety of neurological and biological problems, which has led to a bewildering array of suggested causes for the disorder, including genetics (Bolton & Rutter, 1990), fragile X syndrome (Wahlström, Gillberg, Gustavson, & Holmgren, 1986), phenylketonuria (PKU) (Friedman, 1969), and lactic acidosis (Coleman & Blass, 1985), to name just a few. It is generally recognized that autism is a complex disorder with multiple underlying etiologies.

Most researchers dismiss psychogenic theories of autism. Early psychodynamic theorists (Bettleheim, 1967; Kanner, 1943) attributed the development of this disorder to the child's reaction to cold, unfeeling parents. These parents, often called "emotional refrigerators," were typically very successful professionals who were seen as either too intellectual or too busy to establish an adequate emotional relationship with their infants. On the surface Tommy's parents, both successful professionals, seem to fit this pattern. However, epidemiologic surveys (Ehlers & Gillberg, 1993; Ritvo et al., 1989) have failed to find any differences between parents of autistic children and parents of normal children. It is probable that the preponderance of autism among wealthy, educated families documented in earlier reports simply reflected the fact that these families were more likely to have the intellectual and financial resources to seek sophisticated treatment for their children, and thus their children were more likely to become identified as autistic. As the disorder has become more widely recognized and treatment has become more widely available, this effect has evaporated. Nevertheless, psychogenic theories of childhood autism still retain some popularity. Unfortunately, their primary impact is to intensify the hardships and frustrations of parents by inducing feelings of guilt and failure. In contrast, biomedical theories of autism do not blame the parents for their children's misfortunes, and thus are valuable in helping to alleviate the guilt and despair of these parents as well as providing a framework to conceptualize this disorder.

In the small number of cases where PKU and lactic acidosis are identified soon after birth, special diets can prevent the onset of autism. Otherwise, no effective cure for autism exists at the present time. Educational training and behavior modification have shown some notable improvements in fostering living skills (Howlin & Rutter, 1978; Lovaas, 1987; Lovaas & Bush, 1997), but the gains tend to be limited.

A variety of medications have been and continue to be tried, with mixed results. Early successes reported with fenfluramine (Ritalin) have not been demonstrated in methodologically rigorous studies (DuVerglass, Banks, & Guyer, 1988). Recent trials with novel, or atypical, antipsychotics, most notably riperidone (Risperdal), have shown promise (Findling et al, 1997; Frischauf, 1997), as have studies using naltrexone (ReVia) (Campbell, 1996; Willemsen-Swinkels, Buitelaar, & Van Engeland, 1996).

Treatment for autism remains, at best, a long, difficult, and frustrating process. In all likelihood, effective therapy must involve multiple modalities (Gillberg, 1990; Wakschlag & Leventhal, 1996).

Isolated but widely publicized cases have reported idiot savants (literally "foolish geniuses"), autistics who possess some extraordinarily well-developed ability, usually in the area of mathematical calculation or the manipulation of spatial forms. For example, Dustin Hoffman portrayed an idiot savant in the popular film *Rainman*. Such cases do occur in real life (see Sacks, 1985). Daniel, a 16-year-old student at Tommy's school, could mentally add, subtract, multiply, and even divide 10-digit numbers. He also knew virtually every statistic available for every player who was ever a member of the Green Bay Packers (round drafted into the pros; number of tackles; rushing, receiving, and passing yardage). Two aspects of this phenomenon deserve mention. First, idiot savants make up but a tiny fraction all autistic cases. Second, the abilities of these autistics is usually limited to a narrow range of talents that are rarely of any practical use. For example, despite Daniel's impressive abilities at mental arithmetic, he could not make change for a dollar. Ironically the unique abilities of idiot savants might emphasize the differences between them and most other children and thus can exacerbate their social isolation.

Finally, it is important to note that the behaviors of autistic children, both their disruptive actions and their persistent rejection of social attachments, are very taxing for the people who must deal with them on a regular basis. At Tommy's school the staff often joked that the eight-hour school days, and especially the eight-week summer camp, were more therapeutic for the parents than for the students, and in all likelihood this was true. Treating autistic children is a grueling process with few rewards, and many professionals lose motivation in the face of the slow progress of their students. During Tommy's first two years at the school, two full-time staff members quit, and there was constant turnover in the student volunteer program. The summer camp counselors were especially prone to burnout. Of the twelve camp counselors who worked with Tommy, (all psychology and special education majors from several different colleges), none returned for a second year and only one decided to pursue a career in mental health.

But the option of quitting is not available to parents of autistic children; their choice is to persevere or to institutionalize their child. Recognizing this stress, groups to support parents are being established (Samit, 1996).

REFERENCES

Abelson, J. L., Glitz, D., Cameron, O. G., Lee, M. A., Bronzo, M., & Curtis, G. C. (1991). Blunted growth hormone response to clonidine in patients with generalized anxiety disorder. *Archives of General Psychiatry, 48*, 157–162.

Alcoholics Anonymous. (1976). (3rd. ed.). New York: Alcoholics Anonymous World Services, Inc.

Al-Semaan, Y. (1996). Bromocriptine as adjunctive therapy to clozapine in treatment-resistant schizophrenia. *Canadian Journal of Psychiatry*, 41, 484–485.

American Psychiatric Association. (1968). *Diagnostic and statistical manual of mental disorders* (2nd ed.). Washington, DC: Author.

American Psychiatric Association. (1980). *Diagnostic and statistical manual of mental disorders* (3rd ed.). Washington, DC: Author.

American Psychiatric Association. (1987). *Diagnostic and statistical manual of mental disorders* (3rd ed. rev.). Washington, DC: Author.

American Psychiatric Association. (1994). *Diagnostic and statistical manual of mental disorders* (4th ed.). Washington, DC: Author.

Andreasen, N. C. & Olsen, S. A. (1982). Negative versus positive schizophrenia: Definition and validation. *Archives of General Psychiatry, 39*, 789–794.

Ard, B. N. (1977). Sex in lasting marriages: A longitudinal study. *Journal of Sex Research, 13*, 274–285.

Arnt, J. & Skarsfeldt, T. (1998). Do novel antipsychotics have similar pharmacological characteristics? A review of the evidence. *Neuropsychopharmacology, 18*, 63–101.

Arntz, A. (1994). Treatment of borderline personality disorder: A challenge for cognitive-behavioural therapy. *Behaviour Research and Therapy, 32*, 419–430.

Baer, L., (1994). Factor analysis of symptom substypes of obsessive-compulsive disorder and their relation to personality and tic disorders. *Journal of Clinical Psychiatry, 55* (3, Suppl), 18–23.

229

References

Baer, L., Jenike, M. A., Ricciardi, J. N., Holland, A. D., Seymour, R. J., Minichiello, W. E., & Buttolph, M. L. (1990). Standardized assessment of personality disorders in obsessive-compulsive disorder. *Archives of General Psychiatry, 47,* 826–830.

Baer, L., Rauch, S. L., Ballantine, T., Martuza, R., Cosgrove, R., Cassem, E., Giriunas, I., Manzo, P. A., Dimino, C., & Jenike, M. I. (1995). Cingulotomy for intractable obsessive-compulsive disorder. *Archives of General Psychiatry, 52,* 384–392.

Balon, R. (1994). Buspirone in the treatment of separation anxiety disorder in an adolescent boy. *Canadian Journal of Psychiatry, 39,* 581–582.

Bancroft, J., & Coles, L. (1976). Three years' experience in a sexual problems clinic. *British Medical Journal, 1,* 1575–1577.

Bandura, A. (1986). *Social foundations of thought and action: A social cognitive theory.* Englewood Cliffs, NJ: Prentice-Hall.

Barclay, L. L., Zemcov, A., Blass, J. P., & McDowell, F. H. (1985). Factors associated with duration of survival in Alzheimer's disease. *Biological Psychiatry, 20,* 86–93.

Barrett, P. M., Dadds, M. R., & Rapee, R. M. (1996). Family treatment of childhood anxiety: A controlled trial. *Journal of Consulting and Clinical Psychology, 64,* 333–342.

Beck, A. T., Ward, C. H., Mendelson, M., Mock, J. E., & Erbaugh, J. K. (1961). Reliability of psychiatric diagnosis: II. A study of consistency of clinical judgments and ratings. *American Journal of Psychiatry, 119,* 351–357.

Bell-Dolan, D. (1995). Separation anxiety disorder. In R. T. Ammerman & M. Hersen (Eds.), *Handbook of child behavior therapy in the psychiatric setting* (pp. 217–238). New York: Wiley.

Belloni-Sonzogni, A., Tissot, A., Tettamanti, M., Frattura, L., & Spagnoli, A. (1989). Mortality of demented patients in a geriatric institution. *Archives of Gerontology and Geriatrics, 9,* 193-197.

Benkelfat, C., Ellenbergen, M. A., Dean, P., Palmour, R. M., & Young, S. A. (1994). Mood-lowering effect of tryptophan depletion. *American Journal of Psychiatry, 51,* 687–697.

Berenson, D. (1987). Alcoholics Anonymous: From surender to transformation. *Family Therapy Networker, 11*, 24–31.

Best, S. E., Oliveto, A. H., & Kosten, T. R. (1996). Opioid addiction: Recent advances in detoxification and maintenance therapy. *CNS Drugs, 6*, 301–314.

Bettleheim, B. (1967). *The empty fortress.* New York: Free Press.

Birmaher, B., Waterman, G. S., Ryan, N., Cully, M., Balach, L., Ingram, J., & Brodsky, M. (1994). Fluoxetine for childhood anxiety disorders. *Journal of the American Academy of Child and Adolescent Psychiatry, 33*, 993–999.

Blatt, S. J., & Felson, I. (1993). Different kinds of folks may need different kinds of strokes: The effect of patients' characteristics on therapeutic process and outcome. *Psychotherapy Research, 3*, 245–259.

Blessed, G., Tomlinson, B., & Roth, H. (1968). The association between quantitative measures of dementia and of senile change in the cerebral grey matter of elderly subjects. *British Journal of Psychiatry, 114*, 797–811.

Bliss, E. L. (1984). A symptom profile of patients with multiple personalities, including MMPI results. *Journal of Nervous and Mental Disease, 172*, 197–201.

Bolton, P., & Rutter, M. (1990). Genetic influences in autism. *International Review of Psychiatry, 2*, 67–80.

Boolell, M., Allen, M. J., Ballard, S. A., Gepi-Attee, S., Muirhead, G. J., Naylor, A. M., Osterloh, I. H., & Gingell, C. (1996). Sildenafil: An orally active type 5 cyclic GMP-specific phosphodiesterase inhibitor for the treatment of penile erectile dysfunction. *International Journal of Impotence Research, 8*, 47–52.

Boolell, M., Gepi-Attee, S., Gingell, J. C., & Allen, M. J. (1997). Sildenafil, a novel effective oral therapy for male erectile dys-function. *British Journal of Urology, 78*, 257–261.

Borkovec, T.D., Abel, J. L., & Newman, H. (1995). Effects of psychotherapy on comorbid conditions in generalized anxiety disorder. *Journal of Consulting and Clinical Psychology, 63*, 479–483.

Borkovec, T.D., & Costello, E. (1993). Efficacy of applied relaxation and cognitive-behavioral therapy in the treatment of generalized anxiety disorder. *Journal of Consulting and Clinical Psychology, 61*, 611–619.

Bowden, C. L. (1996). Dosing strategies and time course of response to antimanic drugs. *Journal of Clinical Psychiatry, 57* (Suppl. 13), 4–9.

Bowen, R. C., Offord, D. R., & Boyle, M. H. (1990). The prevalence of overanxious disorder and separation anxiety disorder: Results of the Ontario Child Health Study. *Journal of the American Academy of Child and Adolescent Psychiatry, 29*, 753–758.

Brandsma, J. M., Maultsby, M. C., & Welsh, R. J. (1980). *The outpatient treatment of alcoholism: A review and comparative study.* Baltimore: University Park.

Bryson, S. E., Clark, B. S., & Smith, I. M. (1988). First report of a Canadian epidemiological study of autistic syndromes. *Journal of Child Psychology and Psychiatry, 29*, 433–445.

Buchanan, R. W., Kirkpatrick, B., Heinrichs, D. W., & Carpenter, W. T. (1990). Clinical correlates of the deficit syndrome of schizophrenia. *American Journal of Psychiatry, 147*, 290–294.

Bufe, C. (1991). *Alcoholics Anonymous: Cult or cure?* San Francisco: See Sharp Press.

Burd, L., Fisher, W., & Kerbeshian, J. (1987). A prevalence study of pervasive developmental disorders in North Dakota. *Journal of the American Academy of Child and Adolescent Psychiatry, 26*, 700–703.

Burke, K. C., Burke, J. D., Rae, D. S., & Regier, D. A. (1991). Comparing age at onset of major depression and other psychiatric disorders by birth cohorts in five U.S. community populations. *Archives of General Psychiatry, 48*, 789–795.

Campbell, M. (1996). "Resolved: Autistic children should have a trial of naltrexone": Affirmative rebuttal. *Journal of the American Academy of Child and Adolescent Psychiatry, 35*, 249–250.

Carlson, G. A. (1996). Clinical features and pathogenesis of child and adolescent mania. In K. I. Shulman & M. Tohen (Eds.), *Mood disorders across the lifespan* (pp.127–147). New York: Wiley-Liss.

Carpenter, W. T. (1992). The negative symptom challenge. *Archives of General Psychiatry, 49*, 236–237.

Carpenter, W. T., Conley, R. R., Buchanan, R. W., Breier, A., & Tamminga, C. A. (1995). Patient response and resource management: Another view of clozapine treatment for schizophrenia. *American Journal of Psychiatry, 152*, 827–832.

Carson, R. C. (1969). *Interaction concepts of personality.* Chicago: Aldine.

Centers for Disease Control. (1989). Acquired immunodeficiency syndrome associated with intravenous drug use. *Morbidity and Mortality Weekly Report, 38*, 165–170.

Chen, Y. W., & Dilsaver, S. C. (1996). Lifetime rates of suicide attempts among subjects with bipolar and unipolar disorders relative to subjects with other Axis I disorders. *Biological Psychiatry, 39*, 896–899.

Chethik, M. (1989). *Techniques of child therapy: Psychodynamic strategies.* New York: Guilford.

Cloninger, R. C., Bohman, M., & Sigvardsson, S. (1981). Inheritance of alcohol abuse: Cross-fostering analysis of adopted men. *Archives of General Psychiatry, 38*, 861–868.

Coates, D., & Wortman, C. (1980). Depression maintenance and interpersonal control. In A. Baum & J. E. Singer (Eds.), *Advances in environmental psychology* (vol. 2, pp. 149–182). Hillsdale, NJ: Erlbaum.

Cohen, S., Khan, A., & Cox, G. (1989). Demographic and clinical features predictive of recovery in acute mania. *Journal of Nervous and Mental Disease, 177*, 638–642.

Coleman, M., & Blass, J. P. (1985). Autism and lactic acidosis. *Journal of Autism and Developmental Disorders, 15*, 1–8.

Conte, H. R., Plutchik, R., Karasu, T. B., & Jerrett, I. (1980). A self-report borderline scale: Discriminative validity and preliminary norms. *Journal of Nervous and Mental Disease, 168*, 428–435.

References

Coons, P. M., Bowman, E. S., & Milstein, V. (1988). Multiple personality disorder: A clinical investigation of 50 cases. *Journal of Nervous and Mental Disease, 176,* 519–527.

Coons, P. M., & Milstein, V. (1986). Psychosexual disturbances in multiple personality: Characteristics, etiology, and treatment. *Journal of Clinical Psychiatry, 47,* 106–110.

Cooper, P. J., Soker, S., & Fleming, C. (1996). An evaluation of the efficacy of supervised cognitive behavioral self-help for bulimia nervosa. *Journal of Psychosomatic Research, 40,* 281–287.

Coyne, J. C. (1976). Toward an interactional description of depression. *Psychiatry, 39,* 28–40.

Craighead, W. E., Craighead, L. W., & Ilardi, S. S. (1998). Psychosocial treatments for major depressive disorder. In P. E. Nathan & J. M. Gorman (Eds.), *A guide to treatments that work* (pp. 226–239). New York: Oxford University Press.

Crow, S. J. & Mitchell, J. E. (1996). Integrating cognitive therapy and medications in treating bulimia nervosa. *Psychiatric Clinics of North America, 19,* 755–760.

Crow, T. J. (1980). Molecular pathology of schizophrenia: More than one disease process? *British Medical Journal, 280,* 784–788.

Delbanco, A. & Delbanco, T. (1995, March 20). A.A. at the crossroads. *The New Yorker,* 50–63.

Desmond, D. P., & Maddux, J. F. (1984). Mexican-American heroin addicts. *American Journal of Drug and Alcohol Abuse, 10,* 317–346.

Diaferia, G., Bianchi, I., Bianchi, M. L., Cavedini, P., Erzegovesi, S., & Bellodi, L. (1997). Relationship between obsessive-compulsive personality disorder and obsessive-compulsive disorder. *Comprehensive Psychiatry, 38,* 38–42.

Ditman, K. S., Crawford, G. G., Forgy, E. W., Moskowitz, H., & MacAndrew, C. (1967). A controlled experiment on the use of court probation for drunk arrests. *American Journal of Psychiatry, 124,* 160–163.

Dolan, B. (1991). Cross-cultural aspects of anorexia nervosa and bulimia: A review. *International Journal of Eating Disorders, 10,* 67–79.

Downing, R. W., & Rickels, K. (1985). Early treatment response in anxious outpatients treated with diazepam. *Acta Psychiatrica Scandinavica, 72,* 522–528.

Durham, R. C., & Allan, T. (1993). Psychological treatment of generalized anxiety disorder: A review of the clinical significance of results in outcome studies since 1980. *British Journal of Psychiatry, 163,* 19–26.

Durham, R. C., Allan, T., & Hackett (1997). On predicting improvement and relapse in generalized anxiety disorder following psychotherapy. *British Journal of Clinical Psychology, 36,* 101–119.

DuVerglass, G., Banks, S. R., & Guyer, K. E. (1988). Clinical effects of fenfluramine on children with autism: A review of the research. *Journal of Autism and Developmental Disorders, 18,* 297–308.

Dwyer, J. T., & DeLong, G. R. (1987). A family history study of twenty probands with childhood manic-depressive illness. *Journal of the American Academy of Child and Adolescent Psychiatry, 26,* 176–180.

Edell, W. S. (1984). The Borderline Syndrome Index: Clinical validity and utility. *Journal of Nervous and Mental Disease, 172,* 254–263.

Egeland, J. A., & Hostetter, A. M. (1983). Amish study: I. Affective disorders among the Amish. *American Journal of Psychiatry 140,* 56–61.

Ehlers, S., & Gillberg, C. (1993). The epidemiology of Asperger syndrome: A total population study. *Journal of Child Psychology and Psychiatry and Allied Disciplines, 34,* 1327–1350.

Elkin, I., Shea, M. T., Watkins, J. T., & Imber, S. D. (1990). National Institute of Mental Health Treatment of Depression Collaborative Research Program: General effectiveness of treatments. *Archives of General Psychiatry, 46,* 971–982.

Ellason, J. W., & Ross, C. A. (1995). Positive and negative symptoms in dissociative identity disorder and schizophrenia: A comparative analysis. *Journal of Nervous and Mental Disease, 183,* 236-241.

Ellason, J. W., & Ross, C. A. (1996). Millon Clinical Multiaxial Inventory-II follow-up of patients with dissociative identity disorder. *Psychological Reports, 78,* 707–716.

Ellason, J. W., & Ross, C. A. (1997). Two-year follow-up of inpatients with dissociative identity disorder. *American Journal of Psychiatry, 154,* 832–839.

Fava, M., Rappe, S., Pava, J. A., Nierenberg, R. A., Alpert, J. A., & Rosenbaum, J. F. (1995). Relapse in patients on long-term fluoxetine treatment: Response to increased fluoxetine dose. *Journal of Clincial Psychiatry, 56,* 52–55.

Fichter, M. M., Leibl, C., Kruger, R., & Rief, W. (1997). Effects of fluvoxamine on depression, anxiety, and other areas of general psychopathology in bulimia nervosa. *Pharmacopsychiatry, 30,* 85–92.

Fichter, M. M., & Quadflieg, N. (1997). Six-year course of bulimia nervosa. *International Journal of Eating Disorders, 22,* 361–384.

Findling, R. L., Maxwell, K., Scotese-Wojtila, L., Huang, J., Yamashita, T., & Wiznitzer, M. (1997). High-dose pyridoxine and magnesium administration in children with autistic disorder: An absence of salutary effects in a double-blind, placebo-controlled study. *Journal of Autism and Developmental Disorders, 27,* 467–478.

Flakierska-Praquin, N., Lindstroem, M., & Gillberg, C. (1997). School phobia with separation anxiety disorder: A comparative 20- to 29-year follow-up study of 35 school refusers. *Comprehensive Psychiatry, 38,* 17–22.

Flament, M. F., Whitaker, A., Rapoport, J. L., Davies, M., Berg, C. Z., Kalikow, K., & Sceery, W. (1988). Obsessive-compulsive disorder in adolescence: An epidemiological study. *Journal of the American Academy of Child and Adolescent Psychiatry, 27,* 764–771.

Folstein, M. F., Folstein, S. E., & McHugh, P. R. (1975). "Mini-mental State": A practical method for grading the cognitive state of patients for the clinician. *Journal of Psychiatric Research, 12,* 189–198.

Frank, E. (1996). Long-term treatment of depression: Interpersonal psychotherapy with and without medication. In C. Mundt & M. J. Goldstein (Eds.), *Interpersonal factors in the origin and course of affective disorders* (pp. 303–315). London: Gaskell.

Frank, E., & Anderson, B. P. (1987). Psychiatric disorders in rape victims: Past history and current symptomatology. *Comprehensive Psychiatry, 28,* 77–82.

Frank, E., Anderson, C., & Rubenstein, D. (1978). Frequency of sexual dysfunction in "normal" couples. *New England Journal of Medicine, 299,* 111–115.

Frankel, F. H. (1990). Hypnotizability and dissociation. *American Journal of Psychiatry, 147,* 823–829.

Freud, A. (1926/1946). Introduction to the technique of the analysis of children. In N. Proctor-Gregg (Trans.), *Psychoanalytic techniques for children* (pp. 1–126). London: Imago.

Friedman, E. (1969). The autistic syndrome and phenylketonuria. *Schizophrenia, 1,* 249–261.

Frischauf, E. (1997). Drug therapy in autism. *Journal of the American Academy of Child and Adolescent Psychiatry, 36,* 577.

Gabbard, G. O. (1997). Borderline personality disorder and rational managed care policy. *Psychoanalytic Inquiry,* (Suppl.), 17–28.

Gabbard, G. O., Lazar, S. G., Hornberger, J., & Spiegel, D. (1997). The economic impact of psychotherapy: A review. *American Journal of Psychiatry, 154,* 147–155.

Galaif, E. R., & Sussman, S. (1995). For whom does Alcoholics Anonymous work? *International Journal of the Addictions, 30,* 161–184.

Gauthier, S., Panisset, M., Nalbantoglu, J., & Poirier, J. (1997). Alzheimer's disease: Current knowledge, management, and research. *Canadian Medical Association Journal, 157,*1047–1052.

Gautrin, D., Froda, S., Tetreault, H., & Gauvreau, D. (1990). Canadian projections of cases suffering from Alzheimer's disease and senile dementia of the Alzheimer type over the period 1986–2031. *Canadian Journal of Psychiatry, 35,* 162–165.

References

Geldmacher, D. S. (1997). Donepezil (Aricept) therapy for Alzheimer's disease. *Comprehensive Therapy, 23,* 492–493.

Gershon, E. S., Hamovit, J., Guroff, J. J., Dibble, E., Leckman, J. F., Sceery, W., Targum, S. D., Nurnberger, J. I., Goldin, L. R., & Bunney, W. E. (1982). A family study of schizoaffective, bipolar I, bipolar II, unipolar, and normal control probands. *Archives of General Psychiatry, 39,* 1157–1167.

Gershon, E. S., & Nurnberger, J. I. (1995). Bipolar illness. *American Psychiatric Press Review of Psychiatry, 14,* 405–424.

Ghodse, A. H., Stapleton, J., Edwards, G., & Edeh, J. (1987). Monitoring changing patterns of drug dependence in accident and emergency departments. *Drug and Alcohol Dependence, 19,* 265–269.

Gilbert, P. L., Harris, J. H., McAdams, L. A., & Jeste, D. V. (1995). Neuroleptic withdrawal in schizophrenia patients. *Archives of General Psychiatry, 52,* 173–188.

Gillberg, C. (1990). Autism and pervasive developmental disorders. *Journal of Child Psychology and Psychiatry, 31,* 99–119.

Gleaves, D. H. (1996). The sociocognitive model of dissociative identity disorder: A reexamination of the evidence. *Psychological Bulletin, 120,* 42–59.

Goldberg, J. F., Harrow, M., & Grossman, L. S. (1995). Course and outcome in bipolar affective disorders: A longitudinal follow-up study. *American Journal of Psychiatry, 152,* 379–384.

Goldring, N., & Fieve, R. R. (1984). Attempted suicide in manic-depressive disorder. *American Journal of Psychotherapy, 38,* 373–383.

Golomb, M., Fava, M., Abraham, M., & Rosenbaum, J. F. (1995). Gender differences in personality disorders. *American Journal of Psychiatry, 152,* 579–582.

Goodman, W. K., Price, L. H., Rasmussen, S. A., Mazure, C., Delgado, P., Heninger, G. R., & Charney, D. S. (1989). The Yale-Brown Obsessive-Compulsive Scale: II. Validity. *Archives of General Psychiatry, 46,* 1012–1016.

Goodman, W. K., Price, L. H., Rasmussen, S. A., Mazure, C., Fleischmann, R. L., Hill, C. H., Heninger, G. R., & Charney, D. S. (1989). The Yale-Brown Obsessive-Compulsive Scale: I. Development, use, and reliability. *Archives of General Psychiatry, 46,* 1006–1011.

Goodwin, D. W., Schulsinger, F., Hermansen, L., Guze, S. B., & Winokur, G. A.. (1973). Alcohol problems in adoptees raised apart from alcoholic biological parents. *Archives of General Psychiatry, 28,* 238–243.

Gorman, J. M. (1987). Generalized anxiety disorders. *Modern Problems of Pharmacopsychiatry, 22,* 127–140.

Gottesman, I. I., McGuffin, P., & Farmer, A. E. (1987). Clinical genetics as clues to the "real" genetics of schizophrenia. *Schizophrenia Bulletin, 13,* 23–47.

Gould, R. A., Otto, M. W., Pollack, M. H., & Yap, L. (1997). Cognitive behavioral and pharmacological treatment of generalized anxiety disorder: A preliminary meta-analysis. *Behavioral Therapy, 28,* 285–305.

Graae, F., Milner, J., Rizzotto, L., & Klein, R. G. (1994). Clonazepam in childhood anxiety disorders. *Journal of the American Academy of Child and Adolescent Psychiatry, 33,* 372–376.

Grady, C. L., Haxby, J. V., Horwitz, B., Berg, G., & Rapoport, S. I. (1987). Neuropsychological and cerebral metabolic function in early vs late onset dementia of the Alzheimer type. *Neuropsychologia, 25,* 807–816.

Grady, C. L., Haxby, J. V., Horwitz, B., Sundaram, M., Berg, G., Schapiro, M., Friedland, R. P., & Rapoport, S. I. (1988). Longitudinal study of the early neuropsychological and cerebral metabolic changes in dementia of the Alzheimer type. *Journal of Clinical and Experimental Neuropsychology, 10,* 576–596.

Greenberg, D. (1984). Are religious compulsions religious or compulsive: A phenomenological study. *American Journal of Psychotherapy, 38,* 524–532.

References

Gross, J., & Rosen, J. C. (1988). Bulimia in adolescents: Prevalence and psychosocial correlates. *International Journal of Eating Disorders, 7*, 51–61.

Gunderson, J. G. (1996). Borderline patient's intolerance of aloneness: Insecure attachments and therapist availability. *American Journal of Psychiatry, 153*, 752–758.

Gunderson, J. G., Kolb, J. E., & Austin, V. (1981). The Diagnostic Interview for Borderlines (DIB). *American Journal of Psychiatry, 138*, 896–903.

Hadigan, C. M., Kissileff, H. R., & Walsh, B. T. (1989). Patterns of food selection during meals in women with bulimia. *American Journal of Clinical Nutrition, 50*, 759–766.

Hall, W., Darke, S., Ross, M., & Wodak, A. (1993). Patterns of drug use and risk-taking among injecting amphetamine and opioid drug users in Sydney, Australia. *Addiction, 88*, 509–516.

Hamilton, B. (1994). A systematic approach to a family and school problem: A case of separation anxiety disorder. *Family Therapy, 21*, 149–152.

Hamilton, M. (1967). Development of a rating scale for primary depressive illness. *British Journal of Social and Clinical Psychology, 6*, 278–296.

Hart, K. J., & Ollendick, T. H. (1985). Prevalence of bulimia in working and university women. *American Journal of Psychiatry, 142*, 851–854.

Harvey, A. G., & Rapee, R. M. (1995). Cognitive-behavior therapy for generalized anxiety disorder. *Psychiatric Clinics of North America, 18*, 859–870.

Haxby, J. V., Grady, C. L., Koss, E., Horwitz, B., Heston, L., Schapiro, M., Friedland, R. P., & Rapoport, S. I. (1990). Longitudinal study of cerebral metabolic asymmetries and associated neuropsychological patterns in early dementia of the Alzheimer type. *Archives of Neurology, 47*, 753–760.

Hedges, D. W., Reimherr, F. W., Strong, R. E., Halls, C. H., & Rust, C. (1996). An open trial of nefazodone in adult patients with generalized anxiety disorder. *Psychopharmacology Bulletin, 32*, 671–676.

Henderson, A. S. (1990). The social psychiatry of later life. *British Journal of Psychiatry, 156,* 645–653.

Henderson, J. G., & Pollard, C. A. (1988). Three types of obsessive-compulsive disorder in a community sample. *Journal of Clinical Psychology, 44,* 747–752.

Hester, R. K., & Miller, W. R. (1989). Self-control training. In R. K. Hester & W. R. Miller (Eds.), *Handbook of alcoholism treatment approaches: Effective alternatives* (pp. 141–149). New York: Pergamon.

Hilgard, E. (1988). Professional skepticism about multiple personality. *Journal of Nervous and Mental Disease, 176,* 532.

Hinrichsen, G. A. (1997). Interpersonal psychotherapy for depressed older adults. *Journal of Geriatric Psychiatry, 30, 239–257.*

Horowitz, L. M., & Vitkus, J. (1986). The interpersonal basis of psychiatric symptoms. *Clinical Psychology Review, 6,* 443–469.

Howland, R. H. (1997). Pharmacotherapy of inpatients with bipolar depression. *Annals of Clinical Psychiatry, 9,* 199–202.

Howlin, P., & Rutter, M. (1978). *Treatment of autistic children.* London: Wiley.

Humphreys, K., Moos, R. H., & Finney, J. W. (1996). Life domains, Alcoholics Anonymous, and role incumbency in the 3-year course of problem drinking. *Journal of Nervous and Mental Disease, 184,* 475–481.

Hwu, H.-G., Tan, H., Chen, C.-C., & Yeh, L.-L. (1995). Negative symptoms at discharge and outcome in schizophrenia. *British Journal of Psychiatry, 166,* 61–67.

Hylan, T. R., Crown, W. H., Meneades, L., Heiligenstein, J. H., Melfi, C. A., Croghan, T. W., & Buesching, D. P. (1998). Antidepressant selection and health care costs in the naturalistic setting: A multivariate analysis. *Journal of Affective Disorders, 47,* 71–79.

Imber, S. D., Pilkonis, P. A., Sotsky, S. M., Elkin, I., Watkins, J. T., Collins, J. F., Shea, M. T., Leber, W. R., & Glass, D. R. (1990). Mode-specific effects among three treatments for depression. *Journal of Consulting and Clinical Psychology, 58,* 352–359.

References

Inman, D. J., Bascue, L. O., & Skoloda, T. (1985). Identification of borderline personality disorders among substance abuse inpatients. *Journal of Substance Abuse Treatment, 2,* 229–232.

Jacobs, S., & Kim, K. (1990). Psychiatric complications of bereavement. *Psychiataric Annals, 20,* 314–317.

Johnson, B. D., Wish, E. D., Schmeider, J., & Huizinga, D., (1991). Concentration of delinquent offending: Serious drug involvement and high delinquency rates. *Journal of Drug Issues, 21,* 205–229.

Johnson, C., Tobin, D. L., & Lipkin, J. (1989). Epidemiologic changes in bulimic behavior among female adolescents over a five-year period. *International Journal of Eating Disorders, 8,* 647–655.

Johnston, L. D., O'Malley, P. M., & Bachman, J. G. (1987). Psychotherapeutic, licit, and illicit use of drugs among adolescents: An epidemiological perspective. *Journal of Adolescent Health Care, 8,* 36–51.

Kall, K. I., & Olin, R. G. (1990). HIV status and changes in risk behaviour among intravenous drug users in Stockholm, 1987–1988. *AIDS, 4,* 153–157.

Kanner, L. (1943). Autistic disturbances of effective content. *Nervous Child, 2,* 217–240.

Kanner, L. (1971). Follow-up study of eleven autistic children originally reported in 1943. *Journal of Autism and Childhood Schizophrenia, 1,* 119–145.

Kaplan, H. S. (1974). *The new sex therapy.* New York: Brunner/Mazel.

Karno, M., Golding, J. M., Burnam, M. A., Hough, R. L., Escobar, J. T., Wells, K. M., & Boyer, R. (1989). Anxiety disorders among Mexican-Americans and non-Hispanic whites in Los Angeles. *Journal of Nervous and Mental Disease, 177,* 202–209.

Karno, M., Golding, J. M., Sorenson, S. B., & Burnam, M. A. (1988). The epidemiology of obsessive-compulsive disorder in five U.S. communities. *Archives of General Psychiatry, 45,* 1094–1099.

Kassel, J. D., & Wagner, E. F. (1993). Process of change in Alcoholics Anonymous: A review of possible mechanisms. *Psychotherapy, 30,* 222–234.

Katzman, R. (1993). Education and the prevalence of dementia and Alzheimer's disease. *Neurology, 43*, 13–20.

Kay, S. R., Fiszbein, A., & Opler, L. A. (1987). The Positive and Negative Syndrome Scale (PANSS) for schizophrenia. *Schizophrenia Bulletin, 13*, 261–267.

Keller, M. B., Herzog, D. B., Lavori, P. W., Ott, I. L., Bradburn, I. S., & Mahoney, E. M. (1989). High rates of chronicity and rapidity of relapse in patients with bulimia nervosa and depression. *Archives of General Psychiatry, 46*, 480–481.

Keller, M. B., Hirschfeld, R. M. A., & Hanks, D. (1997). Double depression: A distinctive subtype of unipolar depression. *Journal of Affective Disorders, 45*, 65–73.

Kendall, P. C., & Treadwell, K. R. H. (1996). Cognitive-behavioral treatment for childhood anxiety disorders. In E. D. Hibbs & P. S. Jensen (Eds.), *Psychosocial treatments for child and adolescent disorders: Empirically-based strategies for clinical practice* (pp. 23–41). Washington, D. C.: American Psychological Association.

Kendler, K. B., Silberg, J. L., Neale, M. C., Kessler, R. C., Heath, A. C., & Eaves, L. S. (1991). The family history method: Whose psychiatric history is measured? *American Journal of Psychiatry, 148*, 1501–1504.

Kennedy, B. P., & Minami, M. (1994). The Beech Hill Hospital/Outward Bound Adolescent Chemical Dependency Treatment Program. *Journal of Substance Abuse Treatment, 10*, 395–406.

Kent, J. M., & Gorman, J. M. (1997). Drug treatment of anxiety disorders with comorbidity. In S. Wetzler & W. C. Sanderson (Eds.), *Treatment strategies for patients with psychiatric comorbidity* (pp. 105–134). New York: Wiley.

Kessler, R. C., Rubinow, D. R., Holmes, C., Abelson, J. M., & Zhao, S. (1997). The epidemiology of DSM-III-R bipolar I disorder in a general population survey. *Psychological Medicine, 27*, 1079–1089.

Kiesler, D. J. (1983). The 1982 Interpersonal Circle: A taxonomy for complementarity in human transactions. *Psychological Review, 90*, 185–214.

References

Kiesler, D. J. (1986). Interpersonal methods of diagnosis and treatment. In J. O. Cavenar (Ed.), *Psychiatry* (vol. 1, pp. 1–23). New York: Lippincott.

King, D. J. (1998). Drug treatment of the negative symptoms of schizophrenia. *European Neuropsychopharmacology, 8,* 33–42.

Klein, D. N., Depue, R. A., & Slater, J. F. (1985). Cyclothymia in the adolescent offspring of parents with bipolar affective disorder. *Journal of Abnormal Psychology, 94,* 115–127.

Klerman, G. L., Weissman, M. M., Rounsaville, B. J., & Chevron, S. E. (1984). *Interpersonal psychotherapy of depression.* New York: Basic Books.

Klein, R. G., Koplewicz, H. S., & Kanner, A. (1992). Imipramine treatment of children with separation anxiety disorder. *Journal of the American Academy of Child and Adolescent Psychiatry, 31,* 21–28.

Kluft, R. P. (1984). Aspects of the treatment of multiple personality disorder. *Psychiatric Annals, 14,* 51–55.

Kohut, H. (1977). *The restoration of the self.* New York: International Universities Press.

Kosten, T. R. (1990). Current pharmacotherapies of opioid dependence. *Psychopharmacology Bulletin, 26,* 69–74.

Kozel, N. J., & Adams, E. H. (1986). Epidemiology of drug abuse: An overview. *Science, 234,* 970–974.

Kragh-Sorensen, P., Holm, P., Fynboe, C., Schaumburg, E., Andersen, B., Bech, P., & Pichard, J. (1990). Bromazepam in generalized anxiety: Randomized, multi-practice comparisons with both chlorprothixene and placebo. *Psychopharmacology, 100,* 383–386.

Kramer, M., German, P. S., Anthony, J. C., von Kopff, M., & Skinner, E. A. (1986). Patterns of mental disorders among the elderly residents of Eastern Baltimore. *Journal of the American Geriatrics Society, 33,* 236–245.

Kramer, P. D. (1993). *Listening to Prozac.* New York: Penguin Books.

Kroll, J. (1988). *The challenge of the borderline patient: Competency in diagnosis and treatment.* New York: Norton.

Kullgren, G. (1987). An empirical comparison of three different borderline concepts. *Acta Psychiatrica Scandinavica, 76,* 246–255.

Kumar, V., & Cantillon, M. (1996). Update on the development of medication for memory and cognition in Alzheimer's disease. *Psychiatric Annals, 26,* 280–284.

Kusumakar, V., Yatham, L. N., Haslam, D. R. S., Parikh-Sagar, V., Matte, R., Sharma, V., Silverstone, P. H., Kutcher, S. P., & Kennedy, S. (1997). The foundations of effective management of bipolar disorder. *Canadian Journal of Psychiatry, 42* (Suppl. 2), 69S–73S.

Landrine, H. (1989). The social class-schizophrenia relationship: A different approach and new hypotheses. *Journal of Social and Clinical Psychology, 8,* 288–303.

Last, C. G. (1991). Somatic complaints in anxiety disordered children. *Journal of Anxiety Disorders, 5,* 125–138.

Last, C. G., Francis, G., Hersen, M., Kazdin, A. E., & Strauss, C. C. (1987). Separation anxiety and school phobia: A comparison using *DSM-III* criteria. *American Journal of Psychiatry, 144,* 653–657.

Leary, T. (1957). *Interpersonal diagnosis of personality.* New York: Ronald.

Leckman, J. F., Grice, D. E., Boardman, J., & Zhang, H. (1997). Symptoms of obsessive-compulsive disorder. *American Journal of Psychiatry, 154,* 911–917.

Leitenberg, H., Rosen, J. C., Gross, J. Nudelman, S., & Vara, L. S. (1988). Exposure plus response prevention treatment of bulimia nervosa. *Journal of Consulting and Clinical Psychology, 56,* 535–541.

Libsitz, J. D., Martin, L. Y., Mannuzza, S., Chapman, T. F., Liebowitz, M. R., Klein, D. F., & Fyer, A. J. (1994). Childhood separation anxiety disorder in patients with adult anxiety disorders. *American Journal of Psychiatry, 151,* 927–929.

Lindsay, M., Crino, R., & Andrews, G. (1997). Controlled trial of exposure and response prevention in obsessive-compulsive disorder. *British Journal of Psychiatry, 171,* 135–139.

References

Linehan, M. M. (1993). *Cognitive-behavioral treatment of borderline personality disorder: The dialectics of effective treatment.* New York: Guilford.

Linehan, M. M., Heard, H. L., & Armstrong, H. E. (1993). Naturalistic follow up of a behavioral treatment for chronically parasuicidal borderline patients. *Archives of General Psychiatry, 50,* 971–974.

Ling, W. & Shoptaw, S. (1997). Integration of research in pharmacotherapy for addictive disease: Where are we? Where are we going? *Journal of Addictive Diseases, 16,* 83–102.

Loftus, E. (1993). The reality of repressed memories. *American Psychologist, 48,* 518–537.

Long, J. (1997). Alzheimer's disease and the family: Working with new realities. In T. D. Hargrave & S. M. Hanna (Eds.), *The aging family: New visions in theory, practice, and reality* (pp. 209–234). New York: Brunner/Mazel.

Lord, C., Schopler, E., & Revicki, D. (1982). Sex differences in autism. *Journal of Autism and Developmental Disorders, 12,* 317–330.

Lovaas, O. I. (1987). Behavioral treatment and normal educational and intellectual functioning in young autistic children. *Journal of Consulting and Clinical Psychology, 55,* 3–9.

Lovaas, O. I. & Bush, G. (1997). Intensive behavioral intervention with young children with autism. In N. N. Singh (Ed.), *Prevention and treatment of severe behavior problems: Models and methods in developmental disabilities* (pp. 61–68). Pacific Grove, CA: Brooks/Cole.

Luxenberg, J. S., Haxby, J. V., Creasey, H., Sundaram, M., & Rapoport, S. I. (1987). Rate of ventricular enlargement in dementia of the Alzheimer type correlates with rate of neuropsychological deterioration. *Neurology, 37,* 1135–1140.

Mahler, M. S. (1968). *On human symbiosis and the vicissitudes of individuation.* New York: International Universities Press.

Mann, K., Klinger, T., Noe, S., & Roeschke, J. (1996). Effects of yohimbine on sexual experiences and nocturnal penile tumescence and rigidity in erectile dysfunction. *Archives of Sexual Behavior, 25,* 1–16.

Marks, I. M. (1986). Epidemiology of anxiety. *Social Psychiatry, 21,* 167–171.

Marlatt, G. A. (1983). The controlled drinking controversy: A commentary. *American Psychologist, 38,* 1097–1110.

Martin, J. E. (1990). Bulimia: A review of the medical, behavioural, and psychdynamic models of treatment. *British Journal of Occupational Therapy, 53,* 495–500.

Martin, J. E., & Wollitzer, A. O. (1988). The prevalence, secrecy, and psychology of purging in a family practice setting. *International Journal of Eating Disorders, 7,* 515–519.

Martin, M. K., Giannandrea, P., Rogers, B., & Johnson, J. (1996). Beginning steps of recovery: A challenge to the "come back when you're ready" approach. *Alcoholism Treatment Quarterly, 14,* 45–57.

Martin, R. L. (1989). Update on dementia of the Alzheimer type. *Hospital and Community Psychiatry, 40,* 593–604.

Masters, W., & Johnson, V. (1970). *Human sexual inadequacy.* Boston: Little Brown.

McBride, J. L. (1991). Abstinence among members of Alcoholics Anonymous. *Alcoholism Treatment Quarterly, 8,* 113–121.

McCrady, B. S., & Miller, W. R. (Eds.). (1993). *Research on alcoholics anonymous: Opportunities and alternatives.* Piscataway, NJ: Rutgers Center of Alcohol Study.

McElroy, S. L., Soutullo, C. A., Keck, P. E., & Kmetz, G. F. (1997). A pilot trial of adjunctive gabapentin in the treatment of bipolar disorder. *Annals of Clinical Psychiatry, 9,* 99–103.

McGuffey, E. C. (1997). Alzheimer's disease: An overview for the pharmacist. *Journal of the American Pharmaceutical Association. NS37,* 347–352.

McKay, D., Neziroglu, F., Todaro, J., & Yaryura-Tobias, J. A. (1996). Changes in personality disorders following behavior therapy for obsessive-compulsive disorder. *Journal of Anxiety Disorders, 10,* 47–57.

References

McKisack, C., & Waller, G. (1997). Factors influencing the outcome of group psychotherapy for bulimia nervosa. *International Journal of Eating Disorders, 22,* 1–13.

McMullen, L. M., & Conway, J. B. (1997). Dominance and nurturance in the narratives told by clients in psychotherapy. *Psychotherapy Research, 7,* 83–99.

Merskey, H. (1995). Multiple personality disorder and false memory syndrome. *British Journal of Psychiatry, 166,* 281–283.

Meyer, A. (1957). *Psychobiology: A science of man.* Springfield, IL: Charles C. Thomas.

Miller, N. S., & Verinis, J. S. (1995). Treatment outcome for impoverished alcoholics in an abstinence-based program. *International Journal of Addictions, 30,* 753–763.

Miller, S. D., Blackburn, T., Scholes, G., White, G. L., & Mamalis, N. (1991). Optical differences in multiple personality disorder: A second look. *Journal of Nervous and Mental Disease, 179,* 132–135.

Miller, W. R., & Hester, R. K. (1986). The effectiveness of alcoholism treatment: What research reveals. In W. R. Miller & N. Heather (Eds.), *Treating addictive behaviors: Process and change* (pp. 243–248). New York: Plenum Press.

Mintz, L. B., & Betz, N. E. (1988). Prevalence and correlates of eating disordered behaviors among undergraduate women. *Journal of Counseling Psychology, 35,* 463–471.

Minuchin, S. (1974). *Families and family therapy.* Cambridge, MA: Harvard University Press.

Mitchell, J. E., Hatsukami, D. K., Pyle, R. L., & Eckert, E. D. (1986). The bulimia syndrome: Course of the illness and associated problems. *Comprehensive Psychiatry, 27,* 165–170.

Mitchell, J. E., Raymond, N., & Specker, S. M. (1993). A review of the controlled trials of pharmacotherapy and psychotherapy in the treatment of bulimia nervosa. *International Journal of Eating Disorders, 14,* 229–247.

Moreau, D., & Mufson, L. (1997). Interpersonal psychotherapy for depressed adolescents. *Child and Adolescent Psychiatric Clinics of North America, 6,* 97–110.

Mufson, L., Moreau, D., Weissman, M. M., & Klerman, G. L. (1994). *Interpersonal psychotherapy for depressed adolescents.* New York: Guilford Press.

Muris, P., Merckelbach, H., & Clavan, M. (1997). Abnormal and normal compulsions. *Behaviour Research and Therapy, 35,* 249–252.

Nace, E. P., Saxon, J. J., & Shore, N. (1983). A comparison of borderline and nonborderline alcoholic patients. *Archives of General Psychiatry, 40,* 54–56.

Nakagawa, Marks, I. M., Takei, N., de Araujo, L. A., & Ito, L. M. (1996). Comparisons among the Yale-Brown Obsessive-Compulsive Scale, Compulsion Checklist, and other measures of obsessive-compulsive disorder. *British Journal of Psychiatry, 169,* 108–112.

Newman, S. C., & Bland, R. C. (1994). Life events and the 1-year prevalence of major depressive episode, generalized anxiety disorder, and panic disorder in a community sample. *Comprehensive Psychiatry, 35,* 76–82.

Nicolosi, A., Molinari, S., Musicco, M., Saracco, A., Ziliani, N, & Lazzarin, A. (1991). Positive modification of injecting behavior among intravenous heroin users from Milan and northern Italy, 1987–1989. *British Journal of Addiction, 86,* 91–102.

Nolen-Hoeksema, S. (1990). *Sex differences in depression.* Stanford, CA: Stanford University Press.

O'Connell, R. A., Mayo, J. A., Flatow, L., Cuthbertson, B., & O'Brien, B. E. (1991). Outcome of bipolar disorder on long-term treatment with lithium. *British Journal of Psychiatry, 159,* 123–129.

O'Connor, P. G., & Selwyn, P. A. (1997). Medical issues in the care of opioid-dependent patients. In S. M. Stine & T. R. Kosten (Eds.), *New treatments for opiate dependence* (pp. 199–227). New York: Guilford.

References

Olmsted, M. P., Kaplan, A. S., Rockert, W., & Jacobsen, M. (1996). Rapid responders to intensive treatment of bulimia nervosa. *International Journal of Eating Disorders, 19,* 279–285.

Orford, J. (1986). The rules of interpersonal complementarity: Does hostility beget hostility and dominance, submission? *Psychological Review, 93,* 365–377.

Paillère-Martinot, M.- L., Lecrubier, Y., Martinot, J.- L., & Aubin, F. (1995). Improvement of some schizophrenia deficit symptoms with low doses of amisulpride. *American Journal of Psychiatry, 152,* 130–133.

Pardes, H., Kaufman, C. A., Pincus, H. A., & West, A. (1989). Genetics and psychiatry: Past discoveries, current dilemmas, and future directions. *American Journal of Psychiatry, 146,* 435–443.

Parker, J., Pool, Y., Rawle, R., & Gay, M. (1988). Monitoring problem drug use in Bristol. *British Journal of Psychiatry, 152,* 214–221.

Pauls, D. L., Alsobrook, J. P., II, Goodman, W., Rassmussen, S., & Leckman, J. F. (1995). A family study of obsessive-compulsive disorder. *American Journal of Psychiatry, 152,* 76–84.

Peele, S. (1992). Alcoholism, politics, and burearcracy: The consensus against controlled-drinking therapy in America. *Addictive Behaviors, 17,* 49–62.

Penn, D. L., & Mueser, K. T. (1996). Research update on the psychosocial treatment of schizophrenia. *American Journal of Psychiatry, 153,* 607–617.

Pepper, C. M., Klein, D. N., Anderson, R. L., Riso, L. P., Ouimette, P. C., & Lizardi, H. (1995). DSM-III-R Axis II comorbidity in dysthymia and major depression. *American Journal of Psychiatry, 152,* 239–247.

Peterson, J. A. (1996). Hypnotherapeutic techniques to facilitate psychotherapy with PTSD and dissociative clients. In L. K. Michelson & W. J. Ray (Eds.), *Handbook of dissociation: Theoretical, empirical, and clinical perspectives* (pp. 449–474). New York: Plenum Press.

Pisani, V. D., Fawcett, J., Clark, D. C., & McGuire, M. (1993). The relative contributions of medical adherence and AA meeting attendance to abstinent outcome for chronic alcoholics. *Journal of Studies on Alcohol, 54*, 115–119.

Pope, H. G., & Hudson, J. I. (1989). Are eating disorders associated with borderline personality disorder? A critical review. *International Journal of Eating Disorders, 8*, 1–9.

Pruchno, R. A., Michaels, J. E., & Potashnik, S. L. (1990). Predictors of institutionalization among Alzheimer disease victims with caregiving spouses. *Journals of Gerontology, 45*, S259–S266.

Putnam, F. W., Guroff, J. J., Silberman, E. K., Barban, L., & Post, R. M. (1986). The clinical phenomenology of multiple personality disorder: Review of 100 recent cases. *Journal of Clinical Psychiatry, 47*, 285–293.

Rasmussen, S. A., & Eisen, J. L. (1989). Clinical features and phenomenology of obsessive-compulsive disorder. *Psychiatric Annals, 19*, 67–73.

Rasmussen, S. A., & Eisen, J. L. (1990). Epidemiology of obsessive-compulsive disorder. *Journal of Clinical Psychiatry, 51* (2,Suppl.), 10–13.

Regier, D. A., Boyd, J. H., Burke, J. D., Rae, D. S., Myers, J. K., Kramer, M., Robins, L. N., George, L. K., Karno, M., & Locke, B. Z. (1988). One-month prevalence of mental disorders in the United States: Based on five epidemiologic catchment area sites. *Archives of General Psychiatry, 45*, 977–986.

Regier, D. A., Narrow, W. E., & Rae, D. S. (1990). The epidemiology of anxiety disorders: The Epidemiologic Catchment Area (ECA) experience. *Journal of Psychiatric Research, 24* (2, Suppl.), 3–14.

Renshaw, D. C. (1988). Profile of 2376 patients treated at Loyola Sex Clinic between 1972 and 1987. *Sexual and Marital Therapy, 3*, 111–117.

Rickels, K., Downing, R., Schweizer, E., & Hassman, H. (1993). Antidepressants for the treatment of generalized anxiety disorder: A placebo-controlled comparison of imipramine, trazadone, and diazepam. *Archives of General Psychiatry, 50*, 884–895.

References

Rickels, K., Schweizer, E., Csanalosi, I., Case, W. G., & Chung, H. (1988). Long-term treatment of anxiety and risk of withdrawal: Prospective comparison of clorazepate and buspirone. *Archives of General Psychiatry, 45,* 444–450.

Rittmannsberger, H., & Schony, W. (1986). Prevalence of tardive dyskensia in a population of long-stay schizophrenic inpatients. *Nervenartz, 57,* 116–118.

Ritvo, E. R., Freeman, B. J., Pingree, C., Mason-Brothers, A., Jorde, L., Jenson, W. R., McMahon, W. M., Petersen, P. B., Mo, A., & Ritvo, A. (1989). The UCLA-University of Utah epidemiologic survey of autism: Prevalence. *American Journal of Psychiatry, 146,* 194–199.

Robins, L. N., Helzer, J. E., Crougham, J., & Ratcliff, K. S. (1981). National Institute of Mental Health Diagnostic Interview Schedule: Its history, characteristics, and validity. *Archives of General Psychiatry, 38,* 381–389.

Robins, L. N., Helzer, J. E., Weissman, M. M., Orvaschel, H., Gruenberg, E., Burke, J. D., & Regier, D. A. (1984). Lifetime prevalence rates of specific psychiatric disorders in three sites. *Archives of General Psychiatry, 41,* 949–958.

Rodney, J., Prior, N., Cooper, B., Theodoros, M., Browining, J., Steinberg, B., & Evans, L. (1997). The comorbidity of anxiety and depression. *Australian and New Zealand Journal of Psychiatry, 31,* 700–703.

Rogers, S. L., Farlow, M. R., Doody, R. S., Mohs, R., & Friedhoff, L. T. (1998). A 24-week, double-blind, placebo-controlled trial of donepezil in patients with Alzheimer's disease. Donepezil Study Group. *Neurology, 50,* 136–145.

Rogers, S. L. & Friedhoff, L. T. (1998). Long-term efficacy and safety of donepezil in the treatment of Alzheimer's disease: An interim analysis of the results of a U.S. multicentre open label extension study. *European Neuropsychopharmacology, 8,* 67–75.

Rosen, J. C., Leitenberg, H., Fisher, C., & Khazam, C. (1986). Binge-eating episodes in bulimia nervosa: The amount and type of food consumed. *International Journal of Eating Disorders, 5,* 255–267.

Rosen, R. C. (1996). Erectile dysfunction: The medicalization of male sexuality. *Clinical Psychology Review, 16,* 497–519.

Rosen, R. C., & Lieblum, S. R. (1993). Treatment of male erectile disorder: Current options and dilemas. *Sexual and Marital Therapy, 8,* 5–8.

Rosen, R. C., Lieblum, S. R., & Spector, I. P. (1994). Psychologically based treatment for male erectile disorder: A cognitive-interpersonal model. *Journal of Sex and Marital Therapy, 20,* 67–85.

Rosen, W. C., Mohs, R. C., & Davis, K. C. (1984). A new rating scale for Alzheimer's disease. *American Journal of Psychiatry, 141,* 1356–1364.

Rosenblum, L., Darrow, W., Witte, S., Cohen, J., French, J., Gill, P. S., Potterat, J., Sikes, K., Reich, R., & Hadler, S. (1992). Sexual practices in the transmission of hepatitus B virus and prevalence of hepatitus Delta virus infection in female prostitutes in the United States. *Journal of the American Medical Association, 267,* 2477–2481.

Ross, C. A. (1997). *Dissociative identity disorder: Diagnosis, clinical features, and treatment of multiple personality (2nd ed.).* New York: Wiley.

Ross, C. A., Miller, S. D., Reagor, P., Bjornson, L., Fraser, G. A., & Anderson, G. (1990). Structured interview data on 102 cases of multiple personality disorder from four centers. *American Journal of Psychiatry, 147,* 596–601.

Rutter, M. (1983). Cognitive deficits in the pathogenesis of autism. *Journal of Child Psychology and Psychiatry, 24,* 513–531.

Sacks, O. (1985). *The man who mistook his wife for a hat, and other clinical tales.* New York: Summit Books.

Samit, C. J. (1996). A group for parents of autistic children. In M. Rosenbaum (Ed.), *Handbook of short-term therapy groups* (pp. 23–37). Northvale, NJ: Aronson.

Sanchez-Carbonell, J., Cami, J., & Brigos, B. (1988). Follow-up of heroin addicts in Spain (EMETYST Project): Results one year after treatment admission. *British Journal of Addiction, 83,* 1439–1448.

Sanchez-Craig, M., & Wilkinson, D. A. (1987). Treating problem drinkers who are not severely dependent on alcohol. *Drugs and Society, 1*, 39–67.

Schmidt, E. (1996). Rational Recovery: Finding an alternative for addiction treatment. *Alcoholism Treatment Quarterly, 14*, 47–57.

Schmidt, V., Sloane, G., Tiller, J. & Treasure, J. (1993). Childhood adversity and adult defence style in eating disorder patients: A controlled study. *British Journal of Medical Psychology, 66*, 353–362.

Schou, M. (1997). Forty years of lithium treatment. *Archives of General Psychiatry, 54*, 9–13.

Segraves, R. T., & Segraves, K. B. (1990). Categorical and multi-axial diagnosis of male erectile disorder. *Journal of Sex and Marital Therapy, 16*, 208–213.

Shader, R. I. (1984). Epidemiologic and family studies. *Psychosomatics, 25*, 10–15.

Shaffer, J. W., Nurco, D. N., & Kinlock, T. W. (1984). A new classification of narcotic addicts based on type and extent of criminal activity. *Comprehensive Psychiatry, 25*, 315–328.

Shea, M T., Pilkonis, P. A., Beckham, E., Collins, J. F., Elkin, I., Sotsky, S. M., & Docherty, J. P. (1990). Personality disorders and treatment outcome in the NIMH Treatment of Depression Collaborative Research Program. *American Journal of Psychiatry, 147*, 711–718.

Sheehan, M., Oppenheimer, E., & Taylor, C. (1988). Who comes for treatment? Drug misusers at three London agencies. *British Journal of Addictions, 83*, 311–320.

Shibayama, H., Kasahara, Y., & Kobayashi, H. (1986). Prevalence of dementia in a Japanese elderly population. *Acta Psychiatrica Scandinavica, 74*, 144–151.

Silove, D., Manicavasagar, V., O'Connell, D., & Morris-Yates, A. (1995). Genetic factors in early separation anxiety: Implications for the genesis of adult anxiety disorders. *Acta Psychiatrica Scandinavica, 92*, 17–24.

Silverman, J. M., Li, G., Zaccarrio, M. L., Smith, C. J., Schmeidler, J., Mohs, R. C., & Davis, K. L. (1994). Patterns of risk in first-degree relatives of patients with Alzheimer's disease. *Archives of General Psychiatry, 51,* 577–586.

Small, G. W., Rabins, P. V., Barry, P. P., Buckholtz, N. S., DeKosky, S. T., Ferris, S. H., Finkel, S. I., Gwyther, L. P., Khachaturian, Z. S., Lebowitz, B. D., McRae, T. D., Morris, J. C., Oakley, F., Schneider, L. S., Streim, J. E., Sunderland, T., Teri, L. A., & Tune, L. E. (1997). Diagnosis and treatment of Alzheimer's disease and related disorders: Consensus statement of the American Association for Geriatric Psychiatry and the Alzheimer's Association, the American Geriatrics Society. *Journal of the American Medical Association, 278,* 1363–1371.

Sobell, L. C., Toneatto, A., & Sobell, M. B. (1990). Behavior therapy. In A. S. Bellack & M. Hersen (Eds.), *Handbook of comparative treatments for adult disorders* (pp. 479–505). New York: Wiley.

Sobell, M. B. & Sobell, L. C. (1995). Controlled drinking after 25 years: How important was the great debate? *Addiction, 90,* 1149–1153.

Solomon, D. A., Keitner, G. I., Miller, I. W., Shea, M. T., & Keller, M. B. (1995). Course of illness and maintenance treatments for patients with bipolar disorder. *Journal of Clinical Psychology, 56,* 5–13.

Sommer, S. M. (1997). The experience of long-term recovering alcoholics in Alcoholics Anonymous: Perspectives on therapy. *Alcoholism Treatment Quarterly, 15,* 75–80.

Sotsky, S. M., Glass, D. R., Shea, M. T., Pilkonis, P. A., Collins, J. F., Elkin, I., Watkins, J. T., Imber, S. D., Leber, W. R., Moyer, J., & Oliveri, M. E. (1991). Patient predictors of response to psychotherapy and pharmacotherapy: Findings in the NIMH Treatment of Depression Collaborative Research Program. *American Journal of Psychiatry, 148,* 997–1008.

Spanos, N. P. (1996). *Multiple identities and false memories: A sociocognitive perspective.* Washington, D.C.: American Psychological Association.

References

Spector, I. P., & Carey, M. P. (1990). Incidence and prevalence of the sexual dysfunctions: A critical review of the empirical literature. *Archives of Sexual Behavior, 19*, 389–408.

Spiegel, D. (1986). Dissociating damage. *American Journal of Clinical Hypnosis, 29*, 123–131.

Spiegel, D. (1996). Dissociative disorders. In R. E. Hales & S. C. Yudofsky (Eds.), *The American Psychiatric Press synopsis of psychiatry* (pp. 583–604). Washington, D.C.: American Psychiatric Press.

Spitzer, R. L., Endicott, J., & Gibbon, M. (1979). Crossing the border into borderline personality and borderline schizophrenia: The development of criteria. *Archives of General Psychiatry, 36*, 17–24.

Stein, D. M., & Brinza, S. R. (1988). Bulimia: Prevalence estimates in female junior high and high school students. *Journal of Clinical and Child Psychiatry, 18*, 206–213.

Steinberg, M., Cicchetti, D., Buchanan, J., Rakfeldt, J., & Rounsaville, B. (1994). Distinguishing between multiple personality disorder (dissociative identity disorder) and schizophrenia using the Structured Clinical Interview for DSM-IV Dissociative Dissorders. *Journal of Nervous and Mental Disease, 182*, 495–502.

Steinberg, M., & Hall, P. (1997). The SCID-D diagnostic interview and treatment planning in dissociative disorders. *Bulletin of the Menninger Clinic, 61*, 108–120.

Stinchfield, R. D., Niforopulos, L., & Feder, S. H. (1994). Follow-up contact bias in adolescent substance abuse treatment outcome research. *Journal of Studies on Alcohol, 55*, 285–289.

Strain, E. C., Stitzer, M. L., Liebson, I. A., & Bigelow, G. E. (1993). Methadone dose and treatment outcome. *Drug and Alcohol Dependence, 33*, 105–117.

Strain, E. C., Stitzer, M. L., Liebson, I. A., & Bigelow, G. E. (1996). Buprenorphine versus methadone in the treatment of opioid dependence: Self-reports, urinalysis, and addiction severity index. *Journal of Clinical Psychopharmacology, 16*, 58–67.

Stuart, S., & O'Hara, M. W. (1995). Treatment of postpartum depression with interpersonal psychotherapy. *Archives of General Psychiatry, 52*, 75–76.

Sullivan, H. S. (1953). *The interpersonal theory of psychiatry.* New York: Norton.

Suriyama, T., & Abe, T. (1986). The prevalence of autism in Nagoya, Japan: A total population study. *Journal of Autism and Developmental Disorders, 19*, 87–96.

Swartz, M., Blazer, D., George, L., & Winfield, I. (1990). Estimating the prevalence of borderline personality disorder in the community. *Journal of Personality Disorders, 4*, 257–272.

Swartz, M. S., Blazer, D. G., George, L. K., Winfield, I., Zakaris, J., & Dye, E. (1989). Identification of borderline personality disorder with the NIMH Diagnostic Interview Schedule. *American Journal of Psychiatry, 146*, 200–205.

Sykes, D. K., Leuser, B., Melia, M., & Gross, M. (1988). A demographic analysis of 252 patients with anorexia nervosa and bulimia. *International Journal of Psychosomatics, 35*, 5–9.

Szatmari, P. (1992). The validity of autistic spectrum disorders: A literature review. *Journal of Autism and Developmental Disorders, 22*, 583–600.

Szegedi, A., Wiesner, J., & Hiemke, C. (1995). Improved efficacy and fewer side effects under clozapine treatment after addition of fluvoxamine. *Journal of Clinical Psychopharmacology, 15*, 141–143.

Tan, J. C., & Stoppard, J. M. (1994). Gender and reactions to dysphoric individuals. *Cognitive Therapy and Research, 18*, 211–224.

Tang, M. X., Stern, Y., Marder, K., Bell, K., Gurland, B., Lantigua, R., Andrews, H., Feng, L., Tycko, B., & Mayeux, R. (1998). The APOE-epsilon 4 allele and the risk of Alzheimer's disease among African-Americans, whites, and Hispanics. *Journal of the American Medical Association, 279*, 751–755.

References

Teichman, Y. (1997). Depression in a marital context. In S. Dremen (Ed.), *The family on the threshold of the 21st Century: Trends and implications* (pp. 49–70). Mahwah, NJ: Erlbaum.

Terrier, N. (1991). Behavioural psychotherapy and schizophrenia: The past, the present, and the future. *Behavioural Psychotherapy, 19,* 121–130.

Timko, C., Moos, R. H., Finney, J. W., & Moos, B. S. (1994). Outcome for treatment of alcohol abuse and involvement in Alcoholics Anonymous among previously untreated problem drinkers. *Journal of Mental Health Administration, 21,* 145–160.

Tollefson, G. D., Rampey, A. H., Potvin, J. H., Jenike, M. A., Rush, A. J., Dominguez, R. A., Koran, L. M., Shear, M. K., Goodman, W., & Genduso, L. A. (1994). A multicenter investigation of fixed-dose fluoxetine in the treatment of obsessive-compulsive disorder. *Archives of General Psychiatry, 51,* 559–567.

Trappler, B., Kwong, V., & Leeman, C. P. (1996). Therapeutic effect of clozapine at an unusually high plasma level. *American Journal of Psychiatry, 153,* 133–134.

Tuma, A. H., Siegel, C., Alexander, M. J., & Wanderling, J. (1993). Effects of compliance on outcome independent of pharmacological efficacy in the treatment of opioid dependence: A post hoc regression analysis. *American Journal on Addictions, 2,* 238–249.

Valliant, G. E. (1996). A long-term follow-up of male alcohol abuse. *Archives of General Psychiatry, 53,* 243–249.

Van Denberg, T. F., Schmidt, J. A., & Kiesler, D. J. (1992). Interpersonal circle inventories: Pantheoretical applications to psychotherapy research and practice. *Journal of Psychotherapy Integration, 2,* 77–99.

Van Noppen, B., Steketee, G., McCorkle, B. H., & Pato, M. (1997). Group and multifamily behavioral treatment for obsessive compulsive disorder: A pilot study. *Journal of Anxiety Disorders, 11,* 431–446.

Virag, R. (1997). Intracavernous injections and new medical treatments of impotence. *Revue de Medecine Interne, 18* (Suppl. 1), 31S–35S.

Wahlström, J., Gillberg, C., Gustavson, K.-G., & Holmgren, G. (1986). Infantile autism and the fragile X syndrome: A Swedish population multicenter study. *American Journal of Medical Genetics, 23,* 403–408.

Wakschlag, L. S., & Leventhal, B. (1996). Consultation with young autistic children and their families. *Journal of the American Academy of Child and Adolescent Psychiatry, 35,* 963–965.

Walsh, B. T., Wilson, G. T., Loeb, K. L., Devlin, M. J., Pike, K. M., Roose, S. P., Fleiss, J., & Waternaux, C. (1997). Medication and psychotherapy in the treatment of bulimia nervosa. *American Journal of Psychiatry, 154,* 523–531.

Walsh, D. C., Hingson, R. W., Merrigan, D. M., & Levenson, S. M. (1991). A randomized trial of treatment options for alcohol-abusing workers. *New England Journal of Medicine, 325,* 775–782.

Ward, J., Bell, J., Mattick, R. P., & Hall, W. (1996). Methadone maintenance therapy for opioid dependence: A guide to appropriate use. *CNS Drugs, 6,* 440–449.

Warner, L. A., Kessler, R. C., Hughes, M., Anthony, J. C., & Nelson, C. B. (1995). Prevalence and correlates of drug use and dependence in the United States. *Archives of General Psychiatry, 52,* 219–229.

Watson, C. G., Hancock, M., Gearhart, L. P., Mendez, C. M., Malourh, P., & Raden, M. (1997). A comparative outcome study of frequent, moderate, occasional, and nonattenders of Alcoholics Anonymous. *Journal of Clinical Psychology, 53,* 209–214.

Watters, J. K., Cheng, Y.-T., & Lorvick, J. J. (1991). Drug-use profiles, race, age, and risk of HIV infection among intravenous drug users in San Francisco. *International Journal of Addictions, 26,* 1247–1261.

Webb, J. A., Baer, P. E., & McKelvey, R. J. (1995). Development of a risk profile for intentions to use alcohol among fifth- and sixth-graders. *Psychiatry, 34,* 772–778.

Wechsler, D. (1991). *Manual for the Wechsler Preschool and Primary Intelligence Scale* (3rd ed.). San Antonio: Psychological Corporation.

References

Wechsler, D. (1997). *Manual for the Wechsler Adult Intelligence Scale* (3rd ed.). San Antonio: Psychological Corporation.

Weeke, A., & Vaeth, M. (1986). Excess mortality of bipolar and unipolar manic-depressive patients. *Journal of Affective Disorders, 11,* 227–234.

Weiss, S. W., & Ebert, M. H. (1983). Psychological and behavioral characteristics of normal-weight bulimics and normal-weight controls. *Psychosomatic Medicine, 45,* 293–303.

Weissman, M. M. (1990). Panic and generalized anxiety: Are they separate disorders? *Journal of Psychiatric Research, 24,* 157–162.

Weissman, M. M., Leaf, P. J., Tischler, G. L., Blazer, D. G., Karno, M., Bruce, M. C., & Florio, L. P. (1988). Affective disorders in five United States communities. *Psychological Medicine, 18,* 141–153.

Weissman, M. M., & Markowitz, J. C. (1994). Interpersonal psychotherapy: Current status. *Archives of General Psychiatry, 51,* 599–606.

Weissman, M. M., & Merikangas, K. R. (1986). The epidemiology of anxiety and panic disorders: An update. *Journal of Clinical Psychiatry, 47,* 11–17.

Whitaker, A., Johnson, J., Shaffer, D., Rapoport, J., Kalikow, K., Walsh, B. T., Davies, M., & Braiman, S. (1990). Uncommon troubles in young people: Prevalence estimates of selected psychiatric disorders in a nonreferred adolescent population. *Archives of General Psychiatry, 47,* 487–496.

Willemsen-Swinkels, S. H. N., Buitelaar, J. K., & Van Engeland, H. 1996. The effects of chronic naltrexone treatment in young autistic children: A double-blind placebo-controlled crossover study. *Biological Psychiatry, 39,* 1023–1031.

Wing, L., (1981). Sex ratios in early childhood autism and related conditions. *Psychiatric Research, 5,* 129–137.

Winokur, G., & Crowe, R. R. (1983). Bipolar illness: The sex-polarity effect in affectively ill family members. *Archives of General Psychiatry, 40,* 57–58.

Woerner, M. G., Sheitman, B. B., Lieberman, J. A., & Kane, J. M. (1996). Tardive dyskinesia induced by risperidone? *American Journal of Psychiatry, 153*, 843.

Wu, J. C., Buchsbaum, M. S., Hershey, T. G., Hazlett, E., Sicotte, N., & Johnson, J. C. (1991). PET in generalized anxiety disorder. *Biological Psychiatry, 29*, 1181–1199.

Wurthmann, C., Klieser, E., & Lehmann, E. (1997). Side effects of low dose neuroleptics and their impact on clinical outcome in generalized anxiety disorder. *Progress in Neuro-Psychopharmacology and Biological Psychiatry, 21*, 601–609.

Wylie, K. R. (1997). Treatment outcome of brief couple therapy in psychogenic male erectile disorder. *Archives of Sexual Behavior, 26*, 527–545.

Yager, J., Rorty, M., & Rosotto, E. (1995). Coping styles differ between recovered and nonrecovered women with bulimia nervosa, but not between recovered women and non-eating-disordered control subjects. *Journal of Nervous and Mental Disease, 183*, 86–94.

Yoder, B. (1990). *The resource book.* New York: Simon & Schuster.

NOTES

NOTES

NOTES

NOTES

NOTES

NOTES

NOTES

NOTES

NOTES

NOTES

NOTES

NOTES

NOTES